DUDLEY PUBLIC LIBRARIES

The loan of this book may be renewed if not required by other readers, by contacting the library from which it was borrowed.

5 JAN 2018
6-8-19

D1355485

000002145761

Collins

An imprint of HarperCollins Publishers
Westerhill Road, Bishopbriggs, Glasgow G64 2QT

Copyright © HarperCollins Publishers Ltd 2016
Maps © Collins Bartholomew 2016

First published as The Times Waterways of Britain 2010
Paperback Edition 2016

978 0 00 819547 2
978 0 00 820202 6

10 9 8 7 6 5 4 3 2 1

Printed in China by RR Donnelley APS Co Ltd

Collins ® is a registered trademark of HarperCollins Publishers Ltd

The contents of this publication are believed correct at the time of printing. Nevertheless the publisher can accept no responsibility for errors or omissions, changes in the detail given or for any expense or loss thereby caused.

HarperCollins does not warrant that any website mentioned in this title will be provided uninterrupted, that any website will be error free, that defects will be corrected, or that the website or the server that makes it available are free of viruses or bugs. For full terms and conditions please refer to the site terms provided on the website.

A catalogue record for this book is available from the British Library.

All mapping in this publication is generated from Collins Bartholomew digital databases. Collins Bartholomew, the UK's leading independent geographical information supplier, can provide a digital, custom, and premium mapping service to a variety of markets. For further information: Tel: +44 (0) 208 307 4515 e-mail: collinsbartholomew@harpercollins.co.uk

If you would like to comment on any aspect of this publication, please contact us at the above address or online. e-mail: collinsmaps@harpercollins.co.uk

www.harpercollins.co.uk

 facebook.com/collinsmaps

@collinsmaps

MIX
Paper from
responsible sources
FSC™ C007454

FSC™ is a non-profit international organisation established to promote the responsible management of the world's forests. Products carrying the FSC label are independently certified to assure consumers that they come from forests that are managed to meet the social, economic and ecological needs of present and future generations, and other controlled sources.

Find out more about HarperCollins and the environment at
www.harpercollins.co.uk/green

WATERWAYS
of
BRITAIN

Written by Jonathan Mosse

The Staffordshire & Worcestershire Canal

FOREWORD

What is it that inspires an individual's great passion for and fascination with canals and rivers? For some it is stepping out of their day-to-day existence into a more tranquil world; for others it is the discovery of the great wealth of fundamentally practical, but often awe-inspiring structures and the engineering that created them. The strong community spirit that still exists on these water-filled highways attracts some people; many, quite frankly, just enjoy messing about on boats. For the author, Jonathan Mosse, it was a combination of all of these.

Over thirty years ago he was presented with the challenge of injecting a programme of Personal Development Skills into an already packed residential course, for students pursuing a practical, land-based industries, training programme – agriculture, horticulture, forestry and gamekeeping. In coming to a solution he turned to the waterways. He identified a narrowboat hire company, what was then Alvechurch Boats, based at Bromsgrove and, by coincidence, very close to where L. T. C. Rolt can be said to have kick-started the waterway renaissance which we all benefit from so hugely today. Three brave partners of that company were willing, out of season, to hire twenty or so 12-berth boats, borrowed for a week and to be under the pilotage of a motley crew of teenage boys and girls, many of whom had never seen a canal before, let alone handled a boat.

It was initially envisaged that elements of the programme would be sprinkled throughout the thirteen weeks, where and when a gap could be found. And then, rather in the manner of Paul's conversion on the road to Damascus, the penny dropped: why not make it a feature of the course – unique and truly meaningful, something to be embraced wholeheartedly in a manner that would become unforgettable? After all, that is genuine learning; that is what real life is about within the meaning of 'life skills'.

Many hours were spent planning the trip, devising menus and delegating roles; in getting to grips with map reading, fathoming how to make these strange craft go in vaguely the direction intended (they clearly behaved quite differently to tractors and motor mowers) and making locks fill and empty in the required order; finally arriving back at the starting point with the boats clean and intact. When all the time and experience was assembled end to end, not only had every box on the Personal Development Skills proforma been well and truly ticked, but a group of young people, together with their intrepid supervisory instructors, ventured forth more-rounded people, more aware of the beauty of the countryside they had traversed and, of most significance to this book, in awe of the tremendous feats of engineering that had made their unique and lasting experience possible.

This book introduces its readers to as many of the waterway wonders as the author's students stumbled upon during their time afloat. It does not set out, within the confines of its limited number of pages, to be an exhaustive guide to all and everything about the entire inland waterways system. It is purely a view of Britain's vast and varied canal and river system, and includes a selection of navigations which represent the rich diversity it contains.

CONTENTS

FLORA AND FAUNA

MILEPOSTS

Interspersed with the different waterways throughout this book are a series of 25 Mileposts. Each Milepost is representative of a significant waterway development and several of them are included in the list of what are generally regarded as making up the Seven Waterways Wonders of the World. Taken together they chart the people, places and events that have made an impact on the evolution of the navigable canals and rivers that we enjoy today.

INTRODUCTION

Founded on the careful selection of a variety of significant navigations, *Waterways of Britain* offers a well-rounded view of the contemporary inland waterways system. This picture is built up by delving into their historical past, by a close examination of the present scene, together with a forward glance towards future directions and development. Regarded as the 'quickest way of slowing down', the canals and rivers of Britain evoke a bygone era when life moved at a more leisurely pace.

Yet, even today, Canal & River Trust maintains an incredible 2,200 miles of inland waterways in Britain. An increasing number of people are using these waterways, and others maintained by the Environment Agency or in private ownership, for recreation. As a reader you will hopefully be inspired from within these pages to turn from armchair voyager into towpath spectator (known on the canals as a gongoozler)

Chug *the tug*

Block laying on the Chesterfield Canal

or venture onto the waterways themselves and, as such, grow to become truly absorbed in the wonder of the waterways.

Based on the Grand Cross network of canals as proposed by James Brindley, the first of Britain's waterways engineers, the waterways are described in their regional setting. The introduction to each region is also used to mention those waterways that are not covered in detail but which help to provide a more comprehensive picture of the development and diversity of navigations within the area.

Often a book like this majors on the 'hows' at the expense of the 'whys', so wherever possible an attempt has been made to set a waterway, or its particular features, in context to show why we see what we see today. The twenty-five Mileposts running chronologically throughout the book not only chart significant developments, people or places, but also seek to impart an understanding that is contextual. The short pieces of boxed text provide succinct, significant background to the development of Britain's waterways.

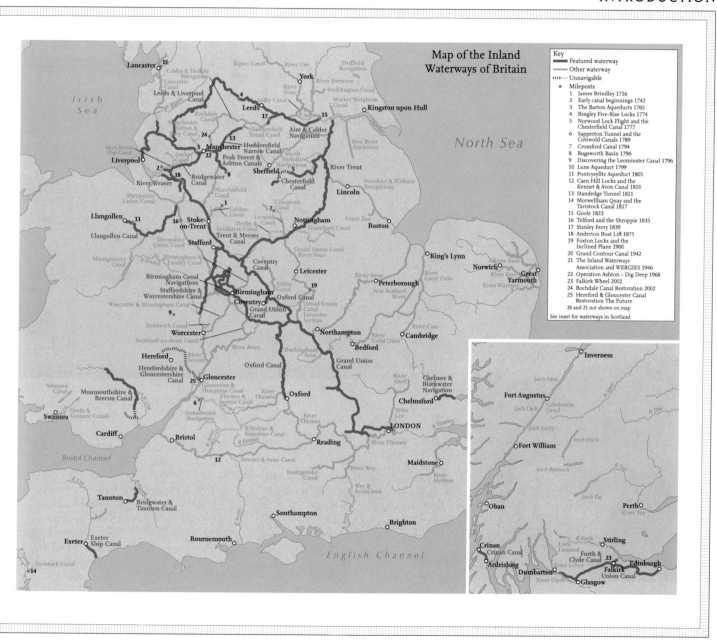

What can be harder to depict and therefore to convey, are the immense social changes that a reliable transport system brought about. It is easier to see how the canals kick-started the Industrial Revolution and how, in turn, much credit for the industrialised nation that we know today can be laid at the collective doors of James Brindley, Francis Egerton, 3rd Duke of Bridgewater, and his agent John Gilbert, as described in Milepost 1. Less simple to take in, is what suddenly being able to travel beyond the parish boundaries for the first time meant for the ordinary villager or townsperson. Being able to reliably move a 70 ton load, with a single horse, that had hitherto struggled to shift 2 tons along a summer-dry cart track (and less than 10 per cent of that in packhorse mode) was a revolution; upping sticks and shifting an entire family away from an economy, based

Vital Spark, *a Clyde Puffer*

Sunset bridge reflection

on casual agricultural labour to the relative security of, say, employment in a foundry was, until then, utterly beyond comprehension.

So next time you cross the Pennines on the M62 – or similar hills on a similar route – and see reservoirs settled deep in steep-sided, flooded valley bottoms, low sun glinting off their peaty waters, do not make the immediate assumption that they provide a drinking water supply to slake a neighbouring city's insatiable thirst. They could well represent an important part of a canal's infrastructure: a source of

water to replace each hungry lock-full lost when a boat makes an ascent of those very hills that your vehicle devours with such consummate ease.

Reflect on the battles between those early waterway promoters, who very often wanted the cheapest job possible, with the quickest return on their shareholders capital, requiring that the engineers they engaged helped realise these ambitions. The cheapest solution, in engineering terms, when confronted with a range of hills, was to build a series of locks up one side and thence down the other. But then, where was the water to come from to replace each lock-full lost on both the ascent and the descent? How much could the navigation depend on reservoirs not emptying totally during the dry summer months? And how much better to replace as many locks as prudence (and some additional capital) would allow, with a tunnel through those self-same hills which would, in turn, provide a long top pound: a reservoir of water in its own right.

Start thinking like this and you are already a canal engineer, a member of an early profession – an entirely new breed: men that were at one moment presented with a unique set of problems, which in the next they promptly turned into challenges. Each challenge was usually approached somewhat differently, on an individual basis, by an individual engineer and solutions were, therefore, evolutionary rather than revolutionary.

Hotel boats, stern detail

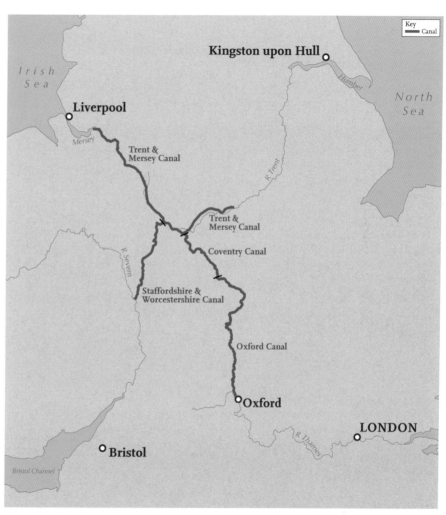

The map (above) shows the Grand Cross network of canals, proposed by James Brindley, linking the ports of Liverpool and Kingston upon Hull in the north to Bristol and London in the south, via existing rivers and a rudimentary canal system. These early waterways formed the skeleton upon which later navigations were grafted, fleshing out this framework to connect with nearly all parts of England and Wales. Brindley's original concept and its subsequent development, has been instrumental in forming the choice of waterways explored within the covers of this book.

James Brindley was Britain's first true canal engineer, and played a crucial part in making possible the canal network that played such an important part in the Industrial Revolution. He was born in 1716 into what was then a relatively poor, tenant farming family at Tunstead, near Buxton in Derbyshire He came from a Quaker background, on his mother's side, although her marriage to a man (also called James) of somewhat hedonistic tendencies had led to a rift that endured for the first ten years of young James' life. When, through the generosity of a great uncle, the family inherited their own holding at Lowe Hill, near Leek in Staffordshire, the change was the making of James senior and provided the opportunity for his son to receive some formal education at the local Quaker school. The fundamental Quaker ethos, of thrift and hard work, will have dictated that the practical side of his education came from the variety of labouring jobs which his parents would have set him to.

Seven years later a further inheritance meant that the family could afford to pay the cost of the indentures incurred as a result of James' apprenticeship with Abraham Bennett, a millwright, based at Sutton in Cheshire, 10 miles from Lowe Hill, where he was to remain for nine more years between 1733 and 1742. Popular belief has it that his early years with Bennett were not an outstanding success and he was left to his own devices in the workshop for long periods of time, whilst his journeymen colleagues were away on other jobs. Gradually, however, he began to demonstrate his capabilities, notably in the salvaging of a paper mill contract, the finer points of which had defeated Bennett's somewhat inebriated powers of comprehension. On his master's death Brindley, having insufficient capital to purchase the business from Bennett's widow, decided to set up on his own in Leek.

Now aged 26, with something of a local reputation for 'his firmness of work', he was prepared to travel far and wide in the search for challenging work. As well as completing repairs on a wide range of mills and machinery, he would always offer advice on how improvements might be made, earning himself the nickname of 'The Schemer'.

Being in the right place at the right time is often the key to success and he was fortunate, while attending a local wedding, to meet John Heathcote, a prosperous mine owner from Clifton, between Manchester and Bolton. Brindley would have listened intently when Heathcote complained about how his Gal Pit coalmine, whilst bearing a rich coal seam, was constantly flooding, earning

Brindley in front of the Barton Aqueduct

it the name of Wet Earth Colliery. Hitherto, no measures had succeeded in stemming the flow of water which was now making a considerable dent in its owner's income. Brindley suggested a solution which was adopted as a remarkable act of faith on Heathcote's part. He devised a series of tunnels, introduced a siphon and a water wheel and successfully pumped the mine dry. The mine went on to employ more than 150 men, staying in production until 1928 – the water wheel lasting a hundred years – and Brindley added a further accolade to his reputation as 'the man who made water run up hill'.

All this suggests that James Brindley understood water and it was this deep and fundamental understanding of the raw ingredient of a waterway, that made him so well placed to design and construct canals. Ability alone is not everything; getting known in the right circles is equally important and the commissions he was now undertaking, especially within the Potteries area, meant that he was mixing with men of power and influence, especially the Wedgwoods – Thomas and John. As their pottery business flourished in Burslem – based on fine porcelain china rather than heavy, brown earthenware – so too did their need for china clay and flint: both materials being, at that time, brought in by packhorse. Likewise the finished goods found their way out to markets by the same means, with the expectation that only some 50 per cent of each consignment would reach its market intact. Clearly a waterway, connecting the area to the rivers Severn and Mersey, would provide an elegant solution to both problems and it was at this point that Brindley came into the picture, providing an initial survey of possible routes for a canal.

As things turned out there was no satisfactory outcome, but it is more than likely that he would have met Thomas Gilbert, Earl Gower's agent. Gower, one of the promoters of the proposed waterway, was the brother-in-law of Francis

POISED FOR REVOLUTION

James Brindley was born into a world of change, although little tangible evidence would have percolated through to the distant fields and woods of his Derbyshire birthplace.

It was a time of the beginnings of sea power and of colonial expansion, of the recent union between Scotland and England and the start of the Hanoverian dynasty. Sir Robert Walpole was soon to become the first British Prime Minister and the American colonies had been identified as a suitable destination for convicts. Poaching had become a capital offence and sat alongside almost 200 other crimes against property – not all carrying such draconian punishments, however.

The country was prospering from the slave trade and religious non-conformism was burgeoning. The population still looked over their collective shoulders towards the plague, some 50 years in the past, but still threatening – via France – to rear its ugly head again. The population of Britain sat at approximately five million and people rarely travelled more than a few miles from their place of birth. To do so entailed encounters with seas of mud in winter time and dust in summer. Crime, in the form of highway robbery, was no respecter of the seasons and travel was, for all but the well off, by foot. Most trade from England's shores was via the ports of Bristol, Exeter, London, Liverpool, Hull and Norwich, with activity centred upon London some tenfold greater than amongst any of its competitors.

Change also extended to the social order and it was not impossible for someone of relatively lowly origins to forge a successful career and become accepted by the gentry. Agrarian revolution was in the air and, what until that time had been largely an agricultural economy, was becoming interlaced with sporadic pockets of industry. It is now clear that the country was primed for further revolution, merely awaiting a suitable catalyst that was to take the form – in James Brindley's capable hands – of a reliable transport system. The ability to move large quantities of goods within the country easily and reliably was a great stimulus to the Industrial Revolution that was to transform first Britain and then the world.

Egerton, 3rd Duke of Bridgewater (*see* Milepost 3) whilst the duke's agent – John Gilbert – was Thomas' younger brother. The duke owned extensive coal mines in Worsley, to the north of the rapidly developing town of Manchester, where there was massive demand for their output. Tentative plans were already afoot for a waterway connection between Worsley and the River Irwell, which in turn led into the city. Operated by a monopolistic navigation company, the river offered an expensive and at times unreliable outlet for the duke's coal and Brindley proposed a direct canal from Worsley into the centre of Manchester, crossing the Irwell on an aqueduct: a solution that was to generate much ridicule on

all sides and the accusation that he 'was building castles in the air'. However, both the duke and his agent were convinced, as was the parliamentary committee before whom the plans for the new scheme were laid. The waterway was constructed on the level, without the aid of locks and, despite one heart-stopping moment, when the aqueduct was filled with water, the navigation went on to be an immense success, halving the price of coal in Manchester on the day it opened in 1761. Brindley's reputation was assured and, as a glance at the table commencing each waterway examined in the pages of this book will show, went on to build many more successful canals before his premature death in 1772, at the age of 56.

THE MIDLANDS

If the northwest saw the birth of the canal system, then it was the Midlands that provided the cradle for its growth. It was here that most of the waterways that went to make up the Grand Cross were developed and it was here that small and hitherto insignificant settlements grew into mighty manufacturing centres, purely through the transport network that these new navigations provided. Looked at logically, who would want to establish industries – reliant on a wide range of raw materials, many of them imported – in the centre of the country, well away from the ports, that would provide an outlet for their finished goods?

The intersection of Brindley's Grand Cross met at Fradley Junction, a little to the north of Birmingham and yet the wealth of minerals – coal, iron ore and limestone – were centred further south, largely around the area that we now know as the Black Country. On their own these waterways were not going to be effective in fuelling the industrial revolution in the Midlands so a 'feeder system' of canals evolved providing direct access to the mines, quarries, iron works and factories. In a short space of time, canal promoters glimpsed the possibility of shortening existing routes; of providing short sections of linking waterway

Farmer's Bridge Locks on the Birmingham Canal Navigations

Brindley statue in Coventry Basin

or providing new, direct routes altogether, these often developing on a piecemeal basis until finally becoming through routes linking major conurbations.

The Grand Union Canal typifies this form of development: a combination of at least eight separate waterways, it provided a direct and far less contorted passage to the Thames – and thence to London markets and the massive dock system for export – than Brindley's tortuous Oxford Canal with its strict adherence to a contour. Likewise the Worcester & Birmingham Canal provided

a more direct route into Birmingham from the River Severn and Bristol Docks and, in conjunction with what was to become the Shropshire Union Canal (now affectionately known as the Shroppie) meant that Cadbury's could now make their chocolate with the milk from the Cheshire dairy plains. The two waterways also guaranteed an uninterrupted supply of imported cocoa, whilst the Droitwich Canals – a further link between the River Severn and Birmingham – provided ready access to the salt used in the burgeoning food processing industry.

Undoubtedly of most significance to the industrial development of the Black Country and its establishment as a centre for manufacturing, was the construction of the Birmingham Canal, connected to the Staffordshire & Worcestershire Canal just to the west of Wolverhampton. This provided an early, direct link to the major ports of Bristol and Liverpool, running through the rich mineral areas flanking Birmingham and virtually passing the gates of many important factories. So busy did it become that Thomas Telford was soon to be commissioned to build a second, less convoluted navigation running parallel and operating in tandem with Brindley's original contour canal. Spurs, such as the Wyrley & Essington Canal, the Daw End Branch, the Walsall Canal, the Netherton Tunnel Branch and the Rushall Canal, were constructed off these two mainlines. Connections were made further afield to the north, to the Coventry Canal and at a second junction with the Staffordshire & Worcestershire Canal. The Birmingham & Fazeley Canal also connected the

Birmingham Canal Navigations – the BCN as they became collectively known – with the Coventry Canal and provided access to the rich coal deposits to the east.

By now a spider's web of canals (boasting more miles of navigable waterway than was to be found in Venice) had been established that, more than anything else, was to be instrumental in forging the Industrial Revolution. Just as the Trent & Mersey Canal enabled pottery production to expand further north in Stoke-on-Trent – centred as much on indigenous skill and enterprise as on a ready supply of essential raw materials – so the evolved waterways network of the Midlands ensured its place at the forefront of manufacture.

Great Haywood Junction

STAFFORDSHIRE & WORCESTERSHIRE CANAL

Construction of this navigation started immediately after that of the Trent & Mersey, to link the Rivers Trent, Mersey and Severn. After this, only the line down to the Thames was necessary to complete the skeleton outline of England's narrow-canal network thereby realising Brindley's Grand Cross. Engineered by James Brindley himself, the Staffordshire & Worcestershire Canal was opened throughout in 1772, at a cost of rather over £100,000 (£10 million today). It stretched 46 miles from Great Haywood on the Trent & Mersey to the River Severn, which it joined at what became the bustling canal town of Stourport.

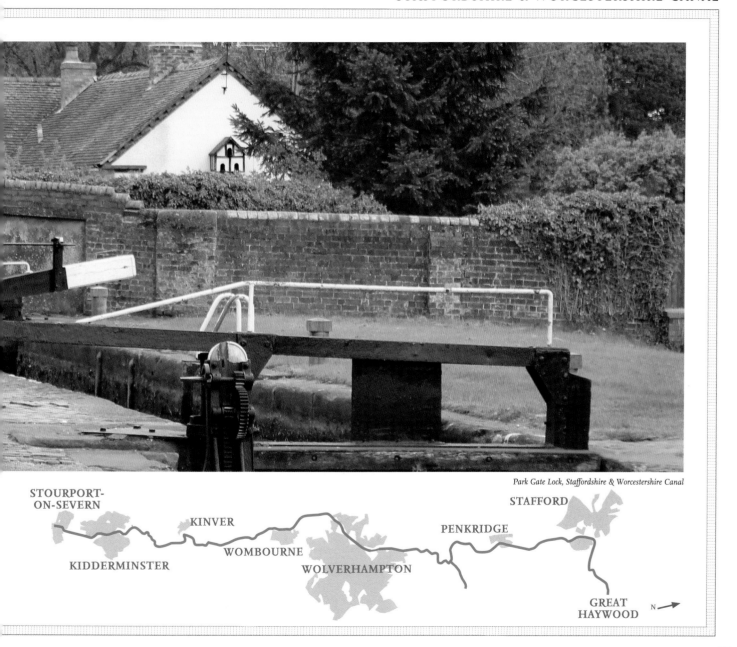

Park Gate Lock, Staffordshire & Worcestershire Canal

STOURPORT-
ON-SEVERN

KIDDERMINSTER

KINVER

WOMBOURNE

WOLVERHAMPTON

PENKRIDGE

STAFFORD

GREAT
HAYWOOD

N

BACKGROUND

The Staffordshire & Worcestershire Canal was an immediate success. It was well placed to bring goods from the Potteries down to Gloucester, Bristol and the West Country; while the Birmingham Canal, which joined it halfway along at Aldersley Junction, fed manufactured goods northwards from the Black Country to the Potteries via Great Haywood. Stourport has always been the focal point of the waterway, for the town owed its birth and rapid growth during the late 18th century to the advent of the canal. It was here that the cargoes were transferred from narrowboats into Severn Trows for shipment down the estuary to Bristol and the southwest.

However, the navigation soon found itself facing strong competition. In 1815 the Worcester & Birmingham Canal opened, offering a more direct but heavily locked canal link between Birmingham and the Severn. The Staffordshire & Worcestershire answered this threat by gradually extending the opening times of the locks, until by 1830 they were open 24 hours a day. When the Birmingham & Liverpool Junction Canal was opened from Autherley to Nantwich in 1835, boats bound for Merseyside from Birmingham naturally began to use this more direct, modern canal, and the Staffordshire & Worcestershire lost a great deal of traffic over its northern length: most of the traffic now passed along only the 1/2-mile stretch of the waterway between Autherley and Aldersley Junctions.

Stourport Basin, Staffordshire & Worcestershire Canal

This was, however, enough for the company, who levied absurdly high tolls for this tiny length.

In 1836 the Birmingham & Liverpool Junction Canal Company, therefore, cooperated with the Birmingham Canal Company to promote a Parliamentary Bill for the Tettenhall & Autherley Canal and aqueduct. This remarkable project was to be a canal flyover, going from the Birmingham Canal right over the profiteering Staffordshire & Worcestershire and locking down into the

Birmingham & Liverpool Junction Canal. In the face of this serious threat to bypass its canal altogether, the canal company gave way and reduced its tolls to a level acceptable to the other two companies. In spite of this setback, the Staffordshire & Worcestershire maintained a good profit, and high dividends were paid throughout the rest of the 19th century. When the new railway companies appeared in the West Midlands, the canal company would have nothing to do with them; but from the 1860s onwards railway competition began to bite, and the company's profits began to slip.

Like the other narrow canals, the Staffordshire & Worcestershire had faded into obscurity as a significant transport route by the middle of the 20th century, although the old canal company proudly retained total independence until it was nationalised in 1947. Today the canal is used for cruising by numerous pleasure craft and for walking and cycling.

AN 18TH-CENTURY VIEW OF STOURPORT

'About 1766, where the river Stour empties itself into the Severn below Mitton stood a little ale house called Stourmouth. Near this Brindley has caused a town to be erected, made a port and dockyards, built a new and elegant bridge, established markets and made it a wonder not only of this county but of the nation at large.'

Treadway Russell Nash, *Collections for the History of Worcestershire* (1782).

THE NAVIGATION

The Staffordshire & Worcestershire Canal is, without doubt, one of the prettiest and most interesting waterways in England. The locks and basins at Stourport are fascinating, having an intriguing combination of all kinds of engineering features and fine buildings, with the famous clock tower looking out over all. There are two sets of locks here, both narrow and broad. Beyond the basins the canal acquires a secluded, unspoilt character. Flanked by discreet houses and walls as it creeps through the town it soon emerges into the country. It follows the west side of a valley, the steep slopes rising sharply from the River Stour. Then the canal's surroundings change, the

hillside on the west bank becoming a dramatic cliff of crumbling red sandstone rising sheer from the canal. Falling Sands and Caldwall locks both enjoy delightful situations at the foot of these cliffs and both have split iron bridges of a type usually associated with the Stratford-on-Avon Canal.

The approach to Kidderminster has changed considerably – what was once an almost claustrophobic route between red-brick mills is now smart developments, with a broad towpath throughout. The cost is the disappearance of some visible canal history. Soon the navigation creeps under a roundabout at the centre of the town to emerge at Kidderminster Lock by the handsome church and wharf crane which overlook the moorings. Nearby is a statue of Richard Baxter, the 17th-century thinker who advocated unity and comprehension in religion.

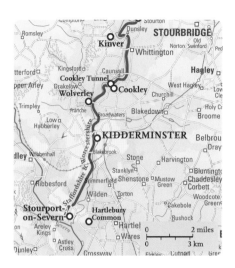

Chief engineer	James Brindley
Assisted by	John Baker, Thomas Dadford (senior), Hugh Henshall, Samuel Simcock.
Significance	Southwestern leg of the Grand Cross.
Started in	1766
Completed in	1772
Length	46 miles
Draught	2' 6"
Headroom	6' 0"
Lock size	72' × 7'
Number of locks	43
Tunnels	2
Aqueducts	5
Goods carried	Finished goods manufactured in the Midlands, raw materials imported into Gloucester and Liverpool, coal, steel, carpets.
Operating authority	Canal & River Trust
Contact details	enquiries.westmidlands @canalrivertrust.org.uk

SAILING DOWN THE SEVERN

It may come as something of a surprise to discover that the longest river in Britain – the River Severn – is so little used by commercial traffic, considering its size and proximity to the industrial Midlands. However, its width belies its depth which throughout history has always been somewhat unreliable. Above Stourport shoals and a rocky, shelving bed have always restricted regular traffic, making it difficult for barges to penetrate above Shrewsbury, into Wales. Downstream, between Tewkesbury and Gloucester, spring tides carry silt up from the estuary which is then trapped by the weirs on the East and West Partings, unable to return with the ebb. Consequently the depth of water is reduced by the silt, causing considerable problems for any commercial craft still determined to exploit this navigation's potential.

This situation is further exacerbated by the extraordinary performance of the Severn Bore: a spring tide *in extremis*. It forces hundreds of tons of unwanted material over the weirs demanding continuous dredging to reinstate the river's depth. Reputedly, one of its more bizarre victims was a 'Blue Peter' camera crew, whose boat was swamped when it was overtaken by the 6ft wave of the bore, whilst filming a surfer riding the bore. Boat and camera went to the bottom, as did plans for screening the event. However, the BBC reckoned without the combined forces of chance and a somewhat bewildered fisherman who, some several weeks later, contacted them with news of a most unusual catch.

THE NAVIGATION

Passing the isolated Wolverley Court Lock, the village of Wolverley on the other side of the valley is marked by its unusual Italianate church standing on a large outcrop of rock. Here the course of the canal becomes really tortuous and narrow as it proceeds up the enclosed and thickly wooded valley, forced into endless diversions by the steep cliffs of friable red sandstone. Vegetation of all kinds clings to these cliffs, giving the impression of jungle foliage. At one point the navigation opens out, becoming momentarily like a normal canal before an impressive promontory of rock compels the canal to double back on itself in a great horseshoe sweep that takes it round to the

Canalside crane at Kidderminster

pretty Debdale Lock. A doorway reveals a cavern cut into the solid rock here; this may have been used as an overnight stable for towing horses. The surroundings of this remarkable waterway do not change as it makes its way through secluded woodlands on its approach to Whittington Lock, the rocky hillside on the east bank steepening as the valley narrows again.

This stretch of the canal begins with yet another delightful scene – on both sides of the canal are cottages, pretty gardens, moored boats and a low bridge. Steep hills rising to over 250ft appear on the east bank. The canal leaves this damp, mossy area and bends round to Kinver Lock. Beyond the particularly pretty Hyde Lock, the canal wanders along the edge of woods on the east side of the valley, where in one place the sandstone, eroded away, is supported on brick pillars. The next lock is at Stewponey, accompanied by a toll house. The Stourbridge Canal leaves at Stourton Junction, north of the wharf: the first of the many locks that carry this canal up towards Dudley and the Birmingham Canal Navigations is just a few yards away. At the far end of the aqueduct over the River Stour is a curious narrowboat-house cut into the rock, known as the Devil's Den, while Prestwood Park is concealed in the woods above the east bank. Beyond the park the canal makes a remote journey through Gothersley and Rocky locks.

Now the outcrops of sandstone appear less frequently and the countryside becomes flatter and more regular. The locks, however, do not disappear, for the canal continues the steady rise up the small valley of the Smestow Brook, through southern Staffordshire towards Wolverhampton. At Greensforge Lock there is an attractive pub, and another of the circular weirs that are found, often hidden behind a wall or a hedge, at many of the locks along this delightful canal.

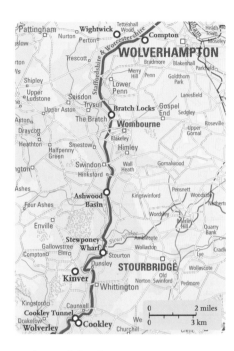

Another wooded, rocky section soon gives way to more open country. Passing through the isolated Hinksford Lock, the navigation bends round to Swindon where the canal is flanked by the tidy gardens of new houses. There are four locks hereabouts – Botterham Lock is a two-chamber staircase with a bridge crossing in the middle.

Now the canal begins to lose its rural character as it encounters the modern outskirts of Wombourne. Beyond is Bumblehole Lock followed by the three Bratch Locks, raising the canal level by over 30ft. From the top there is a good view back down the valley, with the spire of Wombourne Church backed by the great ridge of the Orton Hills to the east.

POINTS OF INTEREST

Stourport-on-Severn When the engineer James Brindley surveyed the line for the Staffordshire & Worcestershire Canal in the early 1760s, he chose to meet the River Severn at the hamlet of Lower Mitton, 4 miles downstream from Bewdley, where the little River Stour flowed into the Severn. Basins and locks were built for the boats, warehouses for the cargoes and cottages for the workmen. The hamlet soon earned the name of Stourport, becoming a busy and wealthy town. Much still remains of Stourport's former glory, for the basins are always full of moored boats, with plenty of other craft passing to and from the river.

Hartlebury Common To the east of Stourport. This is regarded by naturalists as one of the most important surviving areas of heathland in the West Midlands, recognised by the Nature Conservancy Council in 1955 and designated a SSSI. It covers an area of 216 acres rising to a height of 184ft, and consists mainly of dry lowland or scrub heath on river terraces of sand, over a bedrock of Triassic sandstone. There is a pond and marshy areas which support aquatic plants, dragonflies and frogs. Birds to look out for include long-tailed tits, tree pipits and stonechats. Plants to be seen include ling and bell heather, bogbean, marsh cinquefoil, heath milkwort and shepherd's purse.

Kidderminster The town once existed above all else for carpet weaving. The industry was first introduced in 1735, when the town was already a prosperous cloth manufacturing centre. Rowland Hill, founder of the Penny Post, was born here in 1793. His statue, in front of the main post office, commemorates his 'creative mind and patient energy'.

Wolverley A fascinating village on the west side of the Stour valley, once dedicated to the nail-making industry. The church stands on a sandstone rock so steep that the building has to be approached by a zigzag path cut through the constantly eroding stone. Many of the houses close by are partly carved from the rock, their dark back rooms actually caves. Most of the village is clustered just to the north of the church, near the little-used but dignified stone buildings of the Old Court House, which has also seen service as both a grammar school and council offices. The school was endowed in 1629, but most of the buildings date from 1820.

Church of St John the Baptist, Wolverley
A predominant dark red structure built in 1772 in a precise Italianate style, succeeding earlier churches which have stood on this site since Anglo-Saxon times. In legend the Lord of the Manor, a crusader called Attwood, was found in chains in the meadow, having been miraculously transported from a prison after seeing a vision of the Virgin Mary.

Cookley The village is set well above the canal, which passes underneath it in a tunnel. Although it has an attractive situation, Cookley remains a straightforward and workmanlike village. Down in the valley, near the River Stour, there are older, more attractive cottages, and clearly visible are the entrances to caves in the cliff face.

Cookley Tunnel This is 65yds long and is rough-hewn from the living rock. It is unusual, in having a towpath running through it, but this probably reflects the ease with which sandstone can be worked.

Kinver This settlement deservedly has a reputation as a very pretty village. It consists of a long main street of reasonably attractive houses, but its chief glory is its situation – it nestles among high wooded hills, a position that must strike the visitor as remarkable for a village so close to the industries of the west Midlands. Kinver Edge, west of the village, is a tremendous ridge covered in gorse and heather, providing a splendid view of the Cotswold and Malvern Hills. At nearby Holy Austin Rock (probably named after a long-departed Augustinian friar) rooms, windows, cupboards, doorways and chimneys are carved out of the cliffs. One of these houses, which from the inside appears just like normal dwellings (apart from a lack of windows) was in continuous occupation for 150 years until 1935.

Church of St Peter, Kinver Reached by a steep zigzag road, the church overlooks the village and contains several items of interest, including plaques recording the Charter granted by Charles I in 1629 and the Charter granted by Ethelbad in 736, giving '10 cessapis of land to my general Cyniberte for a religious house'.

Stewponey Wharf A fascinating wharf at the head of Stewponey Lock, with a restored octagonal toll office. From near the wharf the long-abandoned Kinver Valley Light Railway used to run from Stourbridge to Kinver following a route close to the canal. Just across the river from the wharf is the impressive bulk of Stourton Castle.

Stourton Castle This building is a curious mixture of building styles and materials and is notable as the birthplace of Cardinal Pole in 1500. A friend of Mary Tudor, Pole became Archbishop of Canterbury in her reign after Cranmer had been burned at the stake.

Ashwood Basin This used to be a railway-connected basin owned by the National Coal Board. After the line was closed the basin was disused for some years, but it has now been enlarged and provides a pleasant mooring site for a large number of pleasure boats in a private marina.

THE NAVIGATION

Leaving The Bratch, the canal wanders through open farmland before arriving at the pleasantly situated Awbridge Lock, accompanied by a fine circular weir.

Ahead, the hills of Wightwick overlook the navigation as it approaches a shallow valley and a busy main road. This valley – in places an artificial cutting – contains the canal right through to the flatter land at Aldersley. Compton Lock marks the end of the 31-lock climb from the River Severn at Stourport, a rise of 294ft. From here northwards, a 10-mile level pound takes the Staffordshire & Worcestershire on to Gailey, where the first of 12 locks begin the fall towards the Trent & Mersey Canal.

Autherley Junction is marked by a big white bridge on the towpath side where a stop lock just beyond marks the entrance to the Shropshire Union (or 'Shroppie' to use its more colloquial name). Leaving

Autherley, the Staffordshire & Worcestershire passes new housing before running through a very narrow cutting in rock, once known as 'Pendeford Rockin' after a local farm, where there is only room for boats to pass in designated places.

The considerable age of this canal is shown by its extremely twisting course, revealed after passing the railway bridge. At one point the canal widens just where Brindley incorporated part of a medieval moat into the canal. Hatherton Junction marks the entrance of the former Hatherton Branch of the Staffordshire & Worcestershire Canal into the main line which used to connect with the Birmingham Canal Navigations. A little further along, a chemical works is encountered, astride the canal in what used to be woodland. This was once called the 'Black Works', as lamp black was produced here.

Gailey Wharf is about a mile further north: it is a small canal settlement that includes a boatyard and a large, round, toll keeper's watch-tower. The canal itself disappears under Watling Street (Thomas Telford's A5 to the motorist) and then rapidly through five locks towards Penkridge. These locks are very attractive, and some are accompanied by little brick bridges. The M6 motorway, and the traffic noise, comes alongside for $1/2$ mile, screening the reservoirs which feed the canal.

THE SHROPPIE'S SURPRISING WATER SUPPLY

When first constructed the Shropshire Union Canal (the Shroppie) relied very heavily on Belvide Reservoir – beside the A5 – for its supplies of water. In its original form the reservoir proved woefully inadequate and its capacity was doubled in 1836 to give a total of 70 million cubic metres of water. Thirty-four years later Barnhurst Sewerage Farm opened at Autherley Junction and, when it later became a treatment works, its entire discharge became available to feed both the Shroppie and the Staffordshire & Worcestershire Canal. Today there is rarely a problem with water shortage on the Shroppie, which can largely be attributed to the regular habits of the good people of Wolverhampton.

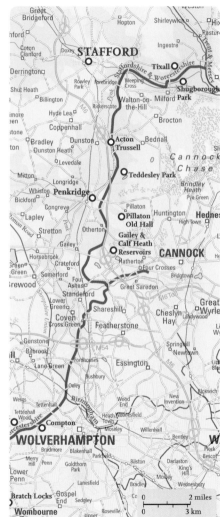

POINTS OF INTEREST

Bratch Locks With their octagonal toll office, attractive situation and unusual layout, these three locks are well known among students of canal engineering and architecture. At first sight they appear curiously illogical, with an impossibly short pound between the bottom of one lock and the top gate of the next; but the secret of their operation is the side ponds hidden behind the towpath hedge, and the culverts that connect these to the intermediate pounds.

Wightwick Pronounced Wittick, this was once a village but is now a suburb of Wolverhampton. There is a hill and plenty of trees, and in spite of the busy road it is a pleasant scene around the canal bridge and the pub.

Wightwick Manor Built between 1887 and 1893 for Theodore Mander, a paint and varnish maker, and designed by Edward Ould. The manor has an exterior that embodies many of the idiosyncrasies of the time. Inside, it is furnished with original wallpapers and fabrics by William Morris and various contributions by the Pre-Raphaelites. The drawing room is perhaps the most richly decorated, with a Jacobean-style ceiling, a 16th-century alabaster carved fireplace and William Morris Dove and Rose silk wall hangings. The Great Parlour is the main room of the house, and gives the impression of a Tudor hall, richly timbered and glowing with stained glass, tiles and porcelain. It contains what is considered to be the finest of Burne-Jones' later works *Love among the Ruins*. Other superb rooms include the kitchen and nursery. The beautiful 17-acre Edwardian gardens were laid out from plans by Alfred Parsons and Thomas Mawson drawn in 1904 and 1910.

Compton A busy village with a modern shopping centre, a pub, and a restaurant by the bridge. The canal lock here was the first that James Brindley built on the Staffordshire & Worcestershire Canal in the late 1760s, but unfortunately the cottage that accompanied it has been demolished.

St Mary & All Saints, Kidderminster

Gailey Wharf, Staffordshire & Worcestershire Canal

Gailey and Calf Heath Reservoirs Half-a-mile east of Gailey Wharf, either side of the M6. These are feeder reservoirs for the canal, though rarely drawn on. The public has access to them as nature reserves to study the wide variety of natural life, especially the long-established heronry which is thriving on an island in Gailey Lower Reservoir.

Pillaton Old Hall Only the gate house and stone-built chapel remain of this late 15th-century brick mansion built by the Littleton family, although there are still traces of the hall and courtyard. The chapel contains a 13th-century wooden carving of a saint.

THE NAVIGATION

Beyond Penkridge, continuing north along the shallow Penk valley, the canal soon reaches Radford Bridge, the nearest point to Stafford, where a branch used to connect with the town via Baswich Lock and the River Sow. The river is still crossed by the main line at Milford via an aqueduct – an early structure by James Brindley, carried heavily on low brick arches.

Entering Tixall Wide – noted for its kingfisher population – the canal now completes its journey to the Trent & Mersey Canal at Great Haywood. This is an amazing and delightful stretch of water – more lake than a canal – said to have been built in order not to compromise the view from Tixall House (alas, no more). Woods across the valley conceal Shugborough Hall while the River Trent is crossed on an aqueduct.

POINTS OF INTEREST

Penkridge The village is bisected by a trunk road, but luckily for the boater most of the village lies to the east of it. The church of St Michael is tall and sombre, and is well kept. A harmonious mixture of styles, the earliest part dates from the 11th century, but the whole was restored in 1881. There is a fine Dutch 18th-century wrought-iron screen brought from Cape Town, and the tower is believed to date from *c*.1500.

Teddesley Park On the east bank of the canal. The hall, once the family seat of the Littletons, was used during the Second World War as a prisoner of war camp, but has since been demolished. Its extensive wooded estate still remains.

Acton Trussell A village overwhelmed by modern housing: much the best way to see it is from the canal. The church stands to the south, overlooking the navigation. The west tower dates from the 13th century, topped by a spire built in 1562.

Stafford This town is well worth visiting, since there is a remarkable wealth of fine old buildings. These include a handsome City Hall complex of ornamental Italianate buildings, *c*.1880. The robust-looking jail is nearby; and the church of St Mary stands in very pleasing and spacious grounds.

Tixall Just to the east of the waterway, before its junction with the Trent & Mersey canal, are the stables and the gatehouse of the long-vanished Tixall Hall. This massive square Elizabethan building dates from 1598 and is fully four storeys high. It stands alone in a field and is considered to be one of the most ambitious gatehouses in the country.

Shugborough Hall The present house dates from 1693, but was substantially altered by James Stuart around 1760 and by Samuel Wyatt around the turn of the 18th century. The National Trust has restored the house at great expense and there are some magnificent rooms and treasures inside.

Shugborough Park There are some remarkable sights in the large park that encircles the hall. Thomas Anson, who inherited the estate in 1720, enlisted in 1744 the help of his famous brother, Admiral George Anson, to beautify and improve the house and the park. In 1762 he commissioned James Stuart, a neo-Grecian architect, to embellish the grounds. 'Athenian' Stuart set to with a will, and the spectacular results of his work can be seen scattered round the landscape.

The Park Farm Within Shugborough Park. Designed by Samuel Wyatt, it contains an agricultural museum, a working mill and a rare breeds centre. Traditional country skills such as bread-making, butter-churning and cheese-making are demonstrated.

Bridge at junction of the Staffordshire & Worcestershire Canal with the River Severn

While the Bridgewater Canal (*see* page 138) can justifiably be said to have kick-started canal building in Britain, it was not the first man-made navigable waterway to be constructed in the 18th century. That accolade can be shared jointly by the Newry Canal, in Northern Ireland, and the Sankey Brook Canal, often known as the St Helens Canal after the major town that it serves.

As early as the 12th century in Ireland waterways were built, aimed at improving links between the country's lakes and rivers. Attempts to improve navigation along Lough Corrib date from 1178, with the building of the Friars' Cut, while in the 17th century various schemes to connect the major rivers were mooted: these had to await the ending of hostilities between James ll and William lll before being realised as a means of promoting economic growth within the country.

The rapid development of Dublin, at the beginning of the 18th century, led to the commensurate increase in demand for coal which, at that time, was shipped in from Britain. Large supplies were available much closer to home in the East Tyrone coalfields, accessible via Lough Neagh, a connecting canal to the sea at Newry and thence down the coast to the city.

Motor barge W. E. Burton *and dumb barges at Alder Root Bridge on St Helens Canal, 1954*

Work on the canal section commenced in 1731, initiated by Edward Pearce, a Dublin architect who had been appointed Surveyor General the previous year. Richard Castle, a French refugee and student of continental waterway construction, subsequently took over from his employer as engineer and, upon his dismissal, was in turn succeeded by Thomas Steers from Liverpool.

The finished navigation was initially 18 miles long (a distance later increased with the construction of a further section of canal, completed in 1769, bypassing a difficult stretch of river approaching Newry), 5ft deep, with fourteen 44ft by 15ft 6in locks, able to take

craft of up to 120 tons. It was a success from the outset and continued until the 1930s when railway competition forced its closure. Its main engineer, Thomas Steers, was also responsible for constructing Liverpool's first docks, engineering the Mersey and Irwell Navigation and for improvement works on the Rivers Douglas and Weaver. His pupil, Henry Berry, was the engineer in charge of constructing the St Helens Canal.

Completed in 1757, two years before the granting of the first Act of Parliament to facilitate the Bridgewater Canal, the original Sankey Navigation linked collieries at Parr and Haydock to the River Irwell at Warrington. Later known as the

Winwick Depot swing bridge on St Helens Canal, 1954

St Helens Canal, as branches extended westwards into the town, the waterway was promoted as a 'river' navigation: an artificial cut being considered too radical a concept at the time. In reality Berry, in conjunction with John Ashton – the principal shareholder – surreptitiously constructed an entirely separate canal alongside the Sankey Brook with broad locks (the first to employ the staircase principle – *see* Milepost 4) built to accommodate traditional Mersey 'flats'. Subsequent extensions further enhanced its success as a navigation, carrying coal for export and bringing in raw materials for the burgeoning local chemical industries, especially glass making, centred on St Helens.

Waddell's Lock, near Gamble's Bridge on the Newry Canal

TRENT & MERSEY CANAL

This early canal was originally conceived, in part, as a roundabout link between the ports of Liverpool and Hull, while passing through the busy area of the Potteries and mid-Cheshire, terminating either in the River Weaver or in the Mersey. One of its prime movers was the famous potter Josiah Wedgwood (1730–95). Like the Duke of Bridgewater a few years previously, he saw the obvious, enormous advantages to his – and others' – industry of cheap, safe and rapid transport which a navigation would offer compared with packhorse carriage (the only alternative then available).

Shardlow on the Trent & Mersey Canal

NORTHWICH

MIDDLEWICH

STOKE-ON-TRENT

NEWCASTLE-UNDER-LYME

STONE

RUGELEY

N

RUGELEY

ALREWAS

BURTON UPON TRENT

CASTLE DONINGTON

LONG EATON

N

BACKGROUND

Josiah Wedgwood was greatly assisted in the promotion of the canal by his friends, notably Thomas Bentley and Erasmus Darwin – grandfather of Charles Darwin. Pamphlets were published, influential support was marshalled and in 1766 the Trent & Mersey Canal Act was passed by Parliament, authorising the building of a navigation from the River Trent at Shardlow to Runcorn Gap, where it would join the proposed extension of the Bridgewater Canal from Manchester.

The ageing James Brindley was appointed engineer for the new waterway. Construction began at once and much public interest was excited in this remarkable project, especially in the great 2,900yd tunnel under Harecastle Hill.

Once opened in 1777 the Trent & Mersey Canal was a great success, attracting much trade in all kinds of commodities. Vast tonnages of china clay and flints for the pottery industry were brought by sea from Devon and Cornwall, then transhipped into canal craft on the Mersey and brought straight to the factories around Burslem, taking finished goods away again. Everyone near the waterway benefited: much lower freight charges meant cheaper goods, healthier industries and more jobs. Agriculture gained greatly from the new supply of water and from stable manure and night soil from the towns and cities.

The Trent & Mersey soon earned its other name (suggested by Brindley) as the Grand Trunk Canal – in the 93 miles between Derwent Mouth and Preston Brook, the navigation gained connections with no fewer than nine other canals or significant branches.

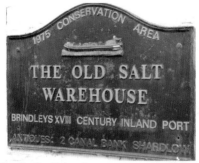

Now Shardlow Heritage Centre

By the 1820s the Trent & Mersey was so busy that the narrow and slowly-sinking tunnel at Harecastle had become a serious bottle-neck for traffic. Thomas Telford was called in: he recommended building a second tunnel beside Brindley's old one. His recommendation was eventually accepted by the company and, in a tremendous burst of energy, the whole tunnel was completed in under three years, in 1827. A much needed towpath (since removed) was also incorporated into this new construction.

Although the Trent & Mersey was taken over in 1845 by the new North Staffordshire Railway Company, the canal flourished until the First World War as a most important trading route. Today there is no trade at all along the canal but it is assured by statute of a future as a pleasure cruising waterway.

There used to be four tunnels in total on the Trent & Mersey apart from the pair at Harecastle. One of these was at Armitage, a 130-yd bore through solid rock. However mining subsidence (the *bête noir* of many industrial waterways) began to affect the tunnel and during 1971–2 it was opened out and a bridge built to carry the main A513 road that crosses at this point.

Bridge 51, Fradley Junction

THE NAVIGATION

The Trent & Mersey Canal begins at Derwent Mouth, some 2$\frac{1}{2}$ miles upstream of the point where the Soar Navigation enters the River Trent at the somewhat complicated waterways junction of Trent Lock. The Trent itself is navigable to Cavendish Bridge, on the outskirts of Shardlow and the 1758 tolls are engraved on a plaque on the bridge – it was washed away in the floods in 1947, and was re-erected in 1960. The first lock on the Trent & Mersey is Derwent Mouth Lock, to the east of Shardlow, one of the most interesting inland canal ports on the whole inland waterway network.

Beyond is the village of Weston-on-Trent, near Weston Lock, where the wooden lock balance beams of the bottom gates, impeded by the bridge, are of necessity short; but they are

LORD BYRON'S UNUSUAL GIFT

The Derby Canal, which left the Trent & Mersey at Swarkestone and joined the River Erewash at Sandiacre, has long been disused. One condition of its building, and a constant drain on its profits, was the free carriage of 5,000 tons of coal to Derby each year, for the use of the poor.

One of the most unusual loads was transported on 19 April 1826, when 'a fine lama, a kangaroo, a ram with four horns, and a female goat with two young kids, remarkably handsome animals' arrived in Derby by canal 'as a present from Lord Byron to a Gentleman whose residence is in the neighbourhood, all of which had been picked up in the course of the voyage of the *Blonde* to the Sandwich Islands in the autumn of 1824'.

Chief engineer	James Brindley
Assisted by	Hugh Henshall
Significance	Northwestern leg of the Grand Cross.
Started in	1766
Completed in	1777
Length	93 miles
Headroom	Varies between 5'9" and 7'
Lock size	Varies between 72' × 14' and 72' × 7'
Number of locks	74
Tunnels	5
Aqueducts	4
Goods carried	Pottery, salt, stone, coal, china clay, flints, iron ore, agricultural lime and manure.
Operating authority	Canal & River Trust
Contact details	enquiries.centralshires @canalrivertrust.org.uk

massively wide. The church and the rectory stand to the north of the village, on a hill with a fine view of the Trent valley.

Leaving Weston, the canal continues along the Trent valley, with low hills to the north and the river, at times very close, to the south. At Swarkestone Lock there is a short arm, used for moorings: this is all that presently remains of the Derby Canal at this end although restoration plans are well advanced. The lock here is very deep, with a fall of almost 11ft. As with the other deep locks, it has very low top gates which incorporate substantial paddles. The village of Barrow upon Trent lies between the canal and the river – the countryside is green and pleasant, with only the occasional train rumbling by to disturb the peace.

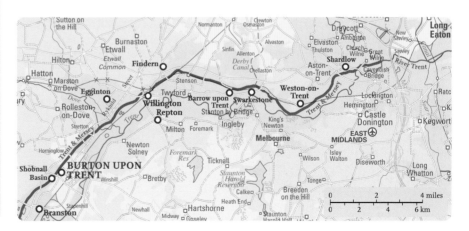

THE NAVIGATION

West of Barrow upon Trent lies Arleston House, an attractive old building with ground-floor walls of stone and the upper tiers of brick. This is followed by Stenson Lock, the last of the wide locks until Middlewich – it has a massive fall of 12ft 4in. Stenson itself is a small farming centre and a popular mooring spot with a large marina. After passing under a railway bridge, the canal changes course and heads off in a southeasterly direction towards Burton upon Trent. The village of Findern is up on a hill to the north. A twelve-arch stone aqueduct carries the canal over the River Dove, beside a handsome four-arch bridge, no longer in use.

The canal then passes along one side of Burton upon Trent, without entering the town. Many of the old canalside buildings have been demolished, but the waterside has been nicely tidied up, making the passage very pleasant. The lovely aroma of brewing – malt and hops – often pervades the town, usually strongest to the west. Dallow Lock is the first of the narrow locks, an altogether easier job of work than the wider ones to the east. The A38 now joins the canal, depriving the would be navigator of any peace. On the hills to the northwest is the well-wooded Sinai Park – the moated 15th-century house here, now a farm, used to be the summer home of the monks from Burton Abbey.

After passing flooded gravel pits and negotiating another tiny brick arch bridge on the approach to Barton-under-Needwood, the canal and the A38, the old Roman road, come very close together – thankfully the settlement of Barton Turn has been bypassed, leaving the main street (the old Roman road of Ryknild Street) wide and empty. It is with great relief that Wychnor Lock, with its diminutive crane and warehouse, is reached – here the A38 finally parts company with the canal, and some

The Clock Warehouse, Shardlow

peace returns. To the west is the little 14th-century Wychnor church. Before Alrewas Lock the canal actually joins the River Trent – there is a large well-marked weir which should be given a wide berth. The canal then winds through the pretty village of Alrewas, passing the old church, several thatched cottages and a charming brick bridge.

The navigation now enters open country at Fradley, and soon reaches its junction with the Coventry Canal. This is an attractive and busy place, with a handsome and famous canal pub, a nature reserve, a boatyard and many moored and interesting craft in the midst of a small flight of locks. Popular with photographers, there are often many gongoozlers (spectators) here, so it is worth ensuring that your lock-operating technique is up to scratch! Leaving all the activity behind, the canal soon enters quiet countryside, climbing through wooded heathland and abruptly changing its course from southwest to northwest, a direction it generally maintains right through to its terminus at Preston Brook, over 67 miles away. The isolated Woodend Lock introduces a further stretch of woodland; beyond this the canal winds towards Handsacre. Armitage soon follows as the railway crosses and the Trent comes very close.

POINTS OF INTEREST

Shardlow Few canal travellers will want to pass through Shardlow without stopping. Everywhere there are examples of large-scale canal architecture, as well as long-established necessities such as canal pubs. By the lock is the biggest and best of these buildings – the 18th-century Trent Mill, now the Clock Warehouse. Restored in 1979, it has a large central arch where boats once entered to unload.

Weston-on-Trent A scattered village that is in fact not very close to the Trent at all! The isolated church is splendidly situated beside woods on top of a hill, its sturdy tower crowned by a short 14th-century spire. Inside are fine aisle windows of the same period. The lock gardens make the approach from the canal particularly attractive.

Swarkestone The main feature of Swarkestone is the 18th-century five-arch stone bridge over the main channel of the River Trent. An elevated causeway then carries the road on stone arches all the way across the Trent's flood plain to the village of Stanton by Bridge. It was at Swarkestone that Bonnie Prince Charlie, in the rising of 1745, gave up his attempt for the throne of England and returned to Scotland and his defeat at Culloden. In a field nearby are the few remains of Sir Richard Harpur's Tudor mansion, which was demolished before 1750. The Summer House, a handsome, lonely building, overlooks a square enclosure called the Cuttle. Jacobean in origin, it is thought that it may have been the scene of bull-baiting, although it seems more likely it was just a 'bowle alley'. The Harpurs moved to Calke following the demolition of their mansion after the Civil War. The pub in the village, and monuments in the church, which is tucked away in the back lanes, are a reminder of the family.

Barrow upon Trent A small, quiet village set back from the canal. A lane from the church leads down to the River Trent. Opposite there is a 'pinfold', once an enclosure for stray animals. The surviving lodge house stands opposite a mellow terrace of old workmen's cottages.

Repton One-and-a-half miles southeast of Willington (over the River Trent) is Repton, one of the oldest towns in England, which was once the capital of Mercia. The crypt below St Wystan's Church was built in the 10th century. One of the finest examples of Saxon architecture in the country, this crypt was completely forgotten until the end of the 18th century when a man fell into it while digging a grave. Repton public school dates from 1557, and there is much of historical interest in the school and the town.

Willington The railway bisects this busy little village on an embankment. There are several pubs, all close together.

Findern A small, quiet village where Jedekiah Strutt, the inventor of the ribbed stocking frame, served a seven-year apprenticeship with the local

Shardlow Lock

wheelwright. At one time the village green was no more than a waste patch used by cars as a short cut, and a parking place. When suggestions were made to turn it into a formal crossroads, the indignant Women's Institute galvanised the villagers into actually uprooting all traces of tarmac from the green and turfing the whole area properly.

Egginton A quiet village lying off the A38. The church, set apart from the village, is pleasingly irregular from the outside, with a large chancel and a squat tower.

Burton upon Trent Known widely for its brewing industry, which originated here in the 13th century, when the monks at Burton Abbey discovered that an excellent beer could be brewed from the town's waters, because of their high gypsum content. At one time there were thirty-one breweries producing three million barrels of ale annually: alas, now only a few remain. The advent of the railways had an enormous effect on the street geography of Burton, as gradually a great network of railways took shape, connecting with each other and with the main line. These branches were mostly constructed at street level, and until recent years it was common for road traffic to be held up by endless goods trains chugging all over the town. Only the last vestiges of this system now remain. The east side of the town is bounded by the River Trent, on the other side of which are pleasant hills.

Shobnall Basin This is all that remains of the Bond End Canal, which gave the breweries the benefit of what was modern transport, before the coming of the railways.

Branston This is apparently the place where the famous pickle originated.

THE NAVIGATION

The A513 crosses the canal on a new bridge where the short, 130-yds long, Armitage Tunnel used to run before its roof was removed in 1971 to combat the subsidence effects of coal being mined nearby. To the west stands Spode House, a former home of the pottery family. The huge power station at Rugeley, tidied up now, comes into view – and takes a long time to recede. North of the town, the canal crosses the River Trent via a substantial aqueduct. It then enters an immensely attractive area full of interest. Accompanied by the River Trent, the canal moves up a narrowing valley bordered by green slopes on either side, Cannock Chase being clearly visible to the south. Wolseley Hall has gone, but Bishton Hall (now a wedding venue) still stands: its elegant front faces the canal near Wolseley Bridge.

The pleasant surroundings continue as the canal passes Colwich. As the perimeter of Shugborough Park is reached the impressive façade of the hall can be seen across the parkland. Haywood Lock and a line of moored craft announce the presence of Great Haywood and the junction with the Staffordshire & Worcestershire Canal (*see* page 16), which joins the Trent & Mersey under a graceful and much photographed towpath bridge. Beyond the junction the Trent valley becomes much broader and more open.

The canal now leaves behind the excitement and interest of Great Haywood to continue its quiet northwesterly passage through a broad valley towards Stone and Stoke-on-Trent. Hoo Mill Lock is a busy spot with many moored boats, and a busy boatyard. North of the lock a main road joins the hitherto quiet canal for a while. To the west is Ingestre Hall: beyond here the locks are broadly spaced and, although roads are never far away, the atmosphere is one of remoteness and peace.

The wooded Sandon Park rises steeply on the north bank as the canal continues in a northwesterly direction, passing through quiet meadows to the little village of Burston. The 100-year-old tower of Aston Church is prominent as the canal passes through the quiet water meadows of the Trent valley. Soon Stone is entered and the locks are somewhat deeper than most on the narrow canals – their average rise is about 10ft. Just above the second lock there is a boatyard and three dry docks: there is another boatyard a few yards further on. Look out for the sculpture of 'Christina' by the bridge. Lock 29 is accompanied by a little tunnel under the road for boat horses, and there are towline rollers at the bridge by lock 30. Stone justifiably calls itself 'a canal town'.

Canal wharf, Stone, with offices of the Trent & Mersey Canal Co. in the background, c.1920

POINTS OF INTEREST

Barton-under-Needwood Many years ago, when there were few roads and no canals in the Midlands, the only reasonable access to this village was by turning off the old Roman road, Ryknild Street: hence, probably, the name Barton Turn. The village is indeed worth turning off for, although unfortunately it is nearly a mile from the canal. A pleasant footpath from Barton Turn Lock leads quietly to the village, which is set on a slight hill. Its long main street has several attractive pubs. The church is battlemented and surrounded by a very tidy churchyard. Pleasantly uniform in style, it was built in the 16th century by John Taylor, Henry VIII's private secretary, on the site of his cottage birthplace. The former Royal Forest of Needwood is to the north of the village.

Wychnor A tiny farming settlement around the church of St Leonards.

Alrewas Just far enough away from the A513, this is an attractive village whose rambling back lanes harbour some excellent timbered cottages. The canal's meandering passage through the village, passing well-tended gardens and a bowling green, and the presence of the church and its pleasant churchyard creates a friendly and unruffled atmosphere. The River Trent touches the village, and once fed the old Cotton Mill (now converted into dwellings), and provides it with a fine background which is much appreciated by fishermen. The somewhat unusual name Alrewas, pronounced 'olrewus', is a corruption of the words Alder Wash – a reference to the many alder trees which once grew in the often-flooded Trent valley and gave rise to the basket weaving for which the village was once famous.

Alrewas Church Mill A spacious building of mainly 13th-century and 14th-century construction,

Bridges at Great Haywood in the 1950s

notable for the old leper window, which is now filled by modern stained glass.

Fradley Junction A long-established canal centre where the Coventry Canal joins the Trent & Mersey. Like all the best focal points on the waterways, it is concerned solely with the life of the canals, and has no relationship with local roads or even with the village of Fradley. The junction bristles with boats as, apart from it being an inevitable meeting place for canal craft, it offers a peaceful mooring spot. Fradley Pool Nature Reserve, teeming with wildlife, is nearby.

King's Bromley There are some pleasant houses and an old mill to be seen here, as well as what is reputed to have been Lady Godiva's early home. The Trent flows just beyond the church, which contains some old stained glass windows. A large cross in the southern part of the churchyard is known locally as Godiva's cross.

Armitage A main road village, whose church is interesting: it was rebuilt in the 19th century in a Saxon/Norman style, which makes it rather dark. The organ is 200 years old and it is enormous: it came from Lichfield Cathedral.

THE NAVIGATION

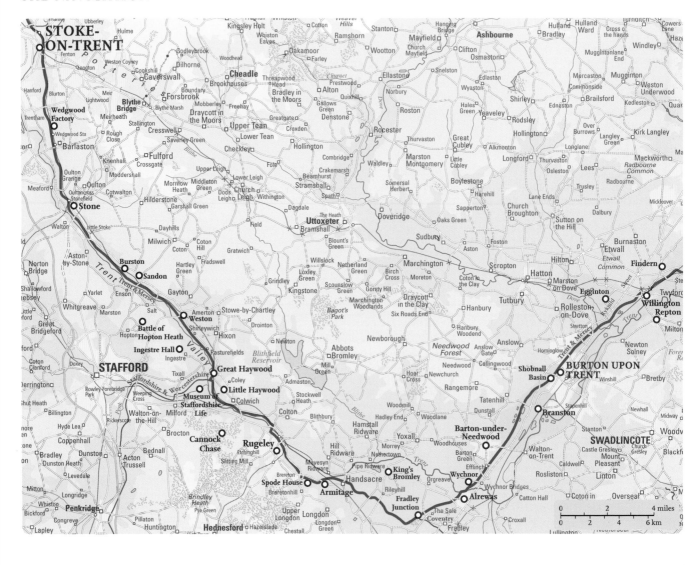

POINTS OF INTEREST

Spode House Spode House and Hawkesyard Priory stand side by side. The priory was founded in 1897 by Josiah Spode's grandson and his niece Helen Gulson when they lived at Spode House. The priory is now known as Hawkesyard Hall, and is a restaurant and spa.

Rugeley A bustling and much redeveloped town, with many shops at the centre. There are two churches by the canal bridge; one is a 14th-century ruin, the other is the parish church built in 1822 as a replacement.

Cannock Chase Covering an area of 26 square miles, and designated as an Area of Outstanding Natural Beauty in 1949, the Chase is all that remains of what was once a Norman hunting ground known as the King's Forest of Cannock. Large parts are recognised as Sites of Special Scientific Interest, and exceptional flora and fauna are abundant. This includes a herd of fallow deer whose ancestors have grazed in this region for centuries. An area of 4½ square miles forms a Country Park, one of the largest in Britain. Near the Sherlock Valley an area was chosen in 1964 as the site of the *Deutscher Soldatenfriedhof*, and was built by the German War Graves Commission. It contains the graves of 2,143 German servicemen from the First World War, and 2,786 from the Second World War. It is an intentionally sombre place. A small area is devoted to the crews of German airships, shot down over the UK in 1916 and 1917.

Little Haywood An elegant residential village with a shop and a pub.

Great Haywood Centre of the Great Haywood and Shugborough Conservation Area, the village is not particularly beautiful, but it is closely connected in many ways to Shugborough Park, to which it is physically linked by the very old Essex Bridge, where the crystal clear waters of the River Sow join the Trent on its way down from Stoke. Haywood Lock is beautifully situated between this packhorse bridge (which is an ancient monument) and the unusually decorative railway bridge that leads into Trent Lane. The lane consists of completely symmetrical and very handsome terraced cottages: they were built by the Ansons to house the people evicted from the former Shugborough village, the site of which is now occupied by the Arch of Hadrian within the park, built to celebrate Anson's circumnavigation of the globe in 1740–4. About 100yds south of Haywood Lock is an iron bridge over the canal. This bridge, which now leads nowhere, used to carry a private road from Shugborough Hall (*see* page 24) which crossed both the river and the canal on its way to the church just east of the railway. This was important to the Ansons, since the packhorse bridge just upstream is not wide enough for a horse and carriage, and so until the iron bridge was built the family had to walk the 300yds to church on Sunday mornings!

Museum of Staffordshire Life This excellent establishment, Staffordshire's County Museum, is housed in the old stables adjacent to Shugborough Hall. Open since 1966, it is superbly laid out and contains all sorts of exhibits concerned with old country life in Staffordshire. Amongst many things it contains an old-fashioned laundry, the old gun-room and the old estate brew-house, all completely equipped. Part of the stables contains harness, carts, coaches and motor cars. There is an industrial annexe up the road, containing a collection of preserved steam locomotives and some industrial machinery.

Ingestre Hall Originally a Tudor building and a former home of the Earls of Shrewsbury, the hall was rebuilt in neo-Gothic style following a fire in 1820. It is surrounded by large attractive gardens, and is now a residential arts centre.

Battle of Hopton Heath An inconclusive Civil War battle fought on 19 March 1643 1½ miles west of Weston. Supported by Roaring Meg – a 29-pound cannon – the Royalists took the initiative, making several bold and effective cavalry charges against the Roundheads. However, the Roundheads' musketry fought back strongly, and after the Royalist leader (the Earl of Northampton) was killed, the Cavaliers weakened and fell back. Eventually both sides were exhausted and nightfall brought an end to the battle. Casualties – at under 200 – were surprisingly light, and neither side could claim victory.

Classic British Waterways van at Fradley Junction

THE NAVIGATION

Stone Locks are soon followed by another flight of four, climbing up the valley to Meaford. The present Meaford Locks replaced an earlier staircase of three, the remains of which can be seen by lock 33. Here the railway line draws alongside, while the valley widens out and becomes flatter and less rural. The railway continues to flank the canal as it approaches the straggling village of Barlaston. Just before Trentham Lock, where there are good moorings, is the Wedgwood Pottery, set back from the canal. The factory is conveniently served by Wedgwood Halt.

Barnton Tunnel, Trent & Mersey Canal

ROLLING QUIETLY ALONG

Perhaps the philosophy, inherent in the travel and general purchasing arrangements, of a couple wending their way home along the Trent & Mersey might reward further study by all of us who travel in faster and more polluting ways in order to satisfy our perceived needs.

We met this retired couple whilst working our respective ways through a particularly recalcitrant flight of locks. They described how they were returning from a trip to Chester which they had just visited with the express purpose of buying a new carpet for their Midlands home. The shopping spree had been eminently successful as witnessed by the polythene clad roll, stretched out below, between the galley and the saloon. There were three days left, of their two-week round trip to run, before carpet and living room were to make their first acquaintance.

When canals first arrived, they did revolutionise the distribution of goods and there were no doubt some who felt that the human and environmental costs were too high. However, the stakes have much increased since then. We now take for granted our right to use the most rapid and polluting means of transport to fly us around the globe. We demand the same choice of food be freshly available on supermarket shelves the whole year round and are unhappy when nature intervenes to shake our expectations. Maybe the fault lies not with nature itself but with our demands of it. It could be that our couple had found a more caring and environmentally-friendly way to lead their lives.

This is a fascinating length of canal, not always (if ever) beautiful but all extremely interesting, passing right through the centre of Stoke-on-Trent, where all was once factories and warehouses – but which are now being rebuilt. Signs of the pottery industry still survive, its most remarkable manifestation being the bottle kilns – the brick furnaces shaped like gigantic bottles about 30ft high that still stand, cold and disused (but, happily, to be preserved), at the side of the canal. The Caldon Canal leaves the main line just above Stoke Top Lock. A statue of James Brindley, who built the Trent & Mersey Canal, stands near the junction. The Trent & Mersey then passes a marina and a pub, built for the National Garden Festival, before heading towards the south portal of the great Harecastle Tunnel. The Roundhouse, the very last remains of the original Wedgwood factory built in 1769, is easily missed – it stands beside the canal bridge.

North of Stoke, the canal swings past what was once the junction with the old Burslem Arm (which headed north for about a 1/4 of a mile and is, hopefully, to be restored) and continues through the flattened remains of an industrial area, before reaching the weathered and evocative red-brick and slate buildings of the Middleport Pottery, with kilns, cranes and cobbles right beside the canal. Before long the navigation passes the open expanse of Westport Park Lake, popular with fishermen, and finally abandons its very twisting course to make a beeline for Harecastle Hill and the famous 2,926yd tunnel.

POINTS OF INTEREST

Weston A regular entrant of Best Kept Village competitions. A pretty village of cottages and new houses, stretching away from St Andrew's church.

Sandon A small estate village clustered near the main gates to Sandon Park. The main road bisecting the place is enough to send any canal boatman scurrying back to the safety of the relative peace and quiet of Sandon Lock.

Burston A hamlet apparently untouched by modern times, in spite of the proximity of three transport routes. Most of the village is set around the village pond. A surprisingly quiet place.

Stone A very busy and pleasant town with strong canal associations, and excellent boating and shopping facilities. The old priory church began to fall down in 1749, so in 1753 an Act of Parliament was obtained to enable the parishioners to rebuild it. The canalside is splendid, with dry docks, wharves and the impressive old Joules brewery buildings having a timeless air. There are always interesting craft to admire.

Wedgwood Factory The pottery firm Josiah Wedgwood and Sons was founded in May 1759, in Burslem, Stoke-on Trent, by the famous Josiah Wedgwood, the Father of English Potters, who came from a small pottery family. By 1766 he was sufficiently prosperous to build a large new house and factory, near Barlaston to the south of Stoke-on-Trent, which he called Etruria – a name suggested by his close friend Dr Erasmus Darwin – and to use the canal, of which he was a promoter, for transport. It was here that he produced his famous Jasper unglazed stoneware with white classical portraits on the surface. He revolutionised pottery-making with his many innovations and after his death in 1795 the company continued to expand. In the 1930s the Wedgwoods decided to build a new factory because mining subsidence had made Etruria unsuitable. The Etruria factory has unfortunately since been demolished but the large new factory began production in 1940 in Barlaston. The factory had six electric tunnel ovens which produced none of the industrial smoke that is commonly associated with the Potteries. The Wedgwood Museum at Barlaston, only a few yards from the canal, has a vast range of exhibits of Wedgwood pottery.

Stoke-on-Trent The city was formed in 1910 from a federation of six towns (Burslem, Fenton, Hanley, Longton, Stoke and Tunstall) but became known as the Five Towns in the novels of Arnold Bennett. The thriving pottery industries are the source of the city's great prosperity. The town hall, in Glebe Street, is an imposing and formal 19th-century building. Opposite the town hall is the parish church of St Peter, which contains a commemorative plaque to Josiah Wedgwood. Festival Park has been built on the site of the old Shelton Steelworks, with a dry ski slope.

Bridges at Great Haywood, 2010

THE NAVIGATION

At the north end of Harecastle Tunnel the navigation passes through Kidsgrove, while beyond is Harding's Wood and the junction with the Macclesfield Canal which, almost immediately, swings back across the Trent & Mersey on Poole Aqueduct. The canal continues to fall through a heavily locked stretch sometimes called 'heartbreak hill' but known simply to the old boatmen as the 'Cheshire Locks'. Two minor aqueducts are encountered, and most of the locks are narrow pairs – the chambers side by side.

The canal now descends the Wheelock flight of eight locks, which are the last paired locks one sees when travelling northwards. The countryside continues to be quiet and unspoilt but unspectacular. The pair of locks half-way down the flight is situated in the little settlement

Boats at Shardlow

Tunnel tug and battery boat waiting to enter the Harecastle Tunnel at Kidsgrove in the 1930s. Both Brindley's and Telford's entrances can be seen.

of Malkin's Bank, overlooked by terraced houses. The boatman's co-op used to be here, in the small terrace of cottages. The adjoining boatyard now specialises in the restoration of traditional working boats. At the bottom of the flight is the village of Wheelock; west of here the navigation curls round the side of a hill before entering the long-established salt-producing area that is based on Middlewich. The 'wild' brine pumping and rock-salt mining that has gone on hereabouts has resulted in severe local subsidence; the effect on the waterway has been to necessitate the constant raising of the banks as lengths of the canal bed sink. This of course means that the affected lengths tend to be much deeper than on ordinary canals making it no place for the non-swimmer. The navigation now begins to lose the rural character it has enjoyed since Kidsgrove. Falling through yet more locks, the waterway is joined by a busy main road which accompanies it into an increasingly flat and industrialised landscape, past several salt works and into Middlewich, where a branch of the Shropshire Union leads off westwards towards that canal at Barbridge. The first 100yds or so of this branch is the Wardle Canal, claimed to be the shortest canal in the country.

POINTS OF INTEREST

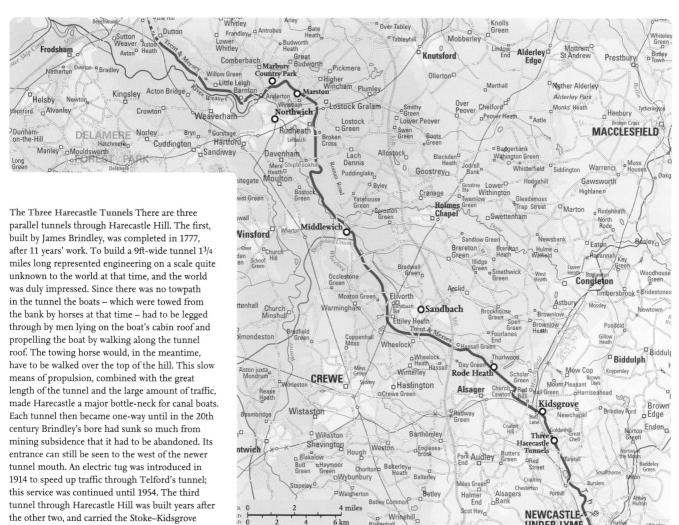

The Three Harecastle Tunnels There are three parallel tunnels through Harecastle Hill. The first, built by James Brindley, was completed in 1777, after 11 years' work. To build a 9ft-wide tunnel 1³/4 miles long represented engineering on a scale quite unknown to the world at that time, and the world was duly impressed. Since there was no towpath in the tunnel the boats – which were towed from the bank by horses at that time – had to be legged through by men lying on the boat's cabin roof and propelling the boat by walking along the tunnel roof. The towing horse would, in the meantime, have to be walked over the top of the hill. This slow means of propulsion, combined with the great length of the tunnel and the large amount of traffic, made Harecastle a major bottle-neck for canal boats. Each tunnel then became one-way until in the 20th century Brindley's bore had sunk so much from mining subsidence that it had to be abandoned. Its entrance can still be seen to the west of the newer tunnel mouth. An electric tug was introduced in 1914 to speed up traffic through Telford's tunnel; this service was continued until 1954. The third tunnel through Harecastle Hill was built years after the other two, and carried the Stoke–Kidsgrove railway line. This tunnel was closed in the 1960s.

THE NAVIGATION

The Trent & Mersey skirts the centre of Middlewich, passing lots of moored narrowboats and through three consecutive narrow locks, arriving at a wide (14ft) lock (which has suffered from subsidence) with a pub beside it. This used to represent the beginning of a wide, almost lock-free navigation right through to Preston Brook, Manchester and Wigan (very convenient for the salt industry when it shipped most of its goods by boat), but Croxton Aqueduct had to be replaced many years ago, and is now a steel structure only 8ft 2in wide. The aqueduct crosses the River Dane, which flows alongside the navigation as both water courses leave industrial Middlewich and move out into fine open country. Initially, this is a stretch of canal as beautiful as any in the country. Often overhung by trees, the navigation winds along the side of a hill as it follows the delightful valley of the River Dane, before finally heading for the industrial outskirts of Northwich, shedding its beauty and solitude once again.

The outlying canal settlement of Broken Cross acts as a buffer between the beauty and solitude of the Dane Valley and the industrial ravages around Northwich. Beyond is another length in which salt mining has determined the nature of the scenery. Part of it is heavily industrial, with enormous Solvay Chemical works dominating the scene; much of it is devastated but rural (just), some of it is nondescript, and some of it is superb countryside. Donkey engines can still be seen in surrounding fields pumping brine. Leaving the vicinity of Lostock Gralam the outskirts of Northwich, one passes Marston and Wincham. Just west of the village, one travels along a 1/2-mile stretch of canal that was only cut in 1958, as the old route was about to collapse into – needless to say – underground salt workings. Beyond the woods of Marbury Country Park lies the short entrance canal to the famous Anderton Boat Lift (*see* page 231) down into

Narrowboats loaded with china clay at Harding's Wood Junction, c.1963

the Weaver Navigation. The main line continues westwards, winding along what is now a steep hill and into (crooked) Barnton Tunnel (*see* page 36). You then emerge onto a hillside overlooking the River Weaver, with a marvellous view straight down the huge Saltersford Locks. Now Saltersford Tunnel (again crooked) is entered: beyond it stretches completely open country again.

This, the northernmost stretch of the Trent & Mersey, is a very pleasant one and delightfully rural. Most of the way the navigation follows the south side of the hills that overlook the

River Weaver. From about 60ft up, one is often rewarded with excellent views of this splendid valley and the very occasional large vessels that ply its length. At one point one can see the elegant Dutton railway viaduct in the distance; then the two waterways diverge as the Trent & Mersey enters the woods preceding the 1,239yd Preston Brook Tunnel. There is a stop lock south of the tunnel just beyond a pretty covered dry dock; there are often fine examples of restored working boats moored here. At the north end of the tunnel a notice proclaims that from here onwards lies the Bridgewater Canal.

POINTS OF INTEREST

Kidsgrove Originally an iron and coal producing town, Kidsgrove was much helped by the completion of the Trent & Mersey Canal.

Rode Heath Canalside village and once the site of a salt works which has now been landscaped and restored as a wildflower meadow.

Sandbach An old market town that has maintained its charm despite the steady growth of its salt and chemical industries. In the cobbled market place on a massive base stand two superb Saxon crosses, believed to commemorate the conversion of the area to Christianity in the 7th century. They suffered severely in the 17th century when the Puritans broke them up and scattered the fragments for miles. After years of searching for the parts, George Ormerod succeeded in re-erecting the crosses in 1816, with new stone replacing the missing fragments.

St Mary's Church, Sandbach A large, 16th-century church with a handsome battlemented tower. The most interesting features of the interior are the 17th-century carved roof and the fine chancel screen.

The Old Hall Hotel, Sandbach An outstanding example of Elizabethan half-timbered architecture, which was formerly the home of the lord of the manor, but is now used as a hotel.

Middlewich A town that since Roman times has been dedicated to salt extraction. Most of the salt produced here goes to various chemical industries. Subsidence from salt extraction has prevented redevelopment for many years, but a big renewal scheme is now in progress. The canalside area is a haven of peace below the busy streets.

St Michael's Church, Middlewich A handsome medieval church which was a place of refuge for the Royalists during the Civil War. It has a fine interior with richly carved woodwork.

Marston A salt-producing village, suffering badly from its own industry. The numerous gaps in this village are caused by the demolition or collapse of houses affected by subsidence.

The Lion Salt Works The Thompson family established an open pan salt works in Marston in 1842, producing fishery salt, bay salt, crystal salt and lump salt. The salt was pumped as wild brine from 45yds beneath the works and evaporated in a large iron pan. The crystals thus formed were raked into tubs to form blocks, and subsequently dried in brick stove houses, before being exported (with the first part of the journey by canal) to India, Canada and West Africa. The works closed in 1986 but, following a £10.2 million restoration, they reopened as a visitor attraction in June 2015.

Marbury Country Park Two-hundred-acre park occupying the landscaped gardens of the former Marbury Hall and estate, once the home of the Barry and Smith-Barry families. Overlooking Budworth Mere, the house was demolished in 1968 and the much-neglected gardens restored to their former glory.

Northwich A rather attractive town at the junction of the Rivers Weaver and Dane. (The latter brings

Trent & Mersey paddle detail

large quantities of sand down into the Weaver Navigation, necessitating a heavy expenditure on dredging.) As in every other town in this area, salt has for centuries been responsible for the continued prosperity of Northwich. The Weaver Navigation has of course been another very prominent factor in the town's history, and the building and repairing of barges, narrowboats, and small seagoing ships has been carried on here for over 200 years. Nowadays this industry has been almost forced out of business by foreign competition, and the last private shipyard on the river closed down in 1971. However, the Weaver and the big swing bridges across it remain a dominant part of the background.

Two very different aqueducts have stood on this site at Barton on Irwell, near Eccles: the first, constructed by James Brindley in 1761, carried the Bridgewater Canal (*see* page 138) over the River Irwell; and its swing-bridge replacement from 1894, still very much in evidence and engineered by Sir Edward Leader Williams. It was designed to provide a clear passage to large vessels using the newly built Manchester Ship Canal, which at this point followed the route of the Irwell.

Brindley's Barton Aqueduct on the Bridgewater Canal (c.1891) before its demolition

Francis Egerton, 3rd Duke of Bridgewater; Brindley's Barton Aqueduct is behind him

Brindley's masterpiece was ground breaking in its day, a wonder of the world and without precedent. It carried the canal in a clay puddle trough around 660ft long over the Irwell. It attracted hordes of onlookers, quite unable to believe their eyes as boats, loaded with coal from the Duke of Bridgewater's Worsley mines, floated gracefully over the turgid waters of the Irwell 39ft below.

As an apprentice to a Cheshire millwright, Abraham Bennett, some 25 years earlier, Brindley had not proved an immediate success, mostly from a lack of supervision in conjunction with a dearth of a formal, structured training. Largely through his own efforts, he unravelled the intricacies of mill construction to the point where it was his

advice that was sought, rather than Bennett's. This prompted one satisfied customer to declare (during the customary adjournment to the local hostelry, in celebration of the successful conclusion of the contract): 'I will wager a gallon of the best ale in the house that before the lad's apprenticeship is out he will be a cleverer workman than any here, whether master or man.'

The contemporary triumph of civil engineering that the Barton Aqueduct represented certainly secured James Brindley's place in canal history and ensured that during the ensuing period of 'canal mania' it was to his door that promoters beat a steady path. To have Brindley's name as engineer, appended to the parliamentary submission, went most of the way to ensuring that the essential Enabling Act was passed. He also became increasingly adept at winning parliamentary committees round to supporting bills, largely through his ability to put over complex engineering concepts, while convincing the members of the viability of the proposal before them. A classic example of his persuasiveness lies between the pages of a pamphlet from 1769 entitled: *Cursory View of the Advantages of an Intended Canal from Chesterfield to Gainsborough* in which the writer eulogises thus: 'so justly famed for his amazing skill in teaching the watery Element to flow in new channels, and over sandy soils, distributing the Bounties of Nature more equally among the Inhabitants of our Island. . . . if then Mr Brindley has confirmed the Practicability of the scheme, let that rest upon the Pillar of his Reputation.'

Presented with the fact that Brindley's masonry masterpiece has been replaced with a pivoting iron trough, many people today are overtaken by feelings of dismay – sometimes bordering on outrage – that such a significant piece of our heritage has gone forever. But, it has often been observed, the march of progress (particularly Victorian progress) is a formidable beast to halt, although it is possible to take heart in the fact that forming the southernmost extremity of today's structure is one of Brindley's original stone arches, somewhat overwhelmed by the girders of its replacement.

Still regarded as a wonder of the waterways, the Barton Swing Aqueduct was designed by Sir Edward Leader Williams and built in the early 1890s in a bold style comparable to contemporary railway engineering. Gates seal off the 235ft-long, 1,450-ton section that swings at right angles to the Ship Canal over a central island. In replacing Brindley's earlier aqueduct, this new design offered an equally ingenious solution to the new problem of how to cross a navigation while avoiding the superstructure of large vessels, in this case by swinging the aqueduct out of the way of boats using the Ship Canal.

Manchester, historically vying with its better placed rival – Liverpool – for a share of the shipping of foreign trade to and from the northwest, had no way of competing with the docks that sprung up along the Mersey estuary during the late 18th and 19th centuries. So, in a bold bid to avoid both high rail and dock charges, a group of Manchester businessmen, in 1885, secured a Parliamentary Bill to construct a canal (one of the last built in this country) enabling ocean-going shipping to penetrate 36 miles, from Eastham on the Mersey almost into the heart of the city. An immediate success, it was only the relentless increase in the size of ships, together with the advent of containerisation, that saw its final demise, rather than the more usual railway competition.

Nearby, the M60 employs a graceful concrete viaduct, soaring to nearly 100ft above the waters of the canalised River Irwell below and in this way meets the needs of a motorway's teeming traffic.

South end of Barton Swing Aqueduct (today) abutting a single arch of Brindley's original

OXFORD CANAL

This was one of the earliest and for many years one of the most important canals in the south of the country. It was authorised in 1769, when the Coventry Canal was in the offing, and was intended to fetch coal southwards from the Warwickshire coalfield to Banbury and Oxford, at the same time giving access to the River Thames. James Brindley was appointed engineer – he built a winding contour canal 91 miles long, which soon began to look thoroughly outdated and inefficient for the carriage of goods. It was subsequently straightened, thereby shortening it by almost 14 miles.

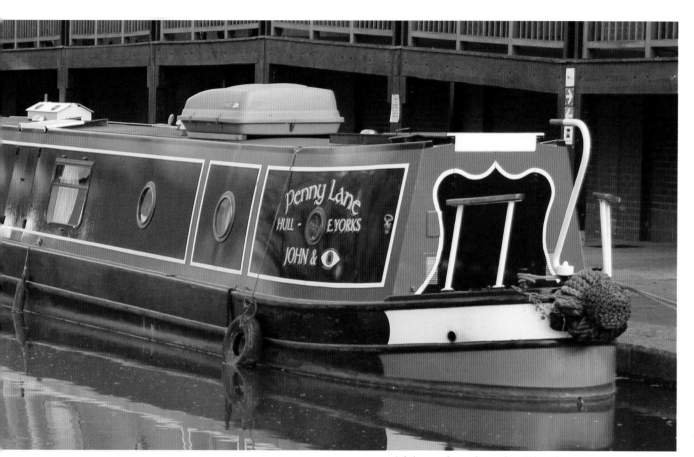

Tooley's Boatyard, at Banbury on the Oxford Canal, now surrounded by a shopping mall

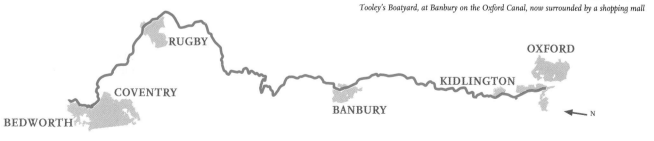

RUGBY

OXFORD

KIDLINGTON

COVENTRY

BANBURY

BEDWORTH

N

BACKGROUND

Brindley died in 1772 before completing the canal and was replaced by Samuel Simcock. He completed the line from Longford (where a junction was made with the Coventry Canal) to Banbury in 1778. After a long pause, the canal was finally brought into Oxford in 1790, and thereafter through-traffic flowed constantly along this important new trade route. It was not, however, connected to the River Thames until 1796.

In 1805 the Grand Junction Canal opened (excepting the tunnel at Blisworth) from London to Braunston, and the Warwick & Napton and Warwick & Birmingham canals completed the new short route from London to Birmingham. This had the natural – and intended – effect of drawing traffic off the Oxford Canal, especially south of Napton Junction. The Oxford company protected itself effectively against this powerful opposition

Narrowboat Anne *takes a quiet break from her travels*

by charging outrageously high tolls for their 5$^{1}/_{2}$-mile stretch between Braunston and Napton, which had become part of the new London–Birmingham through route. Thus the Oxford maintained its revenue and high dividends for many years to come.

By the late 1820s, however, the Oxford Canal had become conspicuously out-of-date with its extravagant winding course: under the threat of various schemes for big new canals which, if built, would render the Oxford Canal almost redundant, the company decided to modernise the northern part of their navigation. Tremendous engineering works were carried out, completely changing the face of the canal north of Braunston. Aqueducts, massive embankments and deep cuttings were built, carrying the canal in great sweeps through the countryside and cutting almost 14 miles off the original 36 miles between Braunston Junction and the Coventry Canal. Much of the old main line

A still winter sunrise

suddenly became a series of loops and branches leading nowhere, crossed by elegant new towpath bridges inscribed 'Horseley Ironworks 1828'. Now most of these old loops are abandoned and weeded up, although their twisting course can still be easily traced. At least one has found a new use as a marina.

This expensive programme was well worthwhile. Although toll rates, and thus revenue, began to fall because of keen competition from the railways, dividends were kept at a high level for years; indeed a respectable profit was still shown right through to the 20th century. Nowadays there is no trade on the canal – but this beautiful waterway has become one of the most popular canals in Britain for pleasure cruising, fishing, cycling and walking. However, water shortages on the long top pound have always presented problems during dry summer months and can, very occasionally, lead to restricted lock opening times on the Claydon and Napton flights.

THE NAVIGATION

The Oxford Canal can be reached from the Thames in two places: one, via Duke's Cut, is convenient but bypasses Oxford altogether; the other, via a backwater under the north end of Oxford Station to the canal at Isis Lock, is more enjoyable. Beyond a disused railway swing bridge, boats continue for 50yds along the backwater and then join the canal by turning sharp left into Isis Lock. The canal continues southwards for 1/4 mile past Worcester College to its terminus near Nuffield College. The original terminal basin, sold to Lord Nuffield in 1936 and eventually infilled, has become a car park. There are now serious proposals to restore it, and bring back life to an otherwise dreary part of this fine city. Isis Lock, with its pretty iron turnover bridge, is wooded and secluded, despite its nearness to the centre of Oxford. The canal proceeds northwards, flanked by houses to the east,

whose gardens run down to the water. Much of this stretch is designated a conservation area, making it an attractive length of urban canal. After passing several wharves the houses give way to industry, while Port Meadow lies to the west. Beyond the railway bridge is Wolvercote, where the canal starts the long climb up to the Midlands. After a series of main road bridges, Duke's Cut branches off to the west to join a backwater of the River Thames, and the canal moves into open country, leaving Oxford behind.

Continuing northwards the waterway runs through lightly wooded fields and meadows to Kidlington, which is hidden from the canal by a low cutting. Keeping Kidlington in the distance, it then joins the Cherwell valley at the pretty canalside village of Thrupp. From here the navigation closely

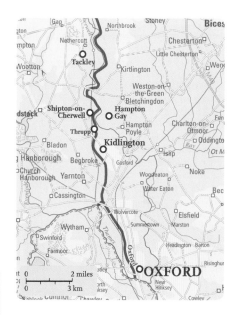

Chief engineer	James Brindley
Assisted by	Samuel Simcock, James King, Robert Whitworth.
Significance	Southeastern leg of the Grand Cross.
Started in	1768
Completed in	1790 (with the completion of Isis Lock into the River Thames).
Length	91 miles as built (later shortened to 77 miles).
Headroom	6'0"
Lock size	70' × 7'
Number of locks	43
Tunnels	4
Significant aqueducts	1
Goods carried	Coal
Operating authority	Canal & River Trust
Contact details	enquiries.southeast @canalrivertrust.org.uk

Narrowboat awaiting repairs

follows the Cherwell and adopts the meandering characteristics of a contour canal. Much of the waterway is tree-lined, while its shallow banks and close relationship with the villages make it seem very river like. At Shipton Weir Lock, whose 1ft rise is made up for by its great width, the Cherwell and the canal merge and share a common course for the next mile. The Cherwell swings away west under an elegant iron bridge, just before Baker's Lock, but soon returns to run parallel to the navigation. Wooded hills now determine the course of the waterway, which passes plenty of villages and places of interest. Only Thrupp yard and the moored maintenance boats, the bridges and the occasional locks give away the fact that this was once a commercial waterway. It is indeed a truly delightful stretch of rural canal.

THE NAVIGATION

The canal continues to follow the Cherwell, winding its way through wooded undulating scenery. The waterway does not intrude at all, in fact it is so well landscaped as to be often invisible from the hills on either side. At first the woods are thick, the overhanging trees forming a tunnel through which the canal passes, bounded by old stone walls. Pigeon Lock marks the centre of the woods, which gradually diminish to reveal rolling farmland to the east and the water meadows of the Cherwell to the west. The canal passes over the route of Akeman Street, and then the trees and the isolation return to conceal the canal from the grounds of Rousham House. As it reaches Lower Heyford the landscape opens out, exposing pretty farmland. The locks continue the rise towards Claydon. Kirtlington and Tackley are set up on ridges away from the canal, but Lower Heyford actually reaches its banks. Here the wharf is now a boatyard and hire boat base.

Continuing north along the Cherwell valley, the canal wanders through water meadows, the high towpath hedge often obscuring the fine views across the valley. As it curves towards Somerton the waterway enters a short cutting and then moves out into open pastureland. Somerton climbs away from the wharf up the hillside to the east, altogether a very attractive situation. Just beyond the bridge four strange sculptured posts are passed, but there are few other intrusions and the canal remains isolated in the middle of the landscape – the locks are generally remote, and set amongst trees, a pattern only broken at Heyford Common Lock. However, the open country continues after Somerton Deep Lock, where the bridge retains its old number, harking back to the great modernisation of the 1820s, when the northern section of the canal was shortened, and the bridges were re-numbered. The canal then pursues a straighter course towards Banbury.

Grantham's Bridge Boat Services, Hillmorton, on the Oxford Canal

ROW, ROW, ROW YOUR BOAT

In the early part of the 20th century it was not uncommon for those who were lucky enough to live by the river to own a camping boat. The Thames Gig was typical of such craft, and could have been 25ft long with a 4ft beam, constructed perhaps by Hammertons of Thames Ditton. Clinker built in mahogany and propelled by two pairs of sculls, it would have two rowing thwarts, passenger seats in the stern and bows, a camping cover and, for comfort, a carpet! A crew of two could propel such a craft at 6 mph over still water for considerable distances, with the added options of a small sail on a mast stepped at the bow if the wind was favourable, or a tow line to haul it from the bank when the current was adverse.

POINTS OF INTEREST

Oxford The town was founded in the 10th century and has been a university city since the 13th century. Today it is a lively cosmopolitan centre of learning, tourism and industry.

Merton College Dates from 1264 and is one of the earliest collegiate foundations that is almost unrestored. The Grove buildings are by Butterfield.

New College Founded by William of Wykeham, Bishop of Winchester, in 1379. The Perpendicular chapel was greatly restored by Sir George Gilbert Scott in the 19th century.

Keble College Built by Butterfield in 1870 entirely in the Victorian Gothic style.

Sheldonian Theatre Built by Sir Christopher Wren in the 17th century under the auspices of Gilbert Sheldon, Archbishop of Canterbury, who disapproved of the annual performances of plays in St Mary's Church. University degrees are awarded here. It has an attractive ceiling by Robert Streeter.

Ashmolean Museum Near Eastern and European archaeology, the Farrer collection of 17th- and 18th-century silver, a display of early coins and drawings by Michelangelo and Raphael.

Kidlington The canal skirts round Kidlington, an extended suburb of Oxford. Parts of an older village survive to the north around the tall-spired church, including Sir William Morton's 17th-century gabled almshouses.

Thrupp A wonderfully romantic canal village, with a terrace of stone houses running along beside the towpath, a pub at one end and an old maintenance yard at the other. The quality of the village makes it an unusual survival of early canal prosperity.

Hampton Gay The church stands by itself, overlooking the River Cherwell, and can only be approached on foot, its seclusion and peace rather disturbed by the railway that almost runs through the churchyard. To the east, half hidden by trees, are the romantic ruins of the manor: gaunt broken stone walls and windows open to the winds.

Shipton-on-Cherwell A village in a magnificent situation: the wooded church overlooks the bridge and the canal, which curls round the foot of the churchyard. Behind, the grey stone manor and farm look out over rolling fields to the west.

Shipton Bridge Just to the east of the village, the scene of a railway disaster on Christmas Eve 1874. Nine carriages fell from the bridge on to the frozen canal below and 34 people were killed. In the 1860s the thighbones of an immense dinosaur, *Cetiosaurus oxoniensis*, were found in the nearby Enslow quarry. They are now in the University Museum, Oxford.

Tackley A residential stone village, spreading down towards the canal to include Nethercott, where there is a small station – Tackley Halt. The church, set on a hill to the south, contains fine monuments.

Boats at Thrupp

THE NAVIGATION

The canal continues through wooded open country with a background of hills to the east. The Cherwell crosses the canal at Aynho Weir Lock before continuing parallel to it and forming a large loop lined by trees as it approaches King's Sutton. Then the tall spire of the church comes into view. Locks continue the rise to Banbury: the very narrow Nell Bridge is one of the oldest, having survived the various road-widening schemes. The railway follows the canal to the east. This pleasant rural stretch of the canal along the Cherwell valley is well punctuated by the characteristic wooden lift bridges: luckily most of these are nowadays left open. Railway and motorway now bracket the canal, intruding into its rural peace. In parts the sinking of the motorway into deep cuttings has helped to lessen its impact, but sadly the steady drone of the traffic is often discernible.

A SPATE OF PROBLEMS

The Oxford Canal and the River Cherwell share a course between Shipton Weir Lock and Baker's Lock, and care should be taken on this section if the river is in spate. William Blake, in his *Strange Adventures of a Houseboat*, published in 1889, recorded how his boat, the *Nameless Barge*, almost came to grief here:

'As this is a candid history, the writer will confess that he was very nearly being the death of all those members of the party who happened to be afloat. Steering at the time, and observing that the heaviest rush of the river was along the western shore, he naturally thought he could cheat the current by edging out towards mid-stream, and proceeded to do so with all imaginary caution. But the moment the heavy weight of water got a grip of the bow, the boat was twisted round, so that the full force of the stream bore down upon her broadside on; while the strain of the tow rope, acting at this awkward angle, proceeded to tilt us over in a very alarming fashion. It was an affair of only a moment or two, for by jamming the tiller over she was presently righted.'

A typical lift bridge on the Oxford Canal

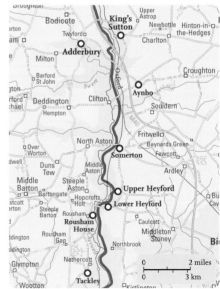

POINTS OF INTEREST

Rousham House A lively picture of fighting during the Civil War is conjured up by the shooting holes made in the doors, which are preserved from the time when a Royalist garrison used the house. It dates from 1635 and was enlarged and its gardens landscaped in 1730 by William Kent.

Lower Heyford Built among woods along the south bank of the Cherwell, and hence the canal. The church, with fine stained glass, overlooks the canal from a slight hill that conceals many of the cottages in a village where motor cars still seem intruders. To the north is a fine and ancient water mill, screened by a line of willow trees.

Upper Heyford A main street of thatched stone cottages falls steeply to the canal, with views across the valley to Steeple Aston. The church overlooks the canal, as does a fine barn.

Somerton A straggling grey stone village winding up the hill to the east of the canal. On the highest point is the church with its Decorated tower: there are good 16th-century tombs inside. In all the villages along the Cherwell valley, the churches are placed on mounds or higher ground, overlooking the valley.

Aynho A self-contained village square sheltered from the road, unchanged and complete in rich stone. New houses have been carefully blended with the old, and peach trees have been trained along the walls of many of the cottages. On the other side of the road is the formal classical façade of Aynho Park, a 17th-century mansion rebuilt by Sir John Soane in the late 18th century, the house is large but restrained, and does not look out of place in a village street. The church beside the house was classicised at the same time: the strange façade added to the nave wall makes it a charming folly.

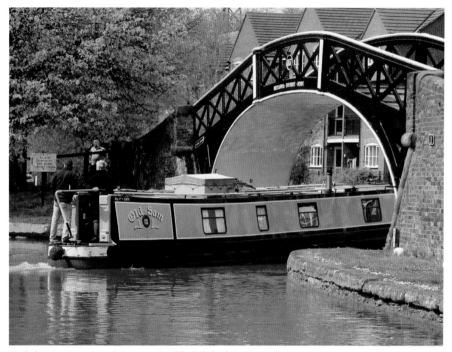

Hawkesbury Junction, or Sutton's Stop – meeting of the Oxford and Coventry canals

King's Sutton An attractive village of narrow streets which wander in every direction. The centre is round a green, at the top of a hill, where rows of thatched cottages, two pubs and the church stand in quiet harmony. The church is superb: beautifully proportioned with a tall, slender spire. The Saxon font, found buried in the churchyard in 1923, has been linked with the baptism in AD662 of St Rumbold who was born at nearby Walton Fields. The spire is a prominent landmark visible to travellers in the area.

Adderbury The large expanse of village green surrounded by splendid houses and overlooked by the old coaching inn gives Adderbury an air of affluence. The church was fortunate in benefiting from the experience of the medieval master mason Richard Winchcombe and is one of the finest examples of Decorated and Perpendicular architecture in the country. Sadly the building was neglected and had to be restored in the 19th century. The graceful spire is one of the famous three that stand in line across the countryside in full view of the Oxford road.

THE NAVIGATION

RALLY AROUND THE OXFORD

Save the Oxford Canal? Who needs to save the Oxford Canal? It is as much an integral part of the network as the Grand Union and the Leeds & Liverpool, and the system would seem bleak without it. But it was not always so . . . .

In 1955 the then British Waterways Board of Survey Report was not at all favourable towards the retention of the narrow canals, and the Oxford was directly under threat. Then, as now, there were thankfully many enthusiasts prepared to direct their skills and energy towards retaining the waterways, and so it was that Joan Marston and the Midlands Branch of the Inland Waterways Association organised a rally at Banbury on 1 August 1955.

Over 50 boats arrived to support the occasion, and estimates of visitors vary between 5,000 and 10,000. The weather was splendid, and the attractions (in addition to the canal) included waterways films, an exhibition, canoe races, a mobile grocery store, a Saturday night reception, a supper dance on Monday, and a beer tent, of course. The *Banbury Guardian* reported 'Never has the town had such a water borne spree'. Those of us who enjoy the Oxford Canal today should be very grateful.

Continuing northwest along the Cherwell valley the canal enters Banbury beside housing estates and an industrial area. It heads through the centre in a flurry of bridges, passing the redeveloped Tooley's Boatyard. Industry remains generally confined to the east – it is not until Hardwick Lock and the M40 bridge are passed that surroundings more typical of the Oxford Canal return, as the navigation swings to the north and hills reappear to the west. Locks continue the steady rise throughout this stretch, and from here on all the locks feature double bottom gates, which make for lighter work. The railway follows the waterway but crosses to the west after Banbury.

Continuing north along the Cherwell valley the canal enters Cropredy, whose stone cottages and wharf have been visible for some time. After the village the high towpath hedge conceals the open fields beyond, although there are views across the valley to the west. Near Varney's and Elkington's

locks the old ridge and furrow field patterns are very pronounced. Soon Claydon comes into sight – here five locks take the navigation to the summit level. Light woods border the canal, which is both shallow and very narrow in places. Near the second lock the remains of the handsome old red-brick stabling for boat horses can be seen.

After Claydon Locks the canal twists and turns. Hills and trees close in, preparing for the cutting that marks the course of the old tunnel. The feeder from Boddington Reservoir, 2^{1}/$_{2}$ miles to the east, enters the waterway to the north of the village. The railway, which moved to the west after Cropredy, reappears beside the navigation. The canal continues along the opened out Fenny Compton Tunnel, now a steep, thickly wooded cutting which ends as it swings in a wide loop eastwards towards Fenny Compton Wharf. The hills retreat for a while, although their influence is still present in the extravagantly indirect course

taken by the waterway, involving a great number of brick-arch accommodation bridges. The navigation first runs west before doubling back on itself and running east to Stoneton Manor, where a steep ridge causes it to resume a north westerly direction towards Napton, Fenny Compton and Wormleighton which are all about 1 mile from the canal.

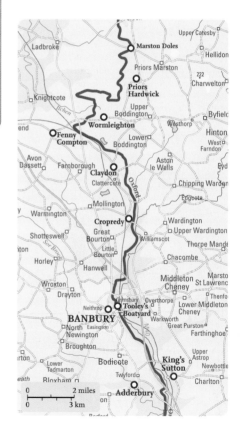

POINTS OF INTEREST

Banbury Originally a wool town, the castle was pulled down by Cromwell's forces in 1646 and now no trace remains. The ancient cross of nursery rhyme fame in the town centre was demolished in 1602, and the present cross is a 19th-century replica. The church was built in 1793 by S. P. Cockrell. The original bake house, which produced the spiced Banbury cakes, survived until 1968.

Tooley's Boatyard This historic boatyard, the last remaining element of the old Banbury canal terminus surviving since 1790, has thankfully been saved. It was here that Tom Rolt's boat *Cressy* was prepared for his honeymoon cruise with his new wife in 1939. This cruise was the basis of

his now classic book *Narrowboat*, which in turn led to the formation of the Inland Waterways Association (*see* page 270) in 1946 aboard *Cressy*, moored at the top of the Tardebigge Flight on the Worcester & Birmingham. Tooley's Boatyard still has a working forge and an operational dry dock (both Scheduled Ancient Monuments), together with all the tools needed to build a wooden narrowboat, and indeed boats are being built and restored here.

Cropredy A quiet village with wandering streets of old brick houses. There is no real centre, but the whole village is very close to the canal. The stately sandstone church contains fine woodwork; the slow swing of the clock pendulum in the belfry seems to echo the sleepy nature of the village, which only bursts into life during the annual Folk Festival. It is held on the second weekend in August and all began in 1979, when Fairport Convention held their farewell concert here.

Battle of Cropredy On 29 June 1644 Cromwell's forces under Waller attacked Cropredy Bridge in an attempt to open a way to Oxford. Despite greatly inferior numbers, the Royalist cavalry managed to scatter Waller's army and capture his artillery, thus protecting Oxford. A plaque on the river bridge recalls the battle.

Claydon Set in a rolling open landscape to the west of the canal, Claydon is an old-fashioned brown-stone village; in spite of some new development it preserves a quiet unpretentious charm. The curiously irregular Church of St James the Great provides a focal point – parts of it date from before the 12th century and the tower, which has a saddle back roof, contains a clock. There is no face, but the hour is chimed.

Fenny Compton The church is partly 14th-century and partly Victorian, with a curious offset tower and a fine graveyard; alongside is a fine brick rectory of 1707. Fenny Compton Tunnel is no more, having been converted into a cutting in 1868.

Wormleighton A manorial village that still retains a feeling of privacy. Its 13th-century brown-stone church contains a Perpendicular screen and Jacobean woodwork. Further up the road from the canal is the early 16th-century brick manor house that must once have been very impressive. South of the house is a grand stone gatehouse dated 1613. A row of Victorian mock-Tudor cottages completes the village.

The Oxford Canal at Thrupp

THE NAVIGATION

The waterway continues northwards through rolling open farmland, with the view to the west concealed by the towpath hedge. At Marston Doles the country opens out and the windmill on top of Napton Hill comes into sight. Here the summit level ends and the canal starts the fall towards the junction. The navigation then swings to the west of Napton Hill, passing Brickyard Bridge, and then turns east to meet the Grand Union at the junction. Marston Doles, at the top of the flight, is a typical canal settlement, but Napton, larger and prosperous, is set to the east on the side of the hill.

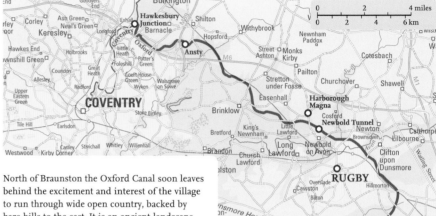

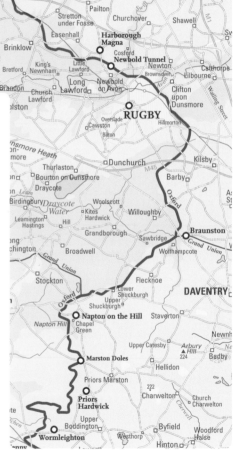

Two-cylinder Gardner engine

North of Braunston the Oxford Canal soon leaves behind the excitement and interest of the village to run through wide open country, backed by bare hills to the east. It is an ancient landscape, and medieval ridge and furrow field patterns are much in evidence. These were created as villagers cleared forested land, and each ploughed strips throwing soil towards the centre. Gradually a collection of strips, all running parallel to each other, made up a furlong or cultura. This was then enclosed by a low bank and an access track (usually difficult to identify today) was created. Fields, consisting of dozens of furlongs, were then sometimes fenced. Skirting round Barby Hill, the waterway swings north east towards Hillmorton and Rugby. The M45 makes a noisy crossing after Barby Hill.

The canal descends Hillmorton Locks and swings in a wide arc around Rugby. The short arm above bottom locks is worth a look, but don't take your boat in. Beyond the old Canal Company buildings, now smart offices, are a range of boatbuilding activities and fully functional dry docks. The River Avon is crossed by an aqueduct, and the Rugby Arm branches to the west.

POINTS OF INTEREST

Priors Hardwick A small, partly deserted but pretty village much of which was pulled down by Cistercian monks in the 14th century. Parts of the squat stone church are 13th-century.

Marston Doles A tiny settlement which owes its existence to the canal – towing horses used to be stabled here. To the north, at the end of a foreshortened arm, are the remains of the pumping house that used to pump water up to the summit from the bottom of the Napton flight.

Napton on the Hill Rising to over 400ft, Napton Hill dominates the immediate landscape. The village is scattered all over the hill, climbing steeply up the sides. The shops and pubs are at the bottom, however, and so only those wishing to enjoy the view or visit the 13th-century church need climb to the top. Legend has it that the church was to be built on the village green but the devil persisted in carrying the building stones to the present site where the church was eventually built. Seven counties can be seen from this high vantage point. Near the church is the restored windmill alone on the hilltop. The canal wanders round the base of the hill, bypassing the village except for the wharf alongside Brickyard Bridge.

Braunston Set up on a hill to the north of the canal, so that the tall spire of Braunston church dominates the valley for miles around. The village is really a long main street a little separate from the canal, with houses of all periods that give the feeling of a spacious market town. A very well-known canal centre, it is no less significant today than when the Oxford and Grand Junction canals were first connected here.

Rugby Originally an Anglo-Saxon farming settlement, Rugby went on to become an important railway town when, in the 19th century, the Midland Counties Railway made a junction with the London & Birmingham Railway Company, becoming a focus for a proliferation of workshops and marshalling yards. It is famous for the invention of Rugby football when in 1823, it is reputed, William Webb Ellis – in picking up the ball – broke the rules of its more staid cousin, soccer. Ellis was a pupil at the well-known public school endowed by a prosperous grocer, Lawrence Sheriff, in 1562. Rugby is also the home of the jet engine, developed by Frank Whittle, who built the first prototype in April 1937.

Newbold Tunnel This 250yd long tunnel was built during the shortening of the canal in the 1820s.

Harborough Magna A quiet red-brick village 1 mile to the north of the canal. The 13th–14th-century church has a Victorian west tower and many Victorian additions, including an interesting stained-glass window depicting Christ rising, with two angels, against a dark blue background.

Brinklow A spacious pre-industrial village built along a wide main street. The church of St John Baptist is of late Perpendicular style, and has some interesting 15th-century stained glass depicting birds, including a peacock. Its sloping floor climbs 12ft from west to east. Alongside is the substantial mound of a motte and bailey castle, built to defend the Fosse Way.

Ansty A tiny village that grew up alongside the canal. To the north are the church of St James and Ansty Hall; the hall is dated 1678 over the doorway. This area has been much altered by the presence of the motorway.

Hawkesbury Junction Hawkesbury Junction is also known as Sutton Stop, after the name of the first lock keeper. It was always a busy canal centre,

Lengthsman's hut

and remains so today, with plenty of narrowboats permanently moored here. There are other things to see here: a fine canal pub, a stop lock and a disused engine house. The latter used to pump water up into the canal from a well. Its engine was installed in 1821, having been previously employed for nearly 100 years at Griff Colliery, a few miles up the canal towards Nuneaton. This Newcomen-type atmospheric steam engine, called *Lady Godiva*, is now in Dartmouth Museum. It ceased work in 1913. Sephtons House and Boatyard used to face the junction. It was here, in 1924, that narrowboat *Friendship* was built. This boat can be seen at the Boat Museum, Ellesmere Port. The whole area is now surrounded by housing.

THE NAVIGATION

Continuing northwest, the canal runs through quiet farmland, and passes the pretty Boat Inn Cottage (no longer a pub) before reaching All Oaks Wood. At Brinklow the navigation passes over an embankment, which was originally an aqueduct; the arches have long been filled in. Only a truncated length of the Brinklow Arm, which once served the village, now remains. The long embankment continues through Stretton Stop and past the Stretton Arm, now used for moorings. Open, rolling fields follow, and then the waterway enters a deep cutting, spanned by the M6 motorway which cuts through this stretch and has greatly altered the landscape. The elegant iron bridges that occur periodically mark the course of the old Oxford Canal, prior to the 1820s shortening. The railway follows the canal to the east.

The open landscape continues beyond Ansty, although the motorway is never far away. Soon the first signs of Coventry appear, with views of pylons and housing estates. The new Wyken Colliery Arm leaves to the west. It was built to replace the old one eaten up by the motorway which comes alongside the canal at this point: it is now used by the Coventry Cruising Club. Sharp bends then lead to the stop lock before Hawkesbury Junction, the end of the Oxford Canal where it joins the Coventry Canal. This last stretch of the Oxford Canal is characterised by the 1820s shortenings: straight cuttings and embankments date from this period, while the cast iron bridges mark the old route.

Lock maintenance

The Bingley Five-Rise Locks, built in 1774 in 'staircase' formation, is a very famous and impressive feature of the canal system near the eastern end of the Leeds & Liverpool Canal (*see* page 156). All five locks are joined together rather than being separated by pounds of 'neutral' water. The top gates of the lowest lock are the bottom gates of the lock above, and so on. There are therefore five chambers and a total of six gates. This means it is not possible to empty a lock unless the one below is itself empty. The resulting rapid descent can be quite daunting as the waterway is able to fall a considerable distance (in this case almost 60ft with a gradient of 1:5) in a relatively short distance.

Of slightly lesser stature but equally impressive, are the subsequent sets of staircase locks below the Five Rise: Bingley Three Rise (with a 30ft drop), Dowley Gap Two Locks (nearly 20ft), Field Three Locks (26ft), Dobson Two Locks, Newlay Three Locks (27ft), Forge Three Locks (23ft 6in.) and, on the approach to the terminal basin in Leeds, Oddy Two Locks (13ft 7in.).

The Bingley stretch of the waterway was opened on 21 March 1774 with the first boat to descend the Five-Rise Locks taking just 28 minutes. The *Leeds Intelligencer* reported: 'From Bingley to about 3 miles downwards the noblest works of the kind

Bingley Five-Rise staircase locks on the Leeds & Liverpool Canal (mid-20th century)

are exhibited viz: A five fold, a three fold and a single lock, making together a fall of 120 feet; a large aqueduct bridge of seven arches over the River Aire and an aqueduct and banking over the Shipley valley . . . this joyful and much wished for event was welcomed with the ringing of Bingley bells, a band of music, the firing of guns by the neighbouring militia, the shouts of spectators, and all marks of satisfaction that so an important an acquisition merits.'

A crowd of some 30,000 people turned out to witness the opening and to partake in some or all of the above merry making. Today it is a popular tourist attraction with many a gongoozler (one who idly observes canalside activity) watching a boat crew labour their way up or down the flight, for many years under the watchful eye of resident lock keeper, Barry Whitelock MBE: an honour awarded to him in the 2006 New Year Honours List for Services to the Inland Waterways in the North.

COVENTRY CANAL

This waterway goes part way to forming the southeastern leg of James Brindley's Grand Cross. Indeed he was the first engineer to be appointed to oversee the undertaking, in 1768, at a salary of £150 per annum for which he committed to devote two months a year to overseeing the canal's construction. His appointment lasted less than the year as his standards of workmanship were considerably higher than those required by the management committee. His dismissal, rather than presenting a setback to the great man, served to further his career, especially when the project stalled at Atherstone after just 16 miles.

The Coventry Canal at Hopwas

FRADLEY
JUNCTION

LICHFIELD

TAMWORTH

FAZELEY

NUNEATON

BEDWORTH

COVENTRY

N

BACKGROUND

The Coventry Canal, whose enabling Act of Parliament was passed in 1768, was promoted by pit owners such as the Parrotts of Hawkesbury and the Newdigates of Arbury with two main objectives: to connect the fast-growing town of Coventry with the new trade route called the Grand Trunk (now the Trent & Mersey Canal) and to provide Coventry with cheap coal from the Bedworth coalfield, 10 miles to the north.

The first, long-term objective was not achieved for some years until the company had overcome financial difficulties, but – wisely – the stretch between Coventry and Bedworth was completed early on, so that the profitable carriage of local coal was quickly established along the canal, in 1769.

By the time the canal reached Atherstone in 1771, all the authorised capital had been spent and James Brindley, the original engineer of the canal, had been sacked. For these reasons – and because of the interminable wrangle with the Oxford Canal Company, whose scheme to link Coventry with southern England had followed hard upon the original Coventry scheme – the Coventry Canal did not reach Fazeley, nearly 12 miles short of its intended terminus at Fradley, until 1790.

By this time, the Birmingham & Fazeley Canal had been built, extending along the Coventry Canal's original proposed line to Whittington Brook, from where the Grand Trunk Canal Company carried it north to Fradley. The Coventry Company later bought this section back, which explains the fact that there is now a detached portion of the Coventry Canal from Whittington Brook to Fradley Junction.

In 1790, the Oxford Canal was also completed through to Oxford and thus to London via the Thames. The profits of the Coventry Canal rose quickly, and rose even higher when the Grand Junction Canal was completed in 1799, shortening the route to London by 60 miles. Other adjoining canals contributed to the Coventry Canal's prosperity: the Ashby, the Wyrley & Essington and the Trent & Mersey. The extension of the Grand Junction Canal via Warwick to Birmingham naturally dismayed the Coventry, but the numerous locks – and high tolls on the stretch of the Oxford Canal between Braunston and Napton Junctions – ensured that a lot of traffic to and from Birmingham still used the slightly longer route via the Coventry and Birmingham & Fazeley Canals, especially after the Oxford Canal was shortened by 14 miles between Braunston and Longford.

The continuous financial success of the Coventry Canal could be attributed both to its being part of so many long-distance routes and to the continued prosperity of the coal mines along its way. Considerable landscaping and reclamation, along with extensive rebuilding, have made this an extremely attractive and interesting route.

Reflections on the Coventry Canal

THE NAVIGATION

The Coventry Canal begins at the large Bishop Street Basin, opened in 1769, near the city centre. It is an interesting situation on the side of a hill, overlooked by tall buildings and attractive old wooden canal warehouses; the warehouses date from 1914, although there were, of course, earlier such buildings on the site. They once stored grain, food and cement, and were well restored in 1984. The old Weighbridge Office is now a shop and information centre, looking out over the basin towards the Vaults, which were used to store coal. The waterway leaves the terminus through an arched bridge, a tiny structure designed to be easily closed with a wooden beam each evening: indeed at one time no boats were allowed to stay in the basin overnight. There was once a toll house here. The navigation now begins to wind through what were busy industrial areas towards Hawkesbury:

Chief engineer	James Brindley (replaced by Thomas Yeoman).
Assisted by	Thomas Dadford senior, Edmund Lingard, Joseph Parker, Thomas Sheasby.
Significance	Forms part of the southeastern leg of the Grand Cross in conjunction with the Oxford Canal.
Started in	1768
Completed in	1790
Length	38 miles
Headroom	6'6"
Lock size	72' × 7'
Number of locks	13
Aqueducts	1
Goods carried	Coal
Operating authority	Canal & River Trust
Contact details	enquiries.centralshires @canalrivertrust.org.uk

Disused engine house at Hawkesbury Junction

it is in places quite narrow, and often flanked by buildings. Just beyond the second bridge are 'Cash's Hundred Houses', an elegant row of weavers' houses, where the living accommodation was on the lower two floors, with the top storey being occupied by looms, driven by a single shaft from a steam engine. There never were 100 houses: only 48 were built, and of these only 37 remain. The waterway then, after various contortions, continues towards Hawkesbury, passing through the outskirts of Coventry. Before it ducks under the motorway, you will notice that the navigation is wider: this was the site of the original junction between the Oxford and Coventry Canals. It was known as Longford Junction. Hawkesbury Junction, their present meeting, contains all the elements expected of such a notable place: plenty of traditional boats, interesting buildings including a fine engine house, a splendid pub and useful facilities for boaters. To the east of the junction is Hawkesbury Hall, at one time the home of mine owner and sponsor of the Coventry Canal, Richard Parrott.

THE NAVIGATION

Leaving Hawkesbury Junction, the waterway passes through Bedworth in a long cutting: the town seems to be composed mainly of vast housing estates, but these make little impression upon the navigation. At Marston Junction the Ashby Canal branches to the east through pleasant countryside, while the Coventry Canal bends due west for a short way before resuming its course towards Nuneaton to the north. There is a pleasant short stretch of open fields, giving a welcome breathing space, before the canal once again enters the suburbs, this time of Nuneaton. The waterway takes a route around the town, marked by a succession of housing estates and well-tended allotments. Continuing northwest out of Nuneaton, the canal winds along the side of a hill into a landscape which is curiously exciting. What were once quarries and spoil heaps are now landscaped, with many transformed into nature reserves. The largest mountain of waste, built with spoil from the old Judkins Quarry, is known as Mount Judd, or locally 'Jees'. This distinctly man-made landscape is broken up with unexpected stretches of open countryside, with fine views away to the north across the Anker valley. The navigation passes below the town of Hartshill: the attractive buildings in the Canal & River Trust yard are crowned by a splendid clock tower, and those travelling on the canal will want to slow right down to enjoy the mellow architecture and old dock. The waterway then continues towards Mancetter, leaving the quarry belt and moving into open rolling country backed by thick woods to the west. The railway closes from the east as the canal approaches Atherstone.

SUTTON'S STOP

Hawkesbury Junction was more commonly known to the boat people as Sutton's Stop. It took this name from a family called Sutton who, during the 1800s, were the toll clerks here.

The Greyhound pub overlooks the junction now as it did then. Corn, oats and maize used to be stored around the back of the pub, as feed for the towing horses. It was often the children's job to bag this up for a trip, lowering the sacks down using a small hand-crane.

Cruising the Coventry Canal

POINTS OF INTEREST

Coventry Recorded as *Couentrev* in the Domesday Book, Coventry's modern history begins with the foundation of a Benedictine priory by Leofric and his wife Godgyfu in 1043, but its fame came with Lady Godiva, who in legend rode naked through the streets, to divert Leofric's anger from the town. This episode is first recorded in the *Flores Historiarum* of 1235. Following the Norman invasion, the town became second in commercial importance to London. Largely destroyed during the Second World War, it is today a modern and well-planned city, although a restored row of medieval buildings can be visited in Spon Street, in the west of the city centre. The origin of the popular phrase 'to send to Coventry', meaning to cold-shoulder or ignore, is uncertain, but there is no reason to connect it with the present population, who seem generally warm and friendly.

Coventry Cathedral Designed by Sir Basil Spence, building began on the new cathedral in 1954 and was completed in 1962. The modern stained-glass windows all reflect their light towards the altar, behind which is a tapestry by Graham Sutherland. The font, a boulder from a hillside near Bethlehem, stands in front of the Baptistry window by John Piper. The whole is topped by a bronze *flèche* (a slender spire with windows), dropped into place by a helicopter and known locally as Radio Coventry.

Cathedral Church of St Michael, Coventry Only the ruins of the old cathedral, destroyed by the Luftwaffe in 1940, still remain. Some of the original stained-glass windows survived. Many interesting artefacts are on display within the ruins.

Longford Bridge It was here, between 1769 and 1865, that members of the nearby Salem Baptist Chapel were baptised in the canal.

Nuneaton A typical Midlands coal mining town. On the site of the Griff Colliery canal arm are the hollows said to be the origin of the Red Deeps in *The Mill on the Floss* by George Eliot, who was born here in 1819.

Arbury Hall Two miles southwest of the canal. Originally an Elizabethan house, it was gothicised by Sir Roger Newdigate 1750–1800 under the direction of Sanderson Miller, Henry Keene and Couchman of Warwick. There are fine pictures, furniture, china and glass and the hall is in a beautiful park setting.

Chilvers Coton Its church dates from 1946 and was designed by H. N. Jepson and built by German prisoners of war.

Bedworth The most impressive parts of this town are its church by Bodley and Garner, 1888–90, and the almshouses built in 1840.

Hartshill Once a mining community, Hartshill has now been swallowed up by Nuneaton, and as such its interest lies mainly in its past. The Romans recognised its strategic importance and there is evidence that they settled here, as both kilns and fragments of pottery have been unearthed. Hugh de Hardreshull chose it as a site for his castle in 1125, the view from the ridge enabling him to see as far as the distant peaks of Derbyshire on a clear day. Below, on the plains, can be counted the towers and steeples of 40 churches. Hartshill's most famous claim is that it was the birthplace of the poet Drayton in 1563, a friend of both Ben Johnson and Shakespeare. Drayton's greatest work was *Polyolbion*, a survey of the country with a son for each county. He died in 1631 and was buried in Westminster.

Hartshill Yard Part of the yard contains a 19th-century carpenter's workshop and blacksmith's forge.

Fradley Junction

Mancetter The church dates from the 13th century, but its best feature is the large collection of 18th-century slate tombstones displaying all the elegance of Georgian incised lettering. There are some almshouses of 1728 in the churchyard, and across the road another row with pretty Victorian Gothic details. The manor, south of the church, is rather over-restored. It was from this house, in 1555, that Robert Glover was led when the Bishop of Lichfield ordered his arrest. A victim of the reign of Mary Tudor, he was seized and taken to the stake, where he was executed alongside a poor cap-maker from Coventry.

THE NAVIGATION

Continuing northwest, the canal skirts to the south of Atherstone, passing Rothens Yard – where coal was once delivered from local colleries – and descends the very attractive Atherstone Locks. The flight of 11 locks is well-cared for and varied, falling through housing, allotments and open countryside. It is just a pity that all of the side ponds on the flight are now sealed off. At the bottom of the flight the River Anker converges with the waterway from the east. Arable land accompanies the canal, lined with oak trees as it passes Grendon, with only the skyline to the west revealing the industrial belt that is approaching. At this distance the horizon looks romantic, an 18th-century vision of industry.

As the navigation turns towards Polesworth, it passes the remains of an iron swing bridge, a curiosity on this canal. The waterway then runs along the side of a hill overlooking the Anker valley. Turning to the west of Polesworth it passes Pooley Hall and an area

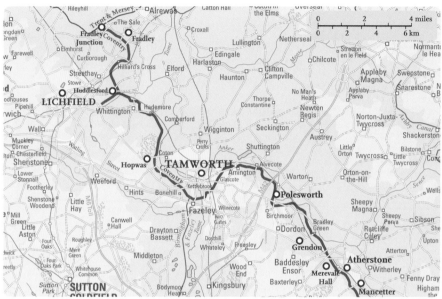

of reclaimed spoil heaps, now pleasant scrubland, with a golf course. Cows graze near Pooley Hall, and wildlife is filling the vacuum left by industry.

At Alvecote Priory the tree-surrounded ruins provide a sudden glimpse of history, while across the waterway is Pooley Field Nature Reserve, firm evidence that the canal has now shed its industrial past. Reaching Tamworth the canal runs through suburban housing, turning in a wide sweep south west past Tamworth towards Fazeley Junction, through the only locks on this stretch, at Glascote. Houses and factories flank the waterway as it passes Kettlebrook Wharf, and then it moves briefly into more open country, crossing the River Tame on an impressive aqueduct. At Fazeley Junction the Coventry Canal meets the Birmingham & Fazeley

Canal and then continues northwest towards Fradley Junction, initially on the Birmingham & Fazeley Canal.

Beyond Whittington the waterway changes from being the Birmingham & Fazeley Canal to the Coventry Canal (see Background, page 60). A stone marks the actual point. At Huddlesford the remains of the eastern end of the Wyrley & Essington Canal, now referred to as the Lichfield Canal and presently used only for moorings, branches to the southwest. The Coventry Canal then runs northwards through flat, open country towards Fradley Junction. There are no locks, but a swing bridge announces your arrival at Fradley. Here the Coventry Canal meets the Trent & Mersey Canal, overlooked by The Swan, a famous canal landmark.

POINTS OF INTEREST

Atherstone A pleasant town, with a strong 18th-century feeling, especially in the open market place in front of the church.

Merevale Hall, Atherstone A large battlemented house, high to the west: a fine example of an early 19th-century mock Tudor mansion. Closer and also to the west, are the remains of the 12th-century abbey and the very pretty 13th-century church which contains fine stained glass, monuments and brasses.

Grendon Grendon is just a small church set in beautiful parkland. The woods and rolling fields are a last refuge before the industrial landscape that precedes Tamworth.

Polesworth The splendid gatehouse and the clerestory are all that remain of the 10th-century abbey, where Egbert, first Saxon King of England, built a nunnery.

Tamworth Tamworth was originally a Saxon settlement, although only earthworks survive from this period. Tamworth Castle has a Norman motte, an Elizabethan timbered hall and Jacobean apartments; it is a splendid mélange of styles.

Hopwas A pretty and tidy village with a green, built on the side of a hill. Anyone walking should look out for the danger flags for Whittington Firing Ranges.

Lichfield Although not on the canal, Lichfield is well worth a visit. It lies at the heart of England and 1,300 years ago it was the centre of the Kingdom of Mercia. It is reputed that around AD300, during the reign of the Roman Emporer Diolectian, 1,000 Christians were martyred in the town and its name means 'field or place of the dead'.

St Chads Cathedral, Lichfield The only English medieval cathedral with three spires. This building, dating from 1195, and replacing an earlier Norman cathedral on the site, was restored to its former medieval splendour by Sir George Gilbert Scott in the latter part of the 19th century following substantial changes to its ordering made by William Wyatt a century earlier.

Huddlesford At Huddlesford Junction the Wyrley & Essington Canal used to join the Coventry Canal. Long abandoned, the first 1/4 mile is used for moorings. This route, which extends west to Ogley Junction on the Anglesey Branch of the Birmingham Canal Navigations, is the subject of an energetic and effective restoration campaign.

Problems of obstruction by the M6 toll road have been overcome with the installation of an aqueduct, but much still remains to be done.

Fradley A small village set to the east of the canal, and well away from the junction. It owed its prosperity to the airfield which is not used as such any more.

Fradley Junction A long-established canal centre where the Coventry Canal joins the Trent & Mersey Canal. There is a boatyard, a Canal & River Trust information centre and café, moorings, a boat club and a popular pub – all in the middle of a five-lock flight.

Coventry Basin (Mr Brindley pores over his next waterway project)

The Chesterfield Canal is explored at length in the northeast region of this book (see page 198) but appears here as a Milepost as one of the finest examples of a Brindley canal, renowned in particular for the restored Thorpe Locks, the collapsed Norwood Tunnel and the now derelict Norwood lock flight, towards its western end.

This canal was surveyed in part by Brindley and also by John Varley who went on to become its resident engineer. Upon Brindley's death, Varley took on overall responsibility for the project, with the former's brother-in-law – Hugh Henshall – becoming inspector of works. In time various dubious contractual arrangements surfaced, involving shoddy workmanship and

Derelict staircase lock west of Norwood Tunnel

the employment of close relatives of John Varley. However, none of this should be allowed to detract from what is surely Brindley's most revered of all waterways. It carries his hallmark at every twist and turn embracing staircase lock flights, giant embankments and a tunnel to equal Harecastle on the Trent & Mersey Canal: Norwood at 2,893 yards in length. This prodigious feat (completed some time after the great engineer's death, as was Harecastle) is merely the gilt atop this waterway 'gingerbread' as leading up to it, both to the east and the west, are two truly amazing flights of locks, many of staircase configuration (see Milepost 4).

Thorpe Locks to the east have been restored to their original glory, leading the navigation out of the old mining village of Shireoaks, across the diminutive River Ryton, and up through the charming settlement of Turnerwood clustered tightly around the navigation, giving its name to the basin and two locks below. Immediately above is a double staircase lock followed shortly by a second double, then come two treble staircase locks separated by several, more conventional single locks. As with the entire Chesterfield Canal, all are narrow locks, seemingly barely wide enough to contain a 6ft 10in. narrowboat.

For a long time the canal reached only as far as Worksop and visions of a renewed connection to the Derbyshire town of Chesterfield remained simply that. Restoration of these highly important Grade II structures have shown what is required if we are to fully appreciate the scope and rugged beauty of our early engineering heritage. Now the challenge remains to restore a similar lock flight on the western side of the watershed: long fallen into complete dereliction and, in many cases, incorporated into garden water features as the accompanying picture shows. Equally challenging is a replacement for Norwood Tunnel which, due to extensive coal mining in the area, gracefully

subsided until, at its final collapse in 1907, a mere 4ft 10in. separated its roof from the water level.

To re-instate the tunnel is a non-starter but to further squirrel the navigation up each side of the watershed, with additional locks is being suggested as the most elegant solution to this problem. However, this only moves the resurrected navigation progressively closer to another problem: six lanes of the M1! As with precedents created in the recent restoration of both the Droitwich and Rochdale canals, there is a solution even to this challenge – making use of an existing culvert under the motorway, originally built to connect fields severed in its construction.

Ingenuity, determination, vision and drive are the stock-in-trade of canal trusts and the Chesterfield Canal Trust is certainly not lacking in any department. It has already undertaken the full restoration of the towpath from its present connection with the River Trent (see page 218) all the way through to Chesterfield itself (some 5 miles of this currently detached western end are in water and in use). There are long-term plans to form a new cruising ring – by making the River Rother, between Chesterfield and Rotherham navigable, thereby linking into the South Yorkshire Navigations and waterways further north and west. Such rings are very popular among boaters, especially hirers, who are understandably reluctant to retrace their steps during the limited period of their cruise.

Funding, especially in these straightened times, will present the major sticking point but with a fair wind, these are all viable possibilities that stand a very good chance of reaching fruition. Only the time scale is in doubt. But funding has, from the very outset of canal construction, presented problems – as in all walks of life – as the driver of both design and the final engineered solution.

A lock and side pound, incorporated into a garden feature, on the derelict flight west of Norwood Tunnel

Fundamental to our canal network in this country, is the gauge of each waterway itself: in other words the dimensions of the craft that can navigate it. This is determined quite simply by the size of the locks and, to a slightly lesser extend, the size of the remaining infrastructure such as bridges.

Presented with the need to make a canal ascend or descend – something Brindley avoided wherever possible, preferring to follow a contour, however much this added to the overall distance – he turned to the pound lock. As a millwright, he had no previous experience and there are accounts of him building his first lock in the grounds of his own house at Turnhurst, near Stafford, by way of experiment. From this he would have established its ideal dimensions, together with the details pertaining to gate, paddle and culvert design.

In balancing function against finance, Brindley arrived at the narrow canals we see today, prevalent throughout a significant part of our inland waterways system. Cheaper to build and operate, being considerably less 'thirsty' than a broad lock, they presented a good compromise that was later to become a straitjacket in the evolution of an artificial navigation system within this country. It is interesting to reflect, therefore, that had broad locks been seen as the preferred option, whether we might have remained in step with continental European countries, as their waterways grew progressively to the 3,000 tonne Large Rhine barge standard that many navigations enjoy today.

BIRMINGHAM CANAL NAVIGATIONS

The Birmingham Canal Company was authorised in 1768 to build a canal from Aldersley on the Staffordshire & Worcestershire Canal to Birmingham. With James Brindley as engineer the work proceeded quickly. The first section, from Birmingham to the Wednesbury collieries, was opened in November 1769, and the whole 22½-mile route was completed in 1772. It was a winding, contour canal, with 12 locks taking it over Smethwick, and another 20 (later 21) taking it down through Wolverhampton to Aldersley Junction. As the route of the canal was through an area of mineral wealth and developing industry, its success was immediate.

Evening on the BCN in central Birmingham

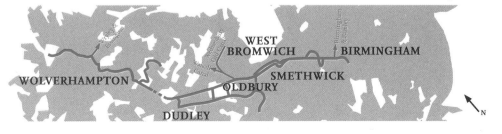

BACKGROUND

Little more than 20 years after completion of the original canal, pressure of traffic caused the summit level at Smethwick to be lowered (thus cutting out six locks – three on either side of the summit), and during the same period branches began to reach out towards Walsall via the Ryder's Green Locks, and towards Fazeley. Out of this very profitable and ambitious first main line there grew the Birmingham Canal Navigations, more commonly abbreviated to BCN.

As traffic continued to increase so did the wealth of the BCN. The pressures of trade made the main line at Smethwick congested and brought grave problems of water supply. Steam pumping engines were installed in several places to recirculate the water, and the company appointed Thomas Telford to shorten Brindley's old main line. Between 1825 and 1838 Telford engineered a new main line between Deepfields and Birmingham, using massive cuttings and embankments to maintain

Telford's Mainline on the left, Brindley's on the right

a continuous level. These improvements not only increased the amount of available waterway (the old line remaining in use) but also shortened the route from Birmingham to Wolverhampton by 7 miles.

Railway control of the BCN meant an expansion of the use of the system, and a large number of interchange basins were built to promote outside trade by means of rail traffic. This was of course quite contrary to the usual effect of railway competition upon canals. Trade continued to grow in relation to industrial development and by the end of the 19th century it was topping $8^{1}/_{2}$ million tons per annum. A large proportion of this trade was local, being dependent upon the needs and output of Black Country industry. After the turn of the century this reliance on local trade started the gradual decline of the system as deposits of raw materials became exhausted. Factories bought from further afield and developed along the railways and roads away from the canals. Yet as late as 1950 there were over a million tons of goods carried on the canals and the system continued in operation until the end of the coal trade in 1967 (although there was some further traffic for the Birmingham Salvage Department), a pattern quite different from canals as a whole. Nowadays there is no recognisable commercial traffic – a dramatic contrast to the roaring traffic on the newer Birmingham motorways.

As trade declined, so parts of the system fell out of use and were abandoned. In its heyday in 1865, the BCN comprised over 160 miles of canal. Today just over 100 miles remain, and much has been done in recent years to tidy these up. This is now having a noticeable effect. Where once there were the old and run-down relics of industry, there is now much new housing and stylish industrial estates. However, the BCN remains an area of retreat for the harassed city dweller and presents new areas of exploration for the canal traveller.

THE NAVIGATION

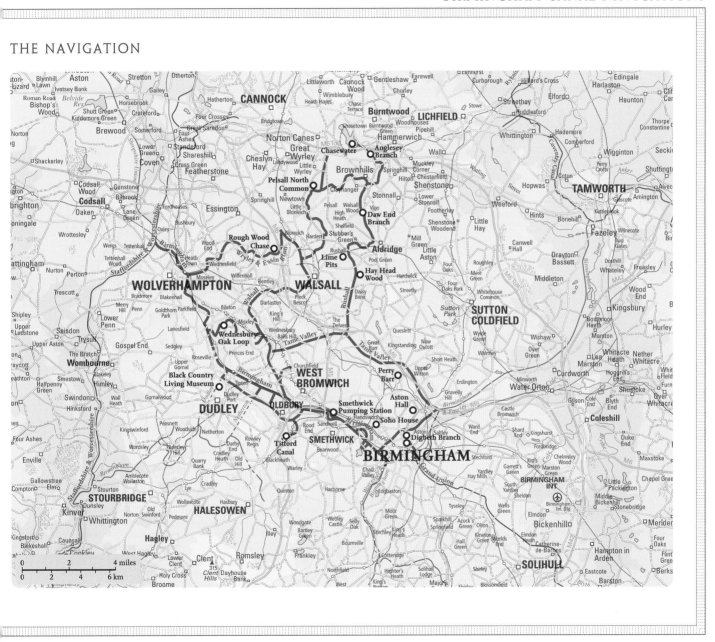

BIRMINGHAM CANAL – OLD AND NEW MAINLINES

The main line of the Birmingham Canal Navigations (BCN) leaves Gas Street Basin, passing immediately under Broad Street Bridge with the towpath continuing beside the canal. North of Broad Street is Deep Cuttings Junction (Old Turn), a canal crossroads where the Old Turn Island was rebuilt in 1985 in a new position. Here the Birmingham & Fazeley Canal swings away to the northeast, immediately passing Cambrian Wharf, beyond which the Farmer's Bridge flight of 13 very tidy locks fall steeply away from the heart of Birmingham. Aston Junction marks the start of the Aston Flight, which falls through 11 locks to Salford Junction, itself dwarfed by the M5 Spaghetti Junction poised, seemingly precariously, above. The Ashted Flight drops through six locks to Typhoo Basin, and on to Bordesley Junction and the start of the Grand Union Canal, heading to London.

OLD MAINLINE

Chief engineer	James Brindley
Significance	Linked Birmingham and the Black Country with the southwestern leg of the Grand Cross.
Started in	1768
Completed in	1772
Length	22½ miles
Headroom	6' 6"
Lock size	70' × 7'
Number of locks	24
Tunnels	2
Aqueducts	2
Goods carried	Coal, iron ore, limestone, cement, imported raw materials, finished goods.
Peak tonnage carried	End of 19th C – over 8,500,000 tons per annum.
Operating authority	Canal & River Trust
Contact details	enquiries.westmidlands@canalrivertrust.org.uk

Old Turn (Deep Cuttings) Junction on the BCN

The main line turns west at Farmer's Bridge, while the short Oozell's Street loop goes to the south, quickly disappearing behind new apartments. This loop, which now houses a boatyard and moorings, and the others further along, are surviving parts of Brindley's original contour canal, now known as the Birmingham Canal Old Main Line. The delays caused by this prompted the Birmingham Canal Company to commission Telford to build a straighter line, the Birmingham Canal New Main Line. This was constructed between 1823 and 1838, and when completed reduced Brindley's old 22½-mile canal to 15 miles. The BCN Society have erected signposts at the main junctions.

The Oozell's Street loop reappears from the south, and then, after two bridges, the Icknield Port loop leaves to the south. This loop acts as a feeder from Rotton Park Reservoir and rejoins after ¼ mile at another canal crossroads – the Winson Green or Soho loop, which leaves the main line opposite the Icknield Port loop. This last loop is the longest of the three, running in a gentle arc for over a mile before rejoining the main line again. It was the only loop to have a towpath throughout its length until the recently completed towpath on the Oozell's Street loop. At its eastern end is Hockley Port, formerly railway-owned but now used for residential moorings. There are houseboats, a community hall, dry docks and workshops.

BIRMINGHAM CANAL – OLD AND NEW MAINLINES

The main line continues towards Smethwick Junction. Here there is a choice of routes: Brindley's old main line swings to the right, while Telford's new main line continues straight ahead – the old line is the more interesting of the two. The two routes run side by side, but the old line climbs to a higher level via the three Smethwick Locks. Here there were two flights of locks, also side-by-side.

Beyond the junction, Telford's new line enters a steep-sided cutting. This 40ft-deep cutting enabled Telford to avoid the changes in level of the old line and thus speed the flow of traffic. The two routes continue their parallel courses, the one overlooking the other, until the lower line passes under the Telford Aqueduct. This elegant single span cast iron structure carries the Engine Branch, a short feeder canal that leaves the old line, crosses the new line and then turns back to the south for a short distance. This arm is named after the first Boulton & Watt steam pumping engine to be bought by the Birmingham Canal Company. This continued to feed the old summit level for 120 years. It was then moved to Ocker Hill for preservation and demonstrations, until the 1950s, when it was finally retired.

The sides of the cutting are richly covered with wild flowers and blackberry bushes and the seclusion of the whole area has turned it into an unofficial nature reserve. The old pumping station at Brasshouse Lane has been restored after years of disuse as part of the new Galton Valley Canal Park development.

The New Main Line continues through natural wilderness to Galton Tunnel. Telford's Galton Bridge crosses the cutting in one magnificent 150ft cast iron span. This bridge is preserved as an ancient monument. The old and the new Birmingham canal lines continue their parallel course, and soon the pleasant semi-rural isolation

of the cutting ends, to be replaced by a complex meeting of three types of transport system. The M5 motorway swings in from the east, carried high above the canal on slender concrete pillars; the railway stays close beside Telford's new line; and the canals enter a series of junctions that seem to anticipate modern motorway practice.

The new line now leaves the cutting and continues in a straight line through industrial surroundings. It passes under Stewart Aqueduct and then reaches Bromford Junction. Here a canal sliproad links the old and the new lines via the three Spon Lane Locks, joining the new at an angle from the east. There is an unusual split bridge at Spon Lane top lock, which was rebuilt in 1986. The old line swings south west following the 473ft contour parallel to the M5, crossing the new line on Stewart Aqueduct. Thus canal crosses canal on the equivalent of a flyover. Spon Lane Locks, the linking sliproad, survive unchanged from Brindley's day and are among the oldest in the country.

The old and the new lines now follow separate courses. The old line continues below the motorway to Oldbury Locks Junction. Here the short Titford Canal climbs away to the south via the six Oldbury Locks; this canal serves as a feeder from Titford Pools to Rotton Park Reservoir. After the junction the old line swings round to the northwest and continues on a parallel course to the new line once again. After Bromford Junction the new line continues its straight course towards Wolverhampton. At Pudding Green Junction the main line goes straight on; the Wednesbury Old Canal forks right to join the Walsall Canal, which in turn joins the Tame Valley Canal at Doebank Junction.

BRINGING IMPORTS TO THE MIDLANDS

Sugar, cocoa beans, soap, tea, metal ingots and tinned food, unloaded at Avonmouth into barges and transhipped into narrowboats at Gloucester, were regular cargoes bound for the Midlands in the early years of the 20th century. Narrowboats, often in groups of twelve, would lock down into the River Severn to be towed by one of the Severn & Canal Carrying Company's tugs as far as Worcester, and sometimes on to Stourport.

Those that had booked the tow were arranged in a double line behind the tug, perhaps it would be the *Alert*, with the tow ropes leading from one stern quarter of the boat ahead to the opposite forequarter of the boat following, thereby allowing each craft steerage.

The narrowboats, on arrival at Diglis Basin, then locked up onto the Worcester & Birmingham Canal, collecting donkeys or mules from the stables to complete their journey to Gas Street Basin and the Birmingham Canal Navigations.

Tardebigge Locks presented a formidable challenge to the crews, who would often urge the donkeys on at the locks, partially opening the gates while the water was still two foot off the level. A block of wood was then inserted between the gates to create an unofficial extra paddle – a practice we would not even contemplate today.

BIRMINGHAM CANAL – OLD AND NEW MAINLINES

At Bradeshall Junction the Gower Branch links the two lines, descending to the lower level of the new line through three locks. To the southwest of Tipton Junction is the branch leading to the Black Country Living Museum and the Dudley Tunnel. The old line turns north at the junction, rejoining the new line at Factory Junction.

At Albion Junction the Gower Branch turns south to join the old line at Bradeshall. At Dudley Port Junction the Netherton Tunnel Branch joins the main line. The Netherton Tunnel Branch goes through the tunnel to Windmill End Junction and from here boats can either turn south down the old Dudley Canal to Hawne Basin, or west towards the Stourbridge Canal, and thus to the Staffordshire & Worcestershire Canal.

North of Dudley Port the New Mainline crosses over the Ryland Aqueduct to reach Tipton, climbing the three Factory Locks immediately before reaching Factory Junction, where it meets the Old Line coming in from the south. Continuing north, the main line pursues its wandering course towards Horseley Fields Junction (its twisting and turning revealing that Brindley's original line was not altered by Telford beyond Deepfields), before winding its way through the heart of industrial Wolverhampton. Factories surround the canal, shutting it off from the rest of the town, but access is not difficult.

Just north of Bilston Road Bridge there is a railway–canal interchange basin (Chillington Wharf), still intact, the sidings running beside the covered wharf. It is a reminder of the busy traffic that once filled the BCN. At Horseley Fields Junction, set in the middle of Wolverhampton, the main line goes straight on. To the east, the Wyrley & Essington Canal starts its meandering contour course towards Brownhills.

Soon after the junction the canal reaches the top lock of the Wolverhampton flight with its attendant BCN cottage, moored narrowboats and moorings, now extending towards the junction by Broad Street Bridge where the canal was diverted in the early 1970s to accommodate road improvements. The original Broad Street Bridge now stands in the Black Country Living Museum. From here 21 locks carry the canal down to join the Staffordshire & Worcestershire Canal at Aldersley Junction. Half the locks are flanked by industry, and railways criss-cross over and around the canal, but gradually this background yields until the last three locks are virtually rural. An extra lock, using just a single bottom gate, was added in 1784 because the original bottom lock was excessively deep. Beyond the bottom lock there is a welcome old-fashioned brick arch bridge, and then the Birmingham Canal main line ends at Aldersley Junction, inconspicuous when approached from the Staffordshire & Worcestershire Canal (see page 16).

CATCHING THE WATER BUS

It is often assumed that canal passenger boats ceased plying the waterways with the coming of the railways, but such a service did exist more recently, albeit briefly, between Aston and Bromford on the Birmingham & Fazeley Canal. When the Dunlop Rubber Company opened its factory at Bromford in 1916, it was then on the rural outskirts of Birmingham and, during the latter part of the First World War and for a while after, motor transport was difficult to organise. As a result the company decided to investigate the practicalities of canal travel, and a single boat, fitted with a 10 hp engine and a rough tarpaulin cover, began a water bus service on 28 April 1919. It was immediately successful and in 1920 a further four boats were added to the fleet, with a smarter livery and a more powerful 16/20 hp petrol engine fitted. These engines were of an original design, being constructed by Mr Hooke of Watercraft Detachable Power Installations, and were mounted on the roof of the boatman's cabin, with the drive being transferred by two shafts – one horizontal, one vertical. The craft were fitted with comfortable cabins, electric lighting and hot water heating. Each carried 100 people, and the whole operation was supervised by J. Lockett, a RNR Chief Petty Officer. The 2½ mile journeys took between 35 and 40 minutes, and were timed to coincide with shifts at the factory. The service came to a premature end around 13 May 1920, when Birmingham Corporation extended its electric tram service along Tyburn Road to the factory gates.

NEW MAINLINE

Chief engineer	Thomas Telford
Significance	Shortened the original Brindley canal by 7 miles.
Started in	1825
Completed in	1838
Length	15 miles
Headroom	6' 6"
Lock size	70' × 7'
Number of locks	24
Tunnels	2
Aqueducts	3
Goods carried	Coal, iron ore, limestone, cement, raw materials, manufactured goods.
Peak tonnage carried	Over 8,500,000 tons in late 19th C.
Operating authority	Canal & River Trust
Contact details	enquiries.westmidlands @canalrivertrust.org.uk

POINTS OF INTEREST

Aston Hall Trinity Road, Birmingham
Built between 1618 and 1635, this one of the last
great houses to be constructed in the spectacular
Jacobean style and is decorated and furnished to
reflect the lifestyle of a wealthy gentleman.

Digbeth Branch This leaves the Birmingham &
Fazeley main line at Aston Junction, and descends
through six locks to Typhoo Basin, where it meets
the former Warwick & Birmingham Canal, which
became part of the Grand Union Canal when the
GUC Company was formed in 1929. There was a
stop lock – called Warwick Bar – at the junction by
Bordesley Basin. One of the lesser-known tunnels
on the canal system is on the Digbeth Branch –
the Ashted.

St Chad's Cathedral, Birmingham Designed
in Gothic revival style by Pugin in 1841, this
was the first Catholic Cathedral to be erected
in England since the Reformation. It possesses
a large collection of medieval artifacts and
carvings, largely assembled by Pugin himself, and
a unique collection of stained glass, metalwork
and vestments made by John Hardman and Co.,
a world-famous firm based in the Jewellery
Quarter.

St Paul's Church, Birmingham Built in 1779 and
centrepiece of the Georgian St Paul's Square,
this Grade I jewel features a painted window, by
Benjamin West, showing the conversion of St Paul.

St Philip's Cathedral, Birmingham Completed in
1725, Birmingham Cathedral is one of the most
beautiful historic buildings in the city centre and
is famous for its four Pre-Raphaelite stained-glass
windows by Sir Edward Burne-Jones. There is a
canal scene on the altar fall, depicting a canal boat,
a lock and a bridge. One of the clergy's vestments
also depicts Smethwick Pumping Station.

THE END OF WINDMILL END

Overlooking the southern portal of Netherton Tunnel stand the gaunt remains of what is known as
Cobbs Engine House. Its actual name is the Windmill End Pumping Station. Sir Horace St Paul
built it in 1831 to drain his mines where, as well as coal, iron stone and clay were extracted. Boilers,
blast furnaces, open-hearth furnaces and brick kilns stood by the canal here, each contributing to
the dirty and poisonous fumes which gave their name to the Black Country. Netherton Tunnel was
opened in 1858 to ease the terrible delays caused by the claustrophobic Dudley and Lapal tunnels,
and soon the engine house stood witness to another scene of water-borne congestion, where
horse-drawn boats vied with each other to enter the tunnel first. To the southeast of Cobbs Engine
House stood a second building housing a smaller engine, which operated a lift in a second shaft.
The machinery here was dismantled in 1928 and shipped to the USA by Henry Ford, who erected
it in his museum at Dearborn, Detroit. What happened to the Cobbs beam engine is not entirely
clear: for some years it appears to have lain derelict before being broken up for scrap. The fate of the
great beam, which had a stroke of 8ft and a rate of 6 or 8 strokes each minute to operate a pump
some 7ft in diameter in a shaft 522ft deep, lifting about 400,000 gallons of water each day, remains
a mystery. Many believe it broke free during removal and fell down the shaft, which was
subsequently infilled.

Smethwick Pumping Station, Birmingham
Restored to full working order, this is the engine
that lifts water from the Telford New Mainline
Canal up to the old Brindley-built Wolverhampton
Level (or Old Mainline). The pump house itself was
built in 1892.

Soho House, Birmingham This was the
elegant Georgian home of the industrialist and
entrepreneur Matthew Boulton from 1766 until
1809 and also the favourite meeting place of the
Lunar Society whose members included Darwin,
Watt and Priestley: they met on the night of the full
moon to enable them to find their way home by
moonlight.

Titford Canal Built in 1837 as part of the original
Birmingham Canal scheme, acting as a feeder to
Spon Lane, the Titford Canal served Causeway
Green. This must have been a very busy canal

in its heyday, with many branches, wharves and
tramways connecting it to the surrounding mines
and engineering works. Today it survives in
shortened form and has the distinction of being
the highest navigable part of the BCN, with a
summit level above Oldbury Locks of 511ft. The
locks are sometimes referred to as the Crow – a
branch which left the canal above the third lock
and served the alkali and phosphorus works of
a local industrialist and benefactor Jim Crow.
The last surviving recirculatory pumphouse
can be seen by the top lock. The waterway now
terminates at the wide expanse of water of
Titford Pools.

Black Country Living Museum, Dudley A superb
outdoor museum built around a reconstructed
canalside village, with a pub, shops and all the
trappings of an inland port and a boat trip into
Dudley Tunnel.

WYRLEY & ESSINGTON CANAL

Opened throughout in 1797, the Wyrley & Essington Canal connected the Birmingham Canal with the Birmingham & Fazeley, running in a meandering contour line from Horseley Fields Junction to Huddlesford on the Coventry Canal (*see page 58*) via Lichfield. In 1954 the main line between Ogley Junction and Huddlesford was abandoned but, in the guise of the Litchfield Canal, is now thankfully being restored.

Leaving the main line at Horseley Fields Junction, the Wyrley & Essington soon establishes its lazy roundabout course to Sneyd Junction, flanked by houses and factories but with enough pleasant breaks of grass and trees to maintain interest. At Wednesfield Junction, beyond a red brick turnover bridge, the

Good cheer at Gas Street Basin, Birmingham

remains of the Bentley Canal can be seen. This was abandoned in 1961. Church Bridge is overlooked by the red brick tower of St Thomas Church. At Lane Head a triangular green is enclosed by terraced cottages on two sides, sometimes grazed by donkeys.

The Wyrley & Essington Canal continues its eccentric course around Rough Wood to join the M6 motorway for a short while, but this is thankfully soon left well behind as Edwards Bridge is approached. At Sneyd Junction the main line turns sharp right under the bridge. Ahead, beyond the derelict lock, the old Wyrley Branch once linked with coal workings and the Essington Branch, at 533ft above sea level the highest point reached on the BCN. It was never successfully operated due to water supply problems. Beyond the wharf buildings and crane the canal makes its journey through Leamore to Birchills Junction, where the Walsall Canal leaves to the south, and the Wyrley & Essington continues, passing factories and car parks. These soon give way to neat rows of suburban houses, and then finally the canal is in open country.

The navigation meanders quietly through suburbs to Pelsall Junction, amidst the flat grassy expanse of Pelsall Wood, where the Cannock Extension Canal leaves to the north. This waterway was built between 1858 and 1863 and once connected with the Staffordshire & Worcestershire Canal. The old basins just before the present terminus used to serve the Brownhills Colliery. It is wholly rural until the boatyards are reached, and is well worth the short diversion. The section to the north of Watling Street was closed in 1963 due to subsidence. It was apparently quite a spectacular length, with massive embankments and vast brick overflow weirs. About 70 boats were left for scrap when it was abandoned. The main line continues on its eccentric course through fields, factories and houses until it approaches Catshill Junction and the wharf at Brownhills.

RUSHALL CANAL

Scout Jamboree on the Walsall Canal, August 1958

Leaving Longwood the character of the route south changes to that of a straight modern canal, revealing that the traveller is now on the Rushall Canal; this was built in 1847 to connect the Daw End Branch with the Tame Valley Canal in order to capture the coal trade from Cannock Mines. After the top two locks the canal passes a golf course; beyond Sutton Road Bridge the banks are lined with canalside gardens, and the towpath is overhung with willow, flowering currant and berberis. Another golf course accompanies the route through the next flurry of locks on this long, drawn-out flight, and still the surroundings are wholly amenable as the navigation makes its way gently to its assignation with the Tame Valley Canal at Rushall Junction. This is truly a fine length of urban canal, which would stand comparison with many others in the country.

POINTS OF INTEREST

Near Farmer's Bridge, Smethwick: a pair of Birmingham Salvage Depot boats being towed by a horse

Daw End Branch The Daw End Branch runs south from the Wyrley & Essington Canal, leaving at Catshill Junction – it was built in 1803 to carry lime from the workings around Daw End and Hay Head – and although constructed originally as a contour canal following the 473ft line, mining and subsidence have frequently left it in a very high, exposed position: this is immediately apparent when approaching Walsall Wood Bridge. Continuing south, the Daw End Branch now finds itself high up on an embankment with very deep clay pits either side, some now partially flooded and landscaped, some still being worked. These dramatic surroundings give way to light industry and new housing, which in turn are followed by a surprisingly rural area which is to last until Walsall's smarter suburbs are reached. There is a remarkable stone cottage and red brick arch at Brawn's Bridge; these red brick arches then appear regularly, enhancing the canal's remote quality. At Longwood Junction the main line of the Daw End Branch used to continue to Hay Head – this is now abandoned and forms part of a nature

reserve. Longwood Boat Club have their moorings at the junction, and their club house is in an old canal building next to BCN house no. 93 at the top lock. With pretty gardens, the whole makes for a charming canal scene.

Anglesey Branch The Anglesey Branch, which heads off east from the Wyrley & Essington Canal at Catshill Junction, last carried coal from the Cannock Mines in 1967, so those who make this worthwhile diversion may be surprised to find that the route is extremely rural, with open country to the north. An elegant cast iron bridge spans Ogley Junction, where the main line of the Wyrley & Essington once descended through locks to join the Coventry Canal at Huddlesford Junction. The route, abandoned in 1954 and now known as the Litchfield Canal, is the subject of an energetic restoration campaign. What was once just a feeder from Chasewater now passes through sandy heathland and under the new M6 toll motorway before terminating at Anglesey Basin, a wide expanse where there are still the remains of loading chutes to be seen.

THOMAS'S LAST WORKING DAYS

It was in May 1955 that the last load of coal was carried from the mines at Anglesey Basin to Townsends Flour Mill at Diglis Basin in Worcester in the narrowboat *Thomas*, skippered by Ray White and pulled by Bob, the horse. The round trip of 103 miles was via Tardebigge, the New Main Line to Pudding Green and onto the Wednesbury Old Canal, then through Ryders Green Junction and down the eight locks to make a right turn at Doebank onto the Tame Valley Canal. A left turn at Rushall Junction brought the climb to Catshill, passing the Travellers Rest pub, once a popular overnight stop, but alas no longer there. After bearing right at Catshill Junction and left at Ogley a whole clutch of moored narrowboats, some full and some empty, would come into view at Anglesey Basin.

Loading at the basin was swift and efficient (some remains of the chutes can still be seen today), with an average of a little under thirty boats being filled daily. *Thomas* carried 27 tons of coal back to Diglis, being towed through Wast Hills Tunnel by the tug, and worked through the Tardebigge flight 'like a bat out of hell'.

Chasewater Built as a canal feeder reservoir, and so efficient was it that at one time its owners, the Wyrley & Essington Canal Company, sold its water to other companies. Just after building, in 1799, the dam collapsed, pouring a torrent of water across Watling Street and into the River Tame at Tamworth. Meadows were left strewn with gravel, and some livestock was drowned, but luckily little other damage was caused. The dam was rebuilt, faced with stone, and has remained stoically intact ever since.

WALSALL CANAL

The Walsall Canal runs from Ryder's Green Junction to Birchills Junction, connecting with the Tame Valley and Wyrley & Essington Canals. Its construction to Walsall was completed in 1799, with the link with the Wyrley & Essington being made via eight locks in 1841. The Wednesbury Old Canal was opened prior to this, in 1769, and still provides the vital link with the Walsall Canal. These two canals remain industrialised, and as such they give some impression of what the BCN was like in its heyday.

The Wednesbury Old Canal leaves the main line at Pudding Green Junction. Immediately after Ryder's Green Junction, where the shortened Ridgeacre Branch heads half-a-mile to the north, eight locks descend to Doebank Junction. Hempole Lane Bridge is one of the few BCN bridges dated in Roman numerals – MDCCCXXV – 1825. Just beyond is the Ocker Hill Tunnel Branch. This once fed water to the Wednesbury Oak Loop. Black and white cast iron bridges mark the junction with the Tame Valley Canal. Beyond the canal reaches what is left of the unnavigable Gospel Oak Branch.

Beyond Foresters Bridge and the railway viaduct the Anson Branch used to fork off northeast – this once connected with the Bentley Canal, which in turn joined the Wyrley & Essington. Now the Walsall Canal is up on an embankment, crossing James Bridge Aqueduct (dated 1797), very exposed but with fine views over distant housing, a car breaker's yard and a cemetery. The M6 motorway zooms overhead and the new ornate gateway to Sister Dora Gardens are passed before reaching Walsall Junction, where the Town Arm branches off below the locks.

Walsall Locks climb away north, enclosed by tall buildings – note especially Albion Flour Mill, dated 1849, with its covered loading bay, at lock 7. Once again traditional paddle gear and big wooden balance beams contribute to the enjoyment of the flight – at the top lock the old Boatman's Rest is visible opposite Thomas's Wharf. Note also the toll office and BCN house no. 206 here. The canal then makes for the Wyrley & Essington, which it joins at Birchills Junction, passing the old brick arch of Raybolds Bridge on the way.

CARING FOR THE BOATMAN'S BODY AND SOUL

The Boatman's Rest at Birchills, which until recently housed the Birchills Canal Museum, was originally one of three institutions operated by the Incorporated Seamen and Boatmen's Friend Society – the other two, at Gas Street Basin and Hednesford, have now been demolished. Caring for the physical and spiritual needs of the boatmen, the halls offered religious services, a clubroom (with no alcohol), overnight accommodation, letter writing and a semblance of education for the boat children. Stables were also provided for the horses.

The Walsall Iron Company's works once stood close to the canal at Birchills, not far from the Boatman's Rest. A furnace in the works, loaded with more molten metal than was prudent, exploded on 15 October 1875, showering 17 men with molten metal and burning them badly. Three of the victims jumped into the canal in an effort to find relief. Although lovingly nursed by Sister Dora (Dorothy Pattison), only two survived the incident. Sister Dora became famous in the area for her nursing skills, and did much to reduce the death rate from industrial accidents, giving Walsall a better track record in this respect than many of the London teaching hospitals. She came from Yorkshire in 1865, taking charge of Walsall's first hospital.

TAME VALLEY CANAL

Opened in 1844 to overcome the long delays which were occurring at Farmer's Bridge Locks, the canal is typified by its direct course, deep cuttings and high embankments. The first $3^{1}/_{2}$ mile section between Doebank Junction and Rushall Junction has the distinction of being the dreariest on the whole BCN.

However, the final approach to Rushall Junction becomes suddenly quite overwhelming, with motorways appearing on all sides and the sweet smells of a sewage farm to spur one on. Leaving the junction, the Tame Valley Canal enters its own secluded world. Colourful suburban gardens are glimpsed here and there before the waterway enters a steep wooded cutting crossed by the high modern Scott Bridge, and the more agreeable Chimney Bridge, a footbridge supported on substantial brick pillars. Emerging from the cutting, the traveller then finds himself on a high embankment, with wide views all around; two aqueducts are crossed.

Soon, however, the canal enters a deep cutting, this time through sandstone some 200 million years old, and propped up here and there with brickwork. After passing the handsome brick arch of Freeth Bridge, Perry Barr Top Lock is reached, set between a fine red brick BCN house (no. 86), old stables and the Gauging Weir House. The lock flight straggles along the canal, and passes through an area of private back gardens, public open spaces and sports fields. Little industry intrudes, although the M6 motorway crosses twice. The Tame Valley Canal joins the Birmingham & Fazeley and Grand Union canals under Spaghetti Junction motorway interchange, where cast iron towpath bridges are dwarfed by flyovers, making a strangely mesmeric scene in complete and utter contrast to the tranquillity of the canals hidden below.

POINTS OF INTEREST

Wednesbury Oak Loop This was the original course of the Old Main Line which followed a contour route around Coseley Hill, and was bypassed in 1837 with the building of Coseley Tunnel. Leaving the main line at Deepfields Junction, the canal passes through what was once a mining area, now landscaped and with wide views to south and north. Beyond Pothouse Bridge, land which at one time reverberated to the sound of iron making is now grassy fields, accompanying the waterway on its last 1/4 mile to the terminus at Canal & River Trust Midlands Regional Workshop. It is to this maintenance yard, where lock gates and boats are made and repaired, that the remaining section of the loop owes its survival. There is now little trace of the length which once connected to the Walsall and Tame Valley canals via the Bradley Locks Branch.

Pelsall North Common, Walsall Originally rough grazing, much of the common was consumed by a great ironworks between 1832 and 1888, which employed 100 people from Pelsall village. Eventually iron prices fell, and the company went into liquidation, with the works being demolished in the late 1920s. A large machine, known as 'the cracker', was used to break up the mounds of foundry waste, and this gave the common its local nickname 'the cracker'. This machine was disposed of shortly after the Second World War. The common covers 137 acres, 92 of which, north of the canal, are designated a local nature reserve. There are areas of valuable lowland heath, pools containing mallard, snipe and mute swans, and many lime-loving plants to the west. Bright green and blue emperor dragonflies can be seen near the canal in summer.

Rough Wood Chase, Walsall In the 12th century Rough Wood was part of Bentley Hay, a district of Cannock Forest. Deer were hunted here, in what

was a Royal Forest, until the 1500s when the king ordered all the trees to be felled. Coal was found in the 1700s, and this was transported by canal to the furnaces of the Black Country. It used to be loaded onto boats by Bentley Wharf Bridge. Today Rough Wood contains fine stands of oak, which in turn support vast numbers of insects, upon which a great variety of birds feed.

Park Lime Pits, Walsall Some 200 years ago this area was a thriving lime quarry, the lime being used as flux in the production of iron. Blocks of limestone were taken to the canal in trucks, to be transported to the furnaces of the Black Country. It is also possible that the Romans may have used stone from here in the building of Watling Street. When quarrying ended some 150 years ago the old workings were landscaped, beech trees were planted and the quarries filled with water. These pools now support coot, moorhen and other waterfowl. Daubenton's bats fly over the water at dusk. Limestone spoil heaps support plants such as burnet-saxifrage and potentilla.

Lime Pits Farm, Walsall This farm adjoins the reserve, and is a pioneering project which is endeavouring to combine nature conservation with productive farming. By following a trail the visitor is introduced to wheat and barley growing, with Jersey cows producing milk. The cattle drink from ponds which also support a variety of birds and insects. There is a wildflower hay meadow, small fields and rich hedgerows, protected from pesticides and fertilisers. Trees have been planted in field corners to provide both shelter and wildlife habitats.

Hay Head Wood, Walsall Another limestone area, with evidence of mine shafts dating from the late 18th century still visible. The lime from here was found to be suitable for cement production,

Bridges at Galton over Telford's Mainline

and much was used in the construction of canal buildings. The pond was once an arm of the canal, built to transport limestone from the mines, and the remains of old wharf buildings can still be made out. Follow the trail in late spring and you will see (and smell) wild garlic, as well as dog's mercury, a plant which loves the lime. Old oak woods support varied birds and insects, and occasionally kingfishers and herons are seen in the remains of the old canal basin.

In the Cotswold, close to Cirencester can be found both the undistinguished site of the source of the River Thames and the Sapperton Tunnel, the longest tunnel of any kind in England when it opened in 1789 as part of the now derelict Thames & Severn Canal. The tunnel is 3,817yds in length (a little over 2 miles) and, like Standedge Tunnel on the Huddersfield Narrow Canal, is now surrounded by two adjacent railway tunnels. The difference lies in the latter's justifiable claim to being the longest, highest and deepest canal tunnel in Britain: statistics that are explored further in Milepost 13. However, what makes this more southerly engineering feat so significant is its bore of 15ft which allows the passage of a wide beam barge, whereas its predecessors had all been constructed to accommodate narrowboats of 7ft beam. It was completed in five years and is, to all intents and purposes, straight – allowing a steerer to see from end to end – having been constructed by the simple expedient of sinking twenty-four vertical shafts from the surface, set out along a straight, marked line.

A little over half the bore runs through solid rock and here the tunnellers made extensive use of gunpowder. In many places the rock formed a natural wall or arch, requiring no additional lining material, which would have been brick or stone. Often fissures in the rock strata caused problems when it came to ensuring that the bed of the navigation held water. The remainder of the length is through Fullers earth, which is notorious for expanding when wet and has been responsible for fairly limited areas of collapse. In some sections of the limestone strata, water levels fluctuate considerably, draining the waterway in summer and raising the water table in winter; everywhere springs abound.

Eisey Lock brickwork

The Cotswold Canals Trust, which has already completed six miles of the waterway through Stroud, is masterminding the complete restoration of the navigation – which presents some formidable challenges – in a partnership that includes local authorities and the Stroudwater Navigation Proprietors. A combination of what was once the Stroudwater Navigation and the Thames & Severn Canal, connecting the two eponymous rivers, the Cotswold Canals (totalling 36 miles) always suffered from water supply problems, exacerbated by severe water loss through the porous Cotswold limestone. By 1927 much of the navigation had fallen into disrepair and it was finally abandoned throughout in 1933.

Their *raison d'être* lay mainly in the cloth industry centred upon the Stroud valley. The numerous mills required coal to fuel their steam-driven machinery and a ready outlet for their finished products. Through transport from the Severn to London was also important and a major inland transhipment port grew up at Brimscombe, where the Stroudwater and the Thames & Severn canals met. Cargoes were transferred from Severn Trows to Thames Barges in much the same way that Morwellham Quay (*see* Milepost 14) once operated and, say, Daventry International Rail Freight Terminal (DIRFT) does today: an immense inland hub where the transfer of containers from road to rail on a hugely increased scale is expedited.

The Coates portal of Sapperton Tunnel under restoration, 1977

This may well be in the form of increased visitor numbers and their potential spending power. Very often the sums add up to a surprisingly high figure and act as a positive spur to moving the project forward. Developers are also well aware that new properties erected beside water – perhaps a restored canal or basin – command a 10–15 per cent premium on the selling price, as do converted waterside buildings such as redundant warehouses.

The Cotswold Canals provide fertile ground for WERGIE activity (*see* Milepost 21 and the accompanying pictures) and sections are once again in water, complete with newly repaired structures, largely due to their tireless activity. Other volunteer groups are also involved in bringing this long abandoned navigation back to life, so that it can truly be viewed as the focus of concerted, community participation.

Eisey Lock prior to 2009, after scrub clearance

Narrowboats unloading over the towpath at Chalford on the Thames & Severn Canal

On the Stroudwater Navigation, whilst there are no plans to restore the most westerly section – between Saul Junction on the Gloucester & Sharpness Canal and the River Severn itself – full reinstatement of the link between the junction and Brimscombe Port is well under way. This activity, in itself, helps to raise awareness not only of the existence of a waterway (albeit in its derelict state) but also draws attention to the economic potential of restoration. One of the many stages that the hopeful canal restoration body has to go through, in the pursuit of funding, is to prepare a cost–benefit analysis to demonstrate how much money the finished waterway will inject into the local economy on an annual basis.

BIRDS

The birds shown on these pages, and the flora and fauna illustrated later in the book, provide just a small glimpse of the marvellous variety and diversity of wildlife to be found around our canals and inland waterways as they form significant wildlife 'corridors'. There are more than 1,000 wildlife conservation sites and 60 SSSIs alongside the waterways network providing habitats for a wide range of species.

However you explore these navigations (and we hope you will, *see* page 288) and at whatever time of year, there is always a creature, wildflower or bird to be spotted, enjoyed or wondered at, whether commonplace or more elusive and in every habitat, from city centre to wild and unkempt corner.

Barn owl

Barn owl A beautiful owl, sadly decidedly scarce in most areas but can be seen along riverbanks and towpaths, usually at dusk or after dark. When caught in the headlights of a car, they appear ghostly white. Their flight is leisurely and slow on rounded wings. Only when seen perched can the orange-buff upperparts, speckled with tiny black and white dots, be appreciated; the facial disc is heart-shaped and white. Barn owls feed mainly on small mammals located by quartering meadows, farmland and verges and they are seen all too often as a road casualty. Sometimes these owls nest in tree holes but, as their name implies, they often use barns and other buildings and readily take to nesting platforms provided for this purpose. The blood-curdling call is one of the most frightening sounds of the countryside at night.

Goldfinch A beautiful, small finch, with bright yellow wingbars and a white rump. The adult has red and white on its face, a black cap extending down the sides of the neck, buffish back and white underparts with buff flanks. The juvenile has brown, streaked plumage but yellow wingbars as in the adult. They are a common and widespread resident in Britain and Ireland (except northern Scotland). Goldfinch favour wasteground and meadows where the narrow, pointed bill is used to feed on seeds of thistles and teasel in particular. The bird builds a neat, deep nest towards the end of a branch. They are usually seen in small flocks which take to the wing with a tinkling flight call. The male's song is twittering but contains call-like elements.

Goldfinch

Grey heron A familiar large, long-legged wetland bird. The adult has a dagger-like, yellow bill and a black crest of feathers. The head, neck and underparts are otherwise whitish except for black streaks on the front of the neck and breast. The back and wings are blue-grey. In flight, the wings are broad and rounded with black flight feathers. Heron employ slow, flapping wingbeats and hold the neck folded in a hunched 's' shape close to the body. The juvenile is similar to the adult but the markings are less distinctive and the plumage more grubby in appearance. Heron are often seen standing motionless for hours on end on long, yellow legs, sometimes with the neck hunched up.

Grey heron

They will occasionally actively stalk prey which comprise mainly amphibians and fish, especially eels. Their call is a harsh and distinctive 'frank'. The birds nest in loose colonies mainly in trees but sometimes in reedbeds.

Kingfisher A dazzlingly attractive bird, although the colours often appear muted when the kingfisher is seen sitting in the shade of vegetation. Orange-red

Kingfisher

underparts and mainly blue upperparts; the electric blue back is seen to best effect when the bird is observed in low-level flight speeding along a river or canal. Invariably seen near water, the bird uses overhanging branches to watch for fish. When a feeding opportunity arises, the kingfisher plunges headlong into the water, catching its prey in its bill: the fish is swallowed whole, head first. Kingfishers sometimes stun their prey first by beating the head on a branch. The birds nest in underground chambers at the end of tunnels excavated in the banks of waterways, dug by both parents.

Lapwing

Lapwing Formerly more numerous but lapwing are still common in many parts of Britain and Ireland and can be seen on the Exe Estuary, particularly in spring. They breed in open, flat country, including undisturbed farmland and coastal marshes, and nest on the ground. After nesting, flocks form and travel to find suitable feeding areas free of frost. In winter the British population is boosted by an influx of continental birds. The lapwing looks black and white at a distance but in good light has a green, oily sheen on the back; winter birds have buffish fringes to their feathers on the back. The spiky

crest feathers are longer in male birds that the females. In flight the lapwing has rounded, black and white wings and a flapping flight. Their call is a loud 'peewit'.

Little egret A common and conspicuous year-round resident on many estuaries and coastal waterways, roosting in colonies. They are an unmistakable, pure white, heron-like bird with black, dagger-like bills and long necks. The legs are long and black, with plastic-yellow feet, often not visible if the bird is wading. In the breeding season the birds acquire head plumes and trailing plumes on their backs. In flight, the trailing legs and yellow feet are conspicuous; the neck held in a hunched 's' shape. An active feeder, often chasing after fish in shallow water and stabbing with great accuracy. At other times, the bird may rest in a hunched-up posture with the head and bill hidden, when it can be confused with a mute swan.

Little egret

THE SOUTH

For the pedant, the south of the country might hold the accolade as birthplace of the canals as we know them today, simply on account of its playing host to the Exeter Canal. The significance of this waterway lies purely in the fact that it is the first recorded navigation to make use of pound locks – erected during the reign of Queen Elizabeth I. The considerably more inefficient flash locks operate by lifting a series of wooden paddles, in a weir-like structure, to enable a boat to change levels; pound locks impound a stretch of water – between two fixed gates – which can be made to rise or fall by letting a controlled amount of water either in or out. Certainly adopting this principle to allow craft to ascend or descend a waterway made a tremendous difference,

Boats moored above Turf Lock on the Exeter Ship Canal

Higher Lock, Bridgwater & Taunton Canal

not least in that it rationed the amount of water required and on a river generally made navigation far more reliable.

Whilst there are records of the Romans dragging craft on rollers across the narrow Cornish isthmus, when trading between Ireland and the Mediterranean, inland navigation in Cornwall – whether utilizing flash or pound locks – has never been greatly exploited and canals in the county have been both short and largely short lived. The Bude Canal, a tub boat canal at 35 miles in length, is one exception although rather than use locks, its builders preferred a system of inclined planes, the underlying principles of which are examined in Milepost 19. Running inland on

the south coast, the Liskeard & Looe Canal was equally short lived and relatively soon after its completion fell victim to railway competition. Further up country, the Tavistock Canal worked hard during its existence and its place in West Country mineral extraction is explored further in Milepost 14.

Grandiose schemes abounded for an inland waterway connection to be made between the Bristol Avon and Exeter, via the ferocious little River Exe but were only in part realised with the construction of the Bridgwater & Taunton and the Grand Western canals which, for a while, met one another at Taunton, linked via seven vertical lifts and one inclined plane – all plagued by mechanical problems and now long defunct.

Calcutt Locks, Grand Union Canal

Traversing the region west to east is, of course, the River Thames, enjoying a special place in the hearts and minds of the British population and metamorphosed as a great patriarchal figure reaching back into the beginnings of time. Lying almost parallel and further to the south, runs the charming Kennet & Avon Canal (featured in Milepost 12) connecting the tidal River Severn at Avonmouth with the Thames at Reading, using the clear chalk stream of the diminutive River Kennet on the final twenty or so miles of its journey towards the city. In the hinterland, and at one time connecting these two waterways, is the now largely abandoned Wiltshire & Berkshire Canal, nearly 69 miles in length, sections of which are now the subject of a vigorous restoration programme.

Along the south and southeast coast there are numerous navigable inlets, often assisted by artificial cuts. London's one waterway link to the south coast lay in the Wey & Arun Canal, connecting a tributary of the Thames, the River Wey (itself a delight and operated by the National Trust), to the English Channel via Arundel and the River Arun. Long abandoned,

this navigation presents a formidable challenge to complete restoration but its dogged band of followers remain intent on seeing its full revival.

Some 12,500 bats, including the largest known colony of Natterer's bats in the UK, have colonised the collapsed Greywell Tunnel on the western end of the Basingstoke Canal, which once connected the River Wey to the waterway's eponymous town. This precludes any attempt to re-open the tunnel and restore the navigation to its full length and the canal, which unusually is in the ownership of two county councils, now terminates beside the melancholy ruins of Odiham Castle, once King John's hunting lodge.

Into the Thames Estuary flow the usually placid waters of the River Medway: a river of contrasts that in its relatively short, course blends tranquillity with commerce, agriculture with industry. Navigable to small craft from Tonbridge, its lower tidal reaches, once the site of vast naval dockyards, played a significant part in British history, particularly on 12–14 June 1667 when a Dutch fleet sailed into the estuary and destroyed some of the Navy's greatest warships: the *Royal James*, the *Royal Oak*, and *Loyal London* amongst others, with the *Royal Charles* being captured. Rudyard Kipling recorded these momentous happenings in a poem which concluded:

> *'For, now De Ruyter's topsails*
> *Off naked Chatham show*
> *We dare not meet him with our fleet,*
> *And this the Dutchmen know.'*

Sunset at Braunston Turn

EXETER SHIP CANAL

The Exe estuary is up to 1¹/₂ miles wide, its deep water channel tortuous, proving difficult for shipping since vessels first traded to Topsham and Exeter. Seaborne trade with the city was further constrained by the construction of a weir during the reign of Edward I. Built above Topsham, ensuring that craft had to unload downstream of the city, the obstruction remained until an inquisition, decreed that a 30ft gap be made. Thirty years later the Earl of Devon, blocked the hole and again all goods to Exeter passed through the town, attracting considerable dues in the process. A canal was the obvious and equitable solution.

Turf Lock and Hotel at the start of the Exeter Ship Canal

EXETER   TURF
(TURF LOCK)   N

BACKGROUND

In 1539 Exeter Corporation obtained an Act of Parliament to remove what were now three weirs across the river, alongside unsuccessful attempts to dredge a series of shoals that had built up in the river and estuary. Passage into the city remained all but impossible so John Trew, of Glamorgan, was engaged to dig a canal, parallel to the river on its west bank. This opened in 1566, at a cost of £5,000. For this he received £225 and a percentage of the tolls.

The original navigation ran from just below the city walls to a connection with the Exe at Matford Brook, although shipping still had to pass Topsham, attracting dues despite the quays not being used. The navigation was 16ft wide, 3ft deep, enabling vessels to carry 16 tons. It is reputed to be the first navigation constructed in this country with pound locks; three in total, utilising guillotine gates. Boats loaded direct from sea-going craft anchored in the estuary but had to contend with an awkward entrance into the canal, only possible on high tide.

THE 1539 ACT

In 1539 Royal Assent was given to 'An Act concerning the amending of the River and Port of Exeter' which stated that it would be lawful to '. . .plucke downe, digge, moyne, banke, and caste upp all and all manner of weyres, rockes, sandes, gravell and noyaunces whatsoever they be in the saide river . . . and make all other thinges requisite and necessarie wherby the saide shippes, boates and vessels may have their sure course and recourse in the said River to & from youre saide Cittie.'

After the Civil War the waterway was in poor condition, suffering water shortages from unauthorised mill abstraction, silting and continuing rivalry with Topsham. In 1676 the Corporation decided on improvements, dredging the canal and extending it south by half a mile, thereby eliminating one mile of awkward river navigation. They built a larger entrance lock and an adjoining transhipment basin able to handle 60-ton craft.

Exeter was becoming an increasingly prosperous city, its wealth founded on the cloth-making industry and again it found the need to enlarge its waterway. In 1698, the Corporation put in hand a scheme to improve the navigation but the engineer in charge absconded with the city funds, leaving an unnavigable canal and the Corporation to complete the task on its own. Completed in 1701, the enlarged waterway measured 50ft wide, 10ft deep and could carry coasters up to 150 tons. The three old locks were removed and replaced by Double Locks, and flood gates were installed at King's Arms. However, it was still approached up a narrow, winding side channel and was only accessible to larger vessels on spring tides.

A decision was taken in 1825 to further improve and extend the canal and, under the direction of James Green, work commenced. He had previously dredged and straightened the navigation and his new strategy was a two-mile extension to Turf; raised banks to allow passage by vessels of 14ft draught and the construction of a deep-water basin in Exeter. The total cost was £113,355, more than a fifth being absorbed by Turf Lock which was built on piles driven through clay and bog to the underlying bedrock.

In the 1840s steam-driven vessels appeared on the canal but because their speed exceeded the 5 mph limit and their wash threatened the banks, they were prohibited from using their own power and had to be towed by horses. This unpopular move was a turning point for the navigation and the tonnage handled began to decline, as shipping unloaded at nearby coastal ports for onward carriage by rail.

Setting sail from Turf Lock

THE NAVIGATION

Exeter Ship Canal with the River Exe estuary beyond

Chief engineer	John Trew
Later improvements completed by	James Green
Significance	Reputed to be the first canal in Britain to use pound locks.
Started in	1563
Completed in	1566
Improved	1677, 1701, 1825
Length	5 miles
Draught	9'9"
Headroom	32'9"
Lock size	122' × 26'3"
Number of locks	2
Goods carried	Paper, leather, wheat, oats, manganese, cloth, sewerage.
Operating authority	Exeter City Council.
Contact details	river-canal@exeter.gov.uk

A mile or so after passing Powderham Castle, Turf Lock with its attendant and isolated hotel are approached: this is the beginning of the Exeter Ship Canal. It is an excellent spot to linger, to enjoy the views and to wonder at this unusual location.

Heading north, the navigation runs alongside the SSSI of Exminster Marshes with river and canal now in close proximity, only separated (in varying degrees according to the state of the tide) by mudflats on the approach to Topsham which is spread out along the river's east bank. The SSSI is home to geese, curlew and widgeon in winter and lapwings, redshank and warblers in the summer.

Ahead is the M5 flyover, built before the leisure potential of the waterway was fully comprehended; it now imposes a 33ft headroom restriction, which is a significant factor in limiting visiting sailing craft.

Bridge Road is crossed and the large volume of traffic carried, over a pair of moveable bridges, leads one to wonder how much 'shipping' the canal can carry before a serious conflict of interests ensues. Ahead is Double Locks, with the attractive and popular pub of the same name sitting beside the bottom gates. The lock is massive, designed not only to raise the level of the canal but also as a passing place. The railway, left behind at Turf Lock, once again exerts itself and the passing trains are a mix of the futuristic Voyagers, the still elegant High Speed 125s, together with a regular procession of the more prosaic local, stopping diesels.

Approaching the city, the terminal basin and activity around the quays invite the visitor to linger before heading upstream beside what is now the River Exe, under the two bridges that form a giant traffic roundabout overhead.

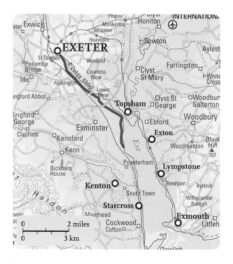

POINTS OF INTEREST

Starcross The central feature of the village is the red sandstone Atmospheric Railway Pumping House, executed by Brunel in Italianate style. This ill-fated venture – one of the great engineer's very few failures – utilised an evacuated iron tube laid between the rails into which a 'shoe' attached to the underside of the locomotive engaged, as would a piston, in a cylinder. Vacuum was created in this tube, ahead of the piston, and the train was thereby sucked along. Obviously the 'leg' attaching shoe to locomotive had to penetrate the tube via a slit and this was where the problems began. Leather flaps were employed to form a seal both ahead and behind the leg and these gave constant trouble,

especially in cold weather. Pumping houses were constructed along the route, of which this one in Starcross is a fine example. Today both railway and road dominate the village whose picturesque cottages are strung along the line of the estuary.

Kenton It is a pretty village, especially the streets behind the main road, with a striking Perpendicular church. The ashlar tower is 120ft high; there are elaborate porches and carvings, and the mullions are in Beer stone. In contrast, the remaining stonework is red sandstone, much patched with grey and white. The pulpit is 15th-century and there is considerable Victorian

restoration. Opposite stands a charming row of late 19th-century almshouses.

Exmouth Exmouth probably first attracted attention when the Danes landed in 1001; the town becoming of consequence at the beginning of the 13th century, by which time a castle had been built to guard the entrance to its sheltered harbour. During the Civil War it was alternately held by Parliamentarians and Royalists, finally falling to the former in March 1646. After a lengthy period of decline, the benefit of its balmy sea air, together with the sheltering hills to the east, was finally recognised and in Victorian times Exmouth became a celebrated seaside resort.

The town developed in an irregular pattern with fine Georgian housing on Beacon Hill overlooking the sea and later building occupying the flat ground at the base of the Beacon, facing the estuary. Further change was initiated by the Hon. Mark Rolle, during the second half of the 19th century, in an attempt to capitalise on the town's popularity – in its heyday it vied with Torquay in its importance as a seaside destination – but this has produced little of architectural importance. The docks were constructed on the southwest point in 1867 and proved to be financially unsuccessful. Notwithstanding, they were rebuilt in 1882 and today, somewhat incongruously, have been developed into a marina, totally encased with upmarket 'New England' style housing.

À la Ronde A 16-sided cottage built in 1798 by Miss Jane Parmiter and her cousin, Mary Parmiter. It was inspired by San Vitale in Ravenna, which they visited as part of their ten year Grand Tour. Built of stone, with lozenge-shaped windows, the central hall – from which rooms radiate – is top-lit by a lantern roof. The gallery is reached by a narrow, grotto-like, shell-lined staircase. The tiled roof was originally thatched.

Turf Hotel seen from the River Exe estuary

POINTS OF INTEREST

Lympstone A charming village set out around the inlet. Winding, narrow cobbled streets, little more than passages, tightly flanked by irregular rows of cottages, rambling down to the water. The delightful red and yellow brick-built clock tower, with a short spire, was erected in 1885 by W. H. Peters in memory of his wife. The clock was designed to face seawards to tell the fishermen the time of the tides. There are two stone limekilns nearby.

Exton Just a few houses sandwiched between the river and main road, lining the estuary and with splendid views. The Royal Marines training camp, complete with its own railway station, lies a little way to the south.

Topsham Delightfully unspoilt, it is not hard to imagine the Topsham of 500 years ago when, as a port and centre for ship building, it was more important than Exeter. Its unique architectural heritage, with shops and housing dating from as early as the 14th century, can be enjoyed on foot.

Moored boats on the Exeter Ship Canal

Secluded canal moorings

A stroll along The Strand provides views of some exquisite examples of 17th- and 18th-century merchant housing, with their characteristic Dutch gables. The nearby Goat Walk is equally charming; with its tiny beach it has been a walking and meeting place over many centuries. In spite of the bustle brought on by the tourist season, the locals remain tolerant, friendly and hospitable.

Exeter Early records for the city mention the construction of a fort, between AD55 and 60, as headquarters for the 2nd Augustan Legion, located at the centre of the present city overlooking the lowest possible crossing of the Exe. It was surrounded by a timber and earth rampart and a ditch; the foundation was exposed during an excavation in 1971, but was subsequently covered over again. The burgeoning Roman town took over much of the plan area of the fortress and spread beyond to be enclosed by a stone wall in the 2nd century. This is the basis of the present city wall which has been extensively rebuilt over the years. Urban life continued to flourish through the following centuries, with the withdrawal of the Roman garrison and the building of a monastery at which St Boniface was educated in the 7th century.

The present High Street follows the line of the Roman main road and the four main medieval gates are sited on Roman gateways. Exeter was occupied by the Danes in AD877 when the chief religious establishment was St Mary Major, which survived in its Victorian form, in the cathedral close, into the 1970s. The city became a See in 1050 and the Norman cathedral was built in the 12th century, later to be much remodelled in medieval times.

POINTS OF INTEREST

From the 15th century onwards, Exeter was the chief cloth marketing town in the southwest and by the 17th century had become one of the richest cities in England. It was a significant port, although imports greatly outweighed exports and it was prey to serious and sustained competition from Topsham, downstream on the Exe estuary. However, the eventual confirmation of its customs rights over the entire estuary during the 17th century, together with the relative success of the canal, restored much of its prosperity and resulted in the construction of the delightful Custom House and development of the City Quays.

Over the 19th century the population almost trebled, aided by the appearance of the railway in 1844. Some 130 years later, the arrival of the M5 was a further improvement in the city's communication links with the rest of the country and a variety of light industries thrive. Exeter lost much of its rich architectural heritage during the pernicious bombings of the 1942 air raids and this has been replaced, in varying degrees, by insensitive redevelopment dating from the 1950s.

Exeter Cathedral Although completed in the 14th century by Bishop Grandisson, the two Norman transept towers date from the building's foundation. It was extensively remodelled by Bishop Bronescombe in the 13th century and the pepperpot roofs replaced the traditional Norman pyramids during further work in the 15th century. There is much original glass in the late 14th-century east window and Sir Gilbert Scott's canopied choir stalls incorporate the oldest set of misericords that survive complete; they were carved 1260–80. The bishop's throne, carved from oak in 1312, is quite exquisite.

Exeter Quay Striking example of an inland port that has developed over the ages to reflect the city's

The River Exe at St David's, Exeter

prosperity, founded on the production of serge cloth. Today it is given over solely to leisure use but this does nothing to detract from the wealth and diversity of the buildings, some dating back to the late 17th century.

The Custom House, completed in 1681, was designed by Richard Allen and enabled Exeter to re-establish its dominance as a port over its long-time rival, Topsham. The building is brick-fronted, with two storeys and five bays and white painted stone quoins. The stairhall, together with some of the downstairs rooms, have superb plasterwork ceilings and the staircase incorporates bulbous, urn-shaped balusters. It remained in continuous use by HM Customs and Excise until 1989.

The warehouses north of the Custom House date from a similar period; cut into the cliffs, they provided bonded stores. The two five-storey warehouses fronting the cliffs date from 1835, and the open fish market is also 19th-century. It incorporated a King's Beam, used for weighing dutiable goods. There are also two further warehouses nearby, built in the late 19th century, and used for storing wine.

Further west, Cricklepit Mill dates from the end of the 17th century and encloses a large waterwheel. It was variously used for fulling, grist production and malting. On the other side of the water, set beside the basin constructed by James Green in 1830, is a large warehouse from the same period.

The Cromford Canal was built to carry coal into the rapidly expanding, industrialised area of Cromford and the Derwent valley, in Derbyshire, and limestone, lead and cotton goods away to neighbouring markets. The waterway obtained its Act of Parliament in 1789. Designed by William Jessop, with help from Benjamin Outram (of tramway fame) it followed a single contour for most of its 14½-mile length, finally descending

ARKWRIGHT'S COTTON MILLS

Before the arrival of Richard Arkwright and his partners in August 1771, the area around Cromford was a scattered community of families who earned their livings in the lead mines. By Christmas of that year Arkwright was already utilising the waters of a local lead mine drain, the Cromford Sough, and of the Bonsall Brook, to power what was soon to become the world's first successful water-powered cotton spinning mill. By 1777 there were two mills in Cromford and further developments were soon to take place in Derby and Matlock Bath. New housing built to accommodate the workers in Cromford featured an additional upper storey which acted as a workroom.

Visiting industrialists from New England were entertained in the recently built Greyhound Hotel. So impressed were they with the developments in Cromford that they returned to America and used Arkwright's mills as a model for their own. By 1783 continental Europe was catching up when its first water-powered cotton spinning mill was erected near Ratingen, Germany. Johann Gottfried Brägelmann created his very own cotton new town and named it Cromford in recognition of Arkwright's innovation.

Wheatcroft & Sons' narrowboats Onward *and* Bristol *moored at the wharf in the Cromford Canal basin*

via 14 locks to its junction with the River Erewash and the Nottingham canals at Langley Mill.

It was initially opposed by the mill owners along the Derwent valley, steadfast in their belief that it would interfere with the valuable water flow of the Derwent that powered their machinery. Outram spent a full year measuring flow rates and was able to allay their fears. In fact arrangements for a water supply to the navigation were finally organised so that the long top pound held a full six days water supply (to feed the 14 locks) which could be replenished during Sunday when the mills were all closed.

There were two major aqueducts, crossing the Rivers Amber and Derwent and one tunnel, Butterley. The Derwent Aqueduct gave trouble and had to be considerably modified: it was finally rebuilt at Jessop's own expense. Although the completed canal cost £42,697, nearly twice the initial estimate, it turned out to be a financial success, doing much to boost the cotton

production of Arkwright's cotton mills. The pure Crich limestone, extracted in the Ecton area, was particularly popular with iron smelters and lead was sent out to many places, passing copper carried in from as far away as Staffordshire. The canal also provided a means of transporting the castings of the Butterley Iron Company which, to this day, are to be found in bridges spanning many of our waterways.

Cast iron canal bridge

CHELMER & BLACKWATER CANAL

Sitting on its own, deep into the extremities of the Essex countryside, the Chelmer & Blackwater is a navigation remote from the remainder of the interconnected British waterways. It joins the county town of Chelmsford, via the River Chelmer, with the Blackwater Estuary a little to the east of Maldon and beside the hamlet of Heybridge exposed to the chill of the east coast breeze. Unlike the majority of its counterparts, it is privately owned by a company of proprietors and managed by a subsidiary of the Inland Waterways Association.

Bugsworth Basin (or Buxworth as it became known out of a sense of politeness during the last century) is at the head of the 14-mile Peak Forest Canal (*see* page 176) and is the only inland interchange basin to survive on Britain's narrow canal system.

The canal line to Bugsworth was built to bring the canal as near as possible to the great limestone quarries at Doveholes, a plate tramway being constructed in 1796 via Chapel Milton to complete the connection. Known as the Peak Forest Tramway, this little line, 6½ miles long, brought the stone down the hills to Bugsworth, where it was transhipped into waiting canal boats. Throughout the history of the line, the wagons on the tramway were drawn exclusively by horse-power – except for a 500yd inclined plane in Chapel-en-le-Frith, where the trucks were attached to a continuous rope so that the descending trucks pulled the empty ones up the 1 in 7½ slope. The tramway was closed by 1926, and the sidings and basins at Buxworth became

The entrance to Bugsworth Basin

disused and overgrown. They have now been fully restored over a period of some three decades and are open to navigation. Construction of the Peak Forest Tramway linked the basin to the limestone and gritstone quarries in Derbyshire whilst, in turn, the canal linked Bugsworth to Manchester and thence to the trans-Pennine canal network.

Gritstone was in particular demand because of its inherent non-slip properties and two substantial seams of the material were found close to Bugsworth Basin during the construction of the tramway. As a 'freestone' it was also easy to cut and work, having no grain. Initially it was used in the construction of the basin infrastructure – for the warehouses, wharfs, bridges, locks and also as sleeper blocks for the tramway. Later it was to find its way much further afield – in the construction of Grimsby fish docks for instance – and was much prized by the Great Central Railway Company, the basin's penultimate owner.

Gritstone tramway sleepers, Bugsworth

Loading wharf beside limekilns, Bugsworth

BRIDGWATER & TAUNTON CANAL

The Bridgwater & Taunton Canal represents a small part of a far more ambitious scheme, the Bristol & Taunton Canal Navigation, for which Rennie gave a quotation in 1811 of no less than £429,990. This was to be part of a ship canal from Bristol to Exeter where it would join up with the long-established Exeter Ship Canal. However, although this sum was forthcoming, very little work seems to have been undertaken and instead, in 1824, an Act of Parliament was obtained to 'abridge, vary, extend and improve the Bristol & Taunton Canal Navigation', which resulted in this much briefer line being adopted.

The Canal Centre at Maunsel Lock

TAUNTON

BRIDGWATER

N

BACKGROUND

The size of the locks was unorthodox at 54' x 13" with a theoretical draught of 3' 0", which meant a normal craft load of only 22 tons. The distance as originally constituted from Firepool Lock, Taunton, to Huntworth was 13$\frac{1}{2}$ miles. Prior to the building of the Bridgwater & Taunton Canal, there already existed a navigation of sorts on the rivers Parrett and Tone providing an alternative route between Taunton and Bridgwater which, however, was prone to drought in summer and floods in winter making it somewhat unreliable.

Mars on Pip Young's Space Walk

In 1837 a further Act was obtained authorising the extension from Huntworth to Bridgwater and the building of the dock and its entrance lock from the River Parrett. This led to the curious anomaly of there being two sets of milestones in close juxtaposition. At the time of its jubilant opening on 25 March 1841, this extension had cost fully £175,000, leaving the proprietors badly out of pocket when the whole waterway and dock complex was later sold to the Bristol and Exeter Railway Company for £64,000 in 1866. When control of the waterway eventually passed to the Great Western Railway, little attempt was made to maintain commercial traffic and the last barge tolls were collected in 1907.

In 1940, at the behest of the War Office, the Bridgwater & Taunton Canal, like the Kennet & Avon (*see* page 154) was turned into a line of defence against the possibility of enemy invasion and pill boxes were erected at strategic points along its banks. The bridges were fixed and strengthened to carry military vehicles.

Little interest was shown in the waterway after nationalisation in 1947, although the Bridgwater Docks continued to operate under the Railway Executive of the British Transport Commission. In 1958 the Bowes Committee Report on waterways put the canal into category C, suitable for redevelopment, and various surveys were carried out, seemingly without any concrete results. The canal passed to the British Waterways Board (BWB) in 1963 but Bridgwater Docks remained in Railways Board ownership. In the meantime the southwestern branch of the Inland Waterways Association (*see* page 270) had begun to consider the canal in terms of restoration and in 1965 the Bridgwater & Taunton Canal Restoration Group was formed. A year later this group became the Somerset Inland Waterways Society, which was formed to work towards restoration of the canal for amenity purposes. A

The Sun on Pip Young's Space Walk

subsequent arrangement, negotiated by BWB, allowed for the extraction of three million gallons of water a day from the canal, providing much needed revenue.

Eventually a partnership between Somerset County Council and the then British Waterways, encouraged by the Somerset Inland Waterways Society, saw full restoration of the navigation and it was opened throughout in 1994. Bridgwater Docks have been developed into a marina, surrounded by new housing, shops and a pub.

THE NAVIGATION

The Bridgwater & Taunton Canal runs through attractive rolling scenery, typical of rural Somerset, starting at Firepool Lock, a junction with the River Tone. This lock, pleasantly situated beside the Tone weir, is the first stage of the canal's northeasterly journey towards Bridgwater and the estuary of the River Parrett.

The canal curves past the railway station, passing under the main Bristol to Exeter line, which follows it closely to Bridgwater. The tall railway warehouse is built on the site of the old junction with the Grand Western Canal. Taunton is quickly left behind as the waterway continues through flat pasture land to Bathpool, where the towpath runs briefly through the churchyard of a small corrugated iron church.

Bathpool Swing Bridge used to be the first obstacle to restoring the navigation east of Taunton, being one of the structures fixed closed during the invasion scare of 1940, when the War Office

destroyed the swinging mechanisms on all the navigation's swing bridges. Contrary to popular opinion, this measure was not so much to prevent navigation by German forces, as to create lines of defence along natural barriers.

Leaving Bathpool the country becomes hilly and more wooded and a modern housing estate accompanies the canal into Creech St Michael. Before the village is the site of the junction with the Chard Canal of which, today, there is little to be seen but to the south the long embankment crossing the Tone flood plain is still clearly visible.

Several small agricultural hamlets flank the waterway on its way to Durston, where the BW maintenance yard is located beside the busy A361 crossing. Beyond, the canal reaches the first lock which begins the descent to Bridgwater. The paddle gear is quite unique, composed of ball-shaped weights and chains to form a counter-balance mechanism.

Following the contours of the land, the waterway continues northwards towards Bridgwater. To the west, low hills rise gradually away from the canal; to the east low-lying farm and marsh land separates the navigation from the River Parrett. This tidal river, a vital drain for the whole area, swings ever nearer to the canal as they approach Bridgwater. To the east the railway line stays close to the navigation until just before Bridgwater, when it turns away to pass east of the town. The course of the waterway is quiet and isolated and there are no villages near the canal.

Standard's Lock drops the navigation to the Bridgwater level and, nearing the town, civilisation returns with a vengeance as traffic roars overhead on the M5 viaduct. After the motorway the towpath crosses to the west and the canal enters Bridgwater

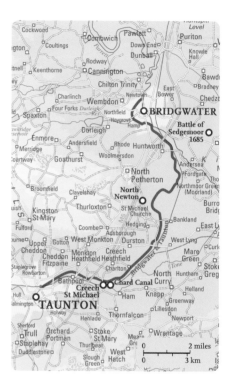

itself. The waterway passes through the town in a cutting, swinging in a wide arc to the west before turning back to the docks and the junction with the Parrett estuary. The smaller outer basin is entered through a twin-bascular lift bridge and then both a ship lock and a canal lock used to allow access to the River Parrett and thus the sea. The river locks have been blocked off, with concrete barriers and so the Bridgwater & Taunton Canal remains just that: an isolated navigation linking its two eponymous towns and nothing else.

Chief engineer	James Hollinsworth
Assisted by	Josiah Easton
Significance	Originally conceived as part of a barge canal linking Bristol and Exeter.
Started in	1822
Completed in	1827 to Huntworth 1841 to Bridgwater Dock
Length	14 miles
Draught	2' 6"
Headroom	7' 1"
Lock size	51' 10" × 13' 7"
Goods carried	Coal, slate, water supply to Bridgwater.
Operating authority	Canal & River Trust
Contact details	enquiries.kennetavon @canalrivertrust.org.uk

POINTS OF INTEREST

Taunton Taunton has long been a rich agricultural market town and an important point on the old trunk route to the West Country. The skyline is dominated by the towers of the churches of St Mary Magdalene and St James. The first, rebuilt in 1862, is 163ft high; its ornamental splendour rather dwarfs the double aisled church. In Middle Street there is an octagonal 18th-century Methodist chapel where Wesley preached when it was first opened. The centre of the town contains an interesting mixture of buildings: 15th-century municipal buildings, the 18th-century Market House, the Victorian Shire Hall and the 20th-century County Hall. Remains of the medieval town can be seen, including fragments of the 13th-century priory.

THE SOMERSET SPACE WALK

It was observed in the 17th century that Taunton was 'the vineyard of the Lord of Hosts and the inhabitants his precious plants'. By the late 17th century, Taunton had two non-conformist chapels – the Baptist Meeting and 'Paul's Meeting', the latter becoming one of the largest congregations in the county.

By way of contrast, an unusual close-up view of the heavens has been provided for us by the Somerset Space Walk, the brainchild of Pip Young. This unique portrayal of our Solar System has been set out to scale along the Bridgwater & Taunton Canal towpath, using the same scale for both the planets and the distances between them. There are no figures to conjure with, just the experience of a journey through space as you walk, cycle or boat along the waterway. See the photographs of the Sun and Mars on page 102.

Entering Higher Lock on the Bridgwater & Taunton

Creech St Michael Although now surrounded by modern housing, the old part of the village still survives. The largely 13th-century church is a sturdy and attractive building; inside there is a fine wagon braced roof.

Chard Canal The Chard Canal was one of the last to be built in England and one of the shortest-lived of all. Work began in 1835 and the 13¹/₂ mile line to Chard from Creech St Michael was opened in 1842. The canal included three tunnels, two major aqueducts, two locks and four inclined planes. It suffered from immediate railway competition and never made any money. Bought by the Bristol and Exeter Railway Company in 1867, it closed the next year.

North Newton An irregular farming village. The eccentric-looking church was rebuilt first in the 17th century and then again in the late 19th. Nothing remains of the original Saxon church, where the Alfred Jewel was found in 1693. This Saxon ornament, the oldest surviving crown jewel, is now displayed in the Ashmolean Museum, Oxford.

POINTS OF INTEREST

Bridgwater Bridgwater is an old market town straddling the River Parrett and formerly an important centre for the cloth trade, which encouraged development of the port from the Middle Ages onwards. The old quay, despite redevelopment, still has an attractive 18th-century flavour. It suffered severely during the Civil War and, in an artillery bombardment in July 1645, lost the greater part of its commercial and domestic buildings, many of which were of timber-frame construction. Elsewhere in the town are signs of 18th-century wealth: the handsome houses in Castle Street, built c.1725, were sponsored by James Bridges, first Duke of Chances. However, little of the medieval town survives. The 13th-century castle was destroyed by the Roundheads as a reprisal for the town's resistance. The Watergate, on the west quay, is the only remaining relic of the castle with a wall 12ft thick. Glass-making briefly flourished in the town when, in 1725, James Bridges built the 125ft Chandos Glass Cone. The venture failed within nine years and the cone, built from rubble from the derelict castle, was converted first to brick making and then to tile manufacture, only closing down during the Second World War.

Admiral Blake Robert Blake was born in Bridgwater in 1598 and represented the town as a Member of Parliament. After a distinguished army career he was appointed by Cromwell as one of his first Generals at Sea and went on to destroy the Dutch fleet in a battle of 1653 and to achieve a resounding victory over the Spaniards in 1657. He is recognised as one of the major influences in establishing the reputation of the Navy – later to become the Royal Navy.

Raising a ground paddle on the Bridgwater & Taunton

Battle of Sedgemoor, 6 July 1685 When Charles II died, he was succeeded by his brother, James II, unpopular due to his Catholic faith. The Duke of Monmouth, an illegitimate son of Charles II, declared himself king, in 1685, in Bridgwater. He landed at Lyme with a few supporters and soon raised an army 4,000 strong, including 800 horsemen under Lord Grey. They moved to Bridgwater, while a Royalist army commanded by Lord Feversham and John Churchill (later the Duke of Marlborough) camped near Westonzoyland, 3 miles east of the town. Monmouth decided on a night attack but lost the element of surprise when caught crossing the Langmoor Rhine, one of the many drainage ditches in the area. A fierce battle broke out in which the artillery played a dominant part. Grey's cavalry tried to outflank Feversham but were prevented by the Bussex Rhine, another deep ditch. Although firing continued all night, Monmouth's cause was already lost. The leaders of the rebellion escaped for a while but the ill-armed rebel army was rounded up, many to be transported or executed on the orders of Judge Jeffreys.

Bridgwater Docks

From time to time local enthusiasm – at the height of the period of so-called 'canal mania' – got the better of common sense and a waterway was conceived that, upon more considered reflection, held little hope of financial success. Part of a far more grandiose plan, the Leominster Canal presents a good example of this phenomenon. Exploring this corner of Herefordshire provides the opportunity to discover clues to the canal's existence, thereby charting its short rise and somewhat longer decline.

Presented to Parliament as the Kington, Leominster and Stourport Canal, work started in 1791 on the construction of the central portion linking the coal mines of Mamble with the sleepy Marches town of Leominster, a distance of some 18½ miles in all. This section did make financial sense and, in common with similar 'coal driven' waterways, halved the price of coal – delivered to the tiny wharf on the northern outskirts of the town – practically overnight when it opened in 1796.

Stourport, to the east of Mamble and the newly established terminus of the Staffordshire & Worcestershire Canal on the River Severn, was

The same inexplicable rise when viewed along the road, just as if it were approaching a bridge.

an obvious goal for this navigation and one that involved a significant lock flight down into the river. Efforts to construct this link stalled on the completion of a ceremonial cut, made on the banks of the Severn on 1 June 1797, with some £25,000 still owing on the previous work.

As originally conceived, this waterway was to run 46 miles from the Welsh borders town of Kington, rising some 48ft before its eventual 496ft descent to the River Severn. The Act of Parliament allowed a total of £190,000 to be raised from share capital. The distinct lack of industry, or any major towns along the proposed route, seemed to worry the promoters not one jot. The initial survey was carried out by Robert Whitworth and slightly varied in a subsequent survey by Thomas Dadford junior. There were 16 locks on the completed section, several aqueducts and two tunnels: Southnet (1,254yd) and Putnall Fields (330yd). Both suffered from construction problems and John Rennie was consulted over Southnet. He criticised Dadford's work, suggesting £20,000 would be needed to rectify matters. He also identified a further sum of £136,000 as being required to complete the Mamble–Leominster section.

Undaunted, the proprietors applied for a second Act of Parliament to raise a further £180,000 which was obtained on 26 April 1796. In parallel with the main thrust, they had put in hand work to the west of Leominster – an aqueduct over the River Lugg and a short length of detached waterway

In this picture the hedge, bordering a minor road, rises from right to left so that by the time it reaches the trees, it is – for no apparent reason – some way above the level of the field, dropping away again into the distance.

Close up picture, clearly showing an embankment, but no evidence of the waterway that it once crossed on a bridge is now visible.

Not all house names are purely fanciful! This really is where the coal from Mamble was unloaded on arrival in Leominster.

running under a by-road just to the north of Kingsland – taking the navigation further towards Kington. These two detached portions remained just that, sitting on their own in splendid isolation, never to be linked either to one another or to the completed portion of the main waterway itself.

So what we are left with today are a series of clues as to the line of the original canal: some obvious and some not quite so clear. Just as it is possible to piece together the route of a pre-Beeching railway – much of it obliterated beneath, say, new housing

Not just an overflowing ditch after heavy rain. This is a very obvious length of the Leominster Canal (near Orleton).

This sign is on the minor road as it leaves Orleton, heading east, towards the canal and railway seen in the picture below.

estates – by poking around in the undergrowth, interpreting the true origins of an apparently muddy ditch, or simply reading house or street names, it is possible to begin piecing together the story of a past and often long forgotten, waterway, as these photographs indicate.

The southern portal of Putnall Fields Tunnel, the brick arch clearly visible. The water level is much higher than normal.

Putnall Fields: the oval shaped hedgeline, stopping abruptly in the middle of the pasture, suggests that there is more here than meets the eye. Below the trees is the tunnel portal shown in the picture on the left.

GRAND UNION CANAL

The Grand Union Canal is unique among English canals in being composed of at least eight separate navigations. This waterway system links London with Birmingham, Leicester and Nottingham. The original – and still the most important – part of the system was the Grand Junction Canal. This was constructed at the turn of the 18th century to provide a short cut between Braunston on the Oxford Canal and Brentford, west of London on the Thames.

Previously, all London-bound traffic from the Midlands had to follow the winding Fazeley, Coventry and Oxford canals down to Oxford and transhipped into lighters to make the 100-mile trip down river to Brentford and London.

Evening settles on Stoke Bruerne

BIRMINGHAM
ROYAL LEAMINGTON SPA
WARWICK
MILTON KEYNES
AYLESBURY
HEMEL HEMPSTEAD
WATFORD
LONDON
SLOUGH

N

BACKGROUND

Up until the 1920s all the canals that now go to make up the Grand Union were owned and operated by quite separate companies: there were five between London and Birmingham alone. The new Grand Junction Canal combined these operations, cutting the distance between the two cities by fully 60 miles and, with its 14ft wide locks and numerous branches to important towns, rapidly became busy and profitable. The building of wide locks to take 70-ton barges was a brave attempt to persuade neighbouring canal companies – the Oxford, Coventry and the distant Trent and Mersey – to widen their navigations and establish a 70-ton barge standard throughout the waterways of the Midlands. Unfortunately, the other companies were deterred by the cost of widening, and to this day those same canals – and many others – can only pass boats 7ft wide. The history of the English canals might have turned out very differently had the Grand Junction's attempt succeeded.

The mere proposal of the building of the Grand Junction Canal was enough to generate and justify plans for other canals linked to it. Before the Grand Junction itself was completed, independent canals were built linking it in a direct line to Warwick and Birmingham, and a little later a connection was established from the Grand Junction to Market Harborough and Leicester, and thence via the canalised River Soar to the Trent. Unfortunately, part of this line was eventually built with narrow locks, thereby sealing the fate of the Grand Junction's wide canals scheme.

Meanwhile, in London in 1812 the Regent's Canal Company was formed to cut a new canal from the Grand Junction's very busy Paddington Arm, round London to Limehouse, where a big dock was planned at the junction with the Thames. This was duly opened in 1820, narrowly escaping conversion at an early stage into a railway, and proved

The Wharf, Braunston

extremely successful. Ten years later a 1$^{1}/_{2}$-mile-long canal – the Hertford Union – was built: this remains a useful short cut from Regent's Canal to the River Lee.

These were the canals that made up the spine of southern England's transport system until the advent of the railways. When in the last century the Regent's Canal Company acquired the Grand Junction and others, the whole system was

integrated as the Grand Union Canal Company in 1929. The new company, aided by the government, in 1932 launched a massive programme of modernisation: widening the 52 locks from Braunston to Birmingham, piling and dredging. But when the grant was all spent, the task was unfinished and broad beam boats never became common on the Grand Union Canal. The great attempt to break loose from narrowboat carrying had failed.

THE NAVIGATION

The Regent's Canal begins at Limehouse Basin (previously known as Regent's Canal Dock) in London's Dockland and climbs up round central London towards Paddington. It is mostly flanked by the backs of houses and factories which usually enclose the canal in a remarkably private and peaceful world of its own. However, the towpath can be followed from Limehouse Basin along the whole length of the Regent's Canal into west London and there are frequent access points.

The entrance to the Regent's Canal and to the River Lee Navigation from the Thames is through Limehouse Lock. The Hertford Union Canal

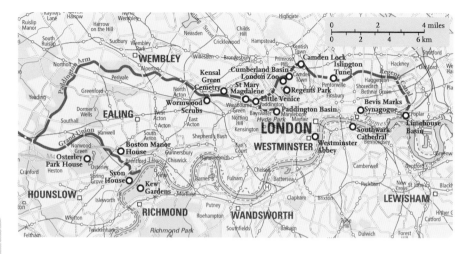

Chief engineer	Various
Assisted by	Various
Significance	Combined eight separate routes to provide a direct link between London and Birmingham.
Started in	Formed in 1929 and 1932
Completed in	1932
Length	137 miles
Headroom	Regent's Canal: 8' 6" Remainder: 7' 6"
Lock size	Regent's Canal: 72' × 14' 6" Brentford–Berkhamsted: 72' × 14' Berkhamsted–Birmingham: 72' × 7'
Number of locks	166
Tunnels	5
Aqueducts	7
Goods carried	Coal, stone, cement, raw materials, manufactured goods.
Operating authority	Canal & River Trust
Contact details	enquiries.london@ canalrivertrust.org.uk

(often known as Duckett's), makes a useful short cut between the Regent's Canal and the Lee Navigation, running along the attractive Victoria Park. The waterway continues to climb, skirting two large basins before plunging under Islington through a 1/2-mile tunnel, then round the back of St Pancras (where there are good views of the Eurostar Terminal to the north of the pinnacles of the St Pancras station façade) and Camden Town, passing Battlebridge Basin, site of the London Canal Museum.

At Camden High Road, the top locks are reached and the long level begins (27 miles of canal without a lock). Near the top lock is a castellated construction: the focus for a youth club. Soon the industrial surroundings melt away and, rounding a right-angled bend, the canal suddenly enters London Zoo and Regent's Park – which look splendid from the water. The navigation continues through a long wooded cutting, then leaves Regent's

Park and skirts the former Marylebone goods yard – now a housing estate – beyond which is the short Maida Hill Tunnel. From here boaters emerge into one of the finest stretches of urban canal in the country. Tree-lined and flanked by fine Regency houses, the Regent's Canal ends gloriously at Little Venice. To the left, under the Westway bridge, is Paddington Basin with its extensive moorings. To the right is the Paddington Arm of the former Grand Junction Canal. The two stop places seen at Little Venice were used for gauging boats for tolls. The Paddington Arm continues west, passing a large housing estate and the backs of houses in Harrow Road, before running along the side of the well-known Kensal Green Cemetery. The huge concrete structure sweeping out over the canal is a further section of the elevated Westway Road. The main Western Region railway tracks run just below the canal, to the south, while at Old Oak Common there are extensive carriage sidings. Beyond them can be seen the towers of Wormwood Scrubs prison.

THE NAVIGATION

Acton Lane Electricity Distribution Station straddles the canal; not far away are the twin townships of Harlesden and Willesden. The navigation crosses the North Circular road on a large aqueduct: a strange contrast between the tranquillity of the waterway and the roaring traffic below. The Paddington Arm continues west through Alperton and Greenford. This is an area where contrasting smells of cooking on a factory scale – representing all corners of the globe – assault the olfactory senses with a vengeance, fighting for acknowledgement from the cruising boater and extending from Acton west as far as Alperton. The surroundings are mostly flat, but Horsenden Hill and Perivale Wood provide a long stretch of beautiful hilly parkland and Greenford Golf Course adjoins the canal. Soon afterwards the navigation turns south into suburban Middlesex.

A busy scene at Limehouse Dock in the 1940s

THE LEE NAVIGATION

In East London commercial traffic on the adjacent Lee Navigation ebbed away over the years. During the mid-1950s horse-drawn lighters were still journeying as far as Hertford, but by 1980 commercial traffic extended no higher than the Enfield Rolling Mills at Brimsdown, with just one tug, the *Vassal*, regularly at work on the river. Powered by a 120hp Gardner diesel engine, she would typically tow a train of two lighters loaded with timber from Bow to Hahn's Wharf at Edmonton. Considerable skill was demonstrated by the skipper, who would propel the first of the train of lighters into a lock under its own momentum, pulling his tug aside at the very last moment.

Stoke Bruerne Top Lock

POINTS OF INTEREST

Limehouse Basin The terminus of the Regent's Canal and of the Lee Navigation where they meet the Thames. Once known as the Regent's Canal Dock, this basin has been developed as a marina. Running underneath is a road tunnel offering easy access to the Canary Wharf development.

Bevis Marks Synagogue, EC3 The interior, representative of so many Nonconformist chapels of the early 18th century, is little changed and the influence of Sir Christopher Wren is also evident. Situated in a secluded courtyard this beautifully preserved building contains a fine collection of Cromwellian and Queen Anne furniture and a magnificent glowing brass candelabra.

Southwark Cathedral, SE1 The cathedral lies on the south bank of the Thames on a site occupied by a church for over 1,000 years. Formerly an Augustinian Priory, it is now a magnificent gothic cathedral, holding five daily services.

Westminster Abbey, SW1 Founded as a Benedictine monastery over 1,000 years ago, the church was rebuilt by Edward the Confessor in 1065 and again by Henry lll in the 13th century in the Gothic style seen today.

Islington Tunnel 960yds long, the tunnel was opened in 1816. In 1826 a towing boat was introduced, which pulled itself to and fro along a chain laid on the canal bed. This system remained until the 1930s. The attractive borough of Islington lies to the north of the tunnel.

Camden Lock A fascinating craft and canal centre, with a busy weekend market, scattered around what was once a timber wharf. Stalls crowd every nook and cranny of the wharf and spill out into several squares south of the canal.

Cumberland Basin, NW1 A small canal basin by the zoo which used to form the junction of the Regent's Canal Main Line with an arm that led off round the park to Cumberland Market near Euston Station. Much of the arm was filled in during the last war and the zoo car park now sits on top of it alongside moored boats.

London Zoo, NW1 The canal passes along the edge of the zoo, one of the largest in the world. Lord Snowdon's aviary can be seen from the canal. The zoo was originally laid out by Decimus Burton in 1827, but since then many famous architects have designed special animal houses.

Regent's Park Originally part of Henry VIII's great hunting forest in the 16th century. In 1811 the Prince Regent planned to connect the park and a new palace via the newly built Regent Street to Carlton House. Although never completed, the design by John Nash is very impressive: the park is surrounded by handsome Regency terraces and gateways. The sanctuary and the northeast corner of the park are excellent points for watching migrant birds, including willow warblers, chiffchaff, white throats, redstarts and redpolls.

Little Venice, W2 Centred on the junction of the Regent's and Grand Junction canals, famous for its elegant houses, colourful residential boats and excellent canalside views. The island and pool were named after Robert Browning. The area is sometimes referred to as Paddington Stop.

Paddington Basin, W2 The basin offers extensive and surprisingly tranquil moorings amidst soaring new office blocks. Today the Basin is best known for its pair of novel pedestrian bridges, seemingly intent in putting form ahead of function: one unrolls like a shy caterpillar, the other mimics an oriental fan!

British Waterways narrowboats (the motor Baldock and butty Lyra) at Little Venice on the Paddington Arm of the Grand Union Canal c.1956

GREAT CENTRAL RAILWAY

On passing the site of the old Great Central Railway's goods yard, beside its Marylebone terminus, it is worth reflecting on this illustrious company's original aims: a railway link from the industrial north via the capital, and an English Channel tunnel into Europe, constructed to a loading gauge compatible with continental railways. And this was in 1899.

Further west, whilst navigating under the concrete spans of the Westway, with its nonstop roar of heavy goods traffic, it is hard to conceive that a plan to resurrect this line – its original loading gauge now capable of conveying, piggy back, fully laden articulated lorries, continental-style – was recently rejected for debate by Parliament.

THE NAVIGATION

Continuing south through the industrial estate, the Paddington Arm soon reaches the junction with the main line of the Grand Union at Bull's Bridge. This was once a large maintenance yard (and formerly the Grand Union Canal Carrying Fleet depot) where maintenance boats were built and repaired. Turning left, the waterway leads east towards Brentford and the Thames past a colourful collection of houseboats; whilst, turning right, the canal goes to Birmingham and beyond. Here the navigation enters the indivisible conurbation of Hayes, Harlington, West Drayton and Yiewsley, passing the site of Colham Wharf where an incised stone from the wharf has been preserved and incorporated into the new building.

Further north, Cowley Lock marks the end of the 27-mile pound and the start of the climb up the Colne valley and the Chiltern Hills. Uxbridge, just

to the north, signals the limit of the outer-suburban belt that surrounds London. Uxbridge Lock has an attractive setting with its lock cottage, a turnover bridge and a tall modern flour mill standing nearby in grounds that are splendidly landscaped down to the water's edge. The Paddington Packet Boat used to run daily from Paddington to Cowley – one of the few passenger boats plying regularly along the Grand Junction Canal. It was pulled by four horses and had precedence over all other boats, so it covered the 15-mile lock-free run in a time that was remarkable at the beginning of the 19th century.

Turning left, this section follows the main line of the Grand Union east from Norwood down to the junction with the Thames at Brentford. At Norwood the 12-lock drop to the River Thames commences and includes the Hanwell flight of six locks. It is in parts an interesting and attractive stretch: Osterley

Grand Union paddle gear at Stockton Locks

THE THAMES BARGE

Around the coasts of Britain every tidal estuary, together with its river navigation, spawned its variant of the sail-driven, cargo-carrying barge. Usually the dimensions and type of rig were determined by the constraints of bridges and locks met on its passage upstream. The Thames barge, however, rarely strayed above Brentford, just to the west of London – from here the Thames was the territory of the inland waterways narrowboats and wide boats. As a result it evolved into a coastal craft with capacities sometimes in excess of 150 tons. To move this tonnage smartly through the water – as smartly as a blunt bow and flat bottom can ever allow – it carried a copious array of additional sail to supplement the predominantly spritsail main. Here the constraining factor was that the boat had to be handled, in its entirety, by one man and a boy.

The activities of the Thames barge were by no means restricted to the Thames and adjoining estuaries. Cargoes were regularly carried north, to east coast ports as far afield as Newcastle upon Tyne and southwest to ports along the English Channel. The flat bottom allowed easy access into shallow estuaries that often dried out completely at low tide. Its capabilities in the open sea are impressive, given its fundamental design, and passages across the Atlantic have been recorded. Under-sail leeboards, pivoting down from the gunwales, enable boats to sail surprisingly close to the wind and to see a racing barge tacking, its traditional mud-brown sails sheeted in tight, is a truly awesome sight.

and Syon parks are nearby. The River Brent joins the canal at the bottom of Hanwell Locks; there is a rare intersection of canal, road and railway at the top of these locks and several of the bridges are of the brick arched type more commonly seen on the rural canals. Near the big M4 embankment is a very attractive cast iron roving bridge, dated 1820. Towards Brentford, the towing path disappears under the roof of a large BW warehouse – an odd experience for walkers and cyclists. Kew Gardens are just across the Thames.

POINTS OF INTEREST

St Mary Magdalene, N7 Sitting almost alongside the canal west of Little Venice and built by Street, 1868–78, the church with its tall Gothic spire is now curiously isolated among modern flats. The richly decorated crypt is very striking.

Kensal Green Cemetery, W10 Opened in 1833, the huge cemetery flanks the canal. The monuments are now all romantically overgrown, and scattered among trees. Water gates set in the wall indicate that at one time coffins for burial could be brought up by barge. Leigh Hunt, Thackeray, Macready, Trollope, Wilkie Collins and Blondin are among the famous buried here.

Wormwood Scrubs, W12 Lying to the south of canal, this expanse of open space has the famous prison on its southern boundary.

Osterley Park House, Isleworth Set in a large park – a superb remodelled mansion with elegant interior decorations by Robert Adam, 1760–80. Gobelins and Beauvais tapestries and fine carpets. There is a fine examples of an Elizabethan stable and a large park.

Boston Manor House, Brentford Tudor and Jacobean house with excellent examples of period ceilings.

Syon House, Brentford Seat of the Duke of Northumberland. Noted for its fine Adam interior and period furniture, also its paintings. Its historical associations go back to the 15th century.

Syon Park Gardens, Brentford Fifty-five acres of Capability Brown gardens. In the grounds are a gardening centre, live butterfly house, and a reptile house.

Kew Gardens, Kew On the south bank of the Thames, opposite Brentford. One of the world's great botanic gardens, with thousands of rare outdoor and hothouse plants. Kew Palace was built in 1631 in the Dutch style.

The Slough Arm At Cowley Peachey Junction, the 5-mile Slough Arm branches off to the west in an almost straight line. Built as late as 1882 (the last canal to be built in Britain except for the New Junction and Manchester Ship canals), it sweeps easily over several aqueducts and through a long cutting. The main traffic on the waterway was bricks made from the copious clay deposits along its length and used to fuel the capital's prodigious construction appetite. In a neat and reciprocal manner boats returned with the city's waste which was used to backfill the brick pits. It can be seen that the canal was built after the rise of the railways and is, perhaps, unique in that it represented the more economic mode of transport.

Iver The church has a Saxon nave with Roman bricks visible in the walls, Norman arches, medieval art and Tudor monuments. The 700-year-old tower owes its great height to the 15th-century bell chamber.

Slough This is the largest town in Berkshire; it is a new town, undistinguished architecturally and remembered more for its wide range of light industries and its immortalization in verse by John Betjeman who wrote (in 1981):

> 'Come, friendly bombs, and fall on Slough
> It isn't fit for humans now
> There isn't grass to graze a cow.'

St Mary's Church is, however, interesting for its stained glass by Kempe and Alfred J. Wolmark; the church was completed in 1876.

Uxbridge The Battle of Britain was directed by the late Air Marshal Lord Dowding from the RAF Headquarters in Uxbridge. The town is perhaps noteworthy for its selection of modern and futuristic buildings in a variety of competing styles.

Fosse Locks, Grand Union

THE NAVIGATION

The main line of the canal continues northwards past the village of Denham and across Harefield Moor, a stretch of common land of considerable interest to naturalists. Denham Lock, with a rise of 11ft 1in, is the deepest on the Grand Union. Leaving Widewater Lock, the canal continues up the Colne valley through a landscape of interesting contrasts which contains woods, mills, lakes and a large sewage works. Black Jack's Lock is beautifully framed by a small mill and a tiny timbered cottage, while Copper Mill Lock is just upstream of an attractive group of canalside buildings.

Old chalk quarries adjoin the canal as it turns northeast towards Rickmansworth. Passing Stocker's Lock with an interesting group of old farm buildings close by – they date from the 16th century – the canal soon reaches Batchworth Lock on the outskirts of Rickmansworth. Here the River Colne comes in from the east and the Chess from the northwest, while the Gade continues to accompany the canal to the northeast. Past

Rickmansworth is Common Moor and north of this is Croxley and the outskirts of Watford. The canal keeps well away from this town and climbs instead into the superb Cassiobury Park, a long and lovely stretch of wooded parkland. A commemorative plaque at Iron Bridge Lock, unveiled by the Duke of Marlborough, is inscribed 1787–1987, to mark 200 years of the Grand Union Canal's existence.

The canal climbs in a northerly direction through Cassiobury Park to Grove Mill, a water mill where the mill stream doubles as a private canal arm. Just north of the mill is the deservedly famous ornamental stone bridge ordered by the Earl of Essex before he would allow the Grand Junction Canal Company to cut a navigation through his park. The canal winds considerably along this valley as it follows the course of the River Gade. The M25 north orbital road and the A41 cross the canal as it approaches the lovely village of Hunton Bridge, while a little further north is Kings Langley.

Ovaltine boat Enid

POINTS OF INTEREST

Denham West of the canal and of the River Colne, Denham is split into two parts: the new part is north of the railway. In the old village is the church set among the cottages. It contains a Doom painting of 1460 and some Renaissance effigies and monuments. Denham Court, which stands in the Colne meadows, and Denham Place, the 17th-century home of the Vansittart family, are both fine examples of English architecture. The original village is quintessential Old England with immense charm, albeit in what has become a very exclusive area of the Home Counties.

Lock-keeper at Denham Deep Lock 87, Uxbridge in the 1930s

Copper Mill An interesting canal settlement. The big mill was once a paper mill, but after the canal was built it turned to making copper sheets for the bottoms of boats. South of here is the unnavigable Troy Cut, which leads to the very ancient Troy Mill.

Harefield Harefield represents the first escape from the stranglehold of outer London suburbia. The church set at the foot of the hill is almost a small museum: Norman masonry, box pews, Georgian pulpit, a huge collection of monuments and work by Grinling Gibbons, Rysbrack and Bacon.

Springwell and Stocker's Locks This stretch is of interest to naturalists: there is a great variety of plants along here and disused watercress beds are nearby. Orchids have been found growing in the adjacent chalk pits.

Rickmansworth Very little of the medieval town remains today: the vicarage in Church Street has late medieval timberwork, but 18th- and 19th-century alterations are intermingled. Despite this, there are several other buildings well worth a look: the 17th-century Bury and the timber-framed but much restored Priory, both lying near the 19th-century Church of St Mary, which lends a wonderful feeling of unity because it is almost entirely the work of one man – Sir Arthur Blomfield.

Cassiobury Park, Watford The canal flows through the park, once part of the 17th-century gardens of the Earls of Essex. The avenue of limes was planted by Moses Cook in 1672 and many of the trees are as old as 300 years. The park stretches for 190 acres and is adjoined by Whippendell Woods.

Abbots Langley The Church of St Lawrence has 12th-century arcades to the nave and a 14th-century

south chapel, an octagonal Perpendicular font and a 14th-century wall painting of Saints Thomas and Lawrence.

Kings Langley Kings Langley derives its name from its royal associations; there are still the remains of a palace in the town.

THE OVALTINE BARGES

In 1864 in Switzerland, Dr George Wander founded the company which was to manufacture Ovaltine. Finding a ready market in England, the company established a factory at Kings Langley, beside what is now the Grand Union Canal. In 1925 they decided to build their own fleet of narrowboats to bring coal to this factory from Warwickshire. Their boats were always immaculately maintained, with the words 'Drink delicious Ovaltine for Health' emblazoned in orange and yellow on a very dark blue background. The last boat arrived at Kings Langley on 17 April 1959.

THE NAVIGATION

The canal begins to climb more steeply to the northwest, passing several large paper mills in Apsley and a quaint double arched bridge. The River Gade leaves the canal for Hemel Hempstead, a handsome modern town (somewhat dominated by the towering office block) standing back from the canal beyond spacious urban parkland known as Boxmoor. The canal turns further west, accompanied now by the little River Bulbourne, heading for Berkhamsted.

The canal enters the town by its back door, stealing inconspicuously through the middle of Berkhamsted, which is the northern limit of the Grand Union as a barge canal. Leaving the conurbation and still climbing up the Chilterns, one passes Northchurch, where a pump draws canal water supplies from a deep borehole in the chalk

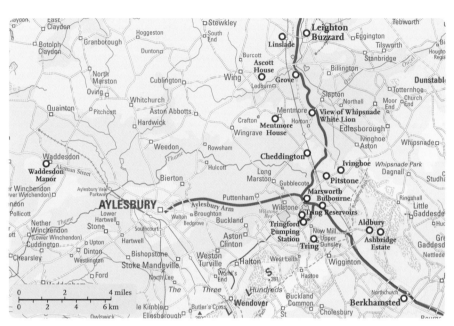

Topping up the water tank at Bascote

beds. The summit level is reached at Cowroast Lock which, in the days before the pump was installed at Northchurch, used to be the scene of long lines of boats tied up in the dry summers as the canal engineers struggled to maintain the water supply in the 3-mile summit level – which was constantly being drained by the use of locks at either end. It is perhaps worth noting that every time a boat crosses this summit level it draws off nearly 200,000 gallons of water.

In the hamlet of Bulbourne are the old Canal Company workshops where traditional wooden lock gate-making was carried out by a small team of craftsmen. Just to the west the Wendover Arm joins the canal, constantly feeding water into the

summit level. This waterway is currently navigable for 1½ miles. In 1989 the Wendover Arm Trust was established with the principal aim of restoring to navigation the full length of the Arm through to Wendover. At Bulbourne Junction, the first of the Marsworth locks begin to wind down the hill past the reservoirs; at the bottom of the flight there is an interesting double-arched bridge, a sight often repeated between here and Stoke Bruerne 33 miles to the north. This type of bridge was built by the Grand Junction Canal Company in the expectation that the locks would later be paired – a programme that was never completed. Due north of the double bridge is Marsworth Junction, once dominated by the old British Waterways workshops, where concrete files were manufactured for bank protection.

POINTS OF INTEREST

Berkhamsted A good-looking large town with buildings of all periods which, until recently, was being shaken apart by the A41 running through the middle. The bypass has provided the community with the chance, once again, to savour the richness and diversity of its architectural heritage. The High Street is dominated by the Church of St Peter, which contains work from practically every period, including a restoration by Butterfield of 1871. There are several brasses. Only the ruins of the Norman castle remain: here William I received the offer of the English crown in 1066.

Ashridge Estate, Berkhamsted Built in 1808 as a large romantic mansion in the Gothic taste by James Wyatt, the house gives an impression of what his famous Fonthill must have been like; the chapel is particularly splendid. The grounds were laid out by Capability Brown, and altered later by Repton.

Aldbury A charming village pond and stocks are sheltered below the hillside which rises to the east towards Ashridge. The monument to the 3rd Duke of Bridgewater (an urn and a Greek Doric column) was erected on the brow of the hill beyond Stocks Road in 1832 to commemorate his pioneering work for the English canals (see page 138).

Tring A settlement founded where Roman Akeman Street intersected the ancient Icknield Way. Today Tring is a delightful mixture of architecture from all periods. There is a natural history museum, given to the nation by Walter Rothschild on his death in 1937, containing a collection of stuffed birds, mammals, insects and reptiles: this is the largest of its kind in the UK made by one individual.

Bulbourne A canalside settlement around the Canal Company workshops which are a well-preserved example of early 19th-century canal architecture,

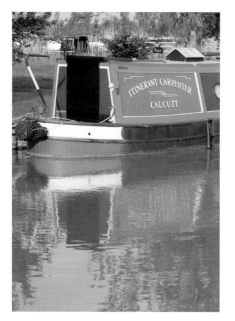

with characteristic fanlights. To the northeast is the long railway cutting built by Robert Stephenson in 1834–8, an engineering feat of the age.

Tringford Pumping Station Near the present terminus of the Wendover Arm. Built by the Grand Junction Canal Company to pump water up from the three reservoirs just down the hill, and from the 100-acre Wilstone reservoir over to the west. This water, plus the supply from springs in Wendover was – and still is – fed down the arm into the Tring summit level. Originally the pumping station housed big beam engines, but these were replaced in the 20th century by heavy diesels. Now quiet, smooth, electric motors perform this vital task, lifting some four million gallons of water each day.

The system was recently overhauled, having been in constant use since 1929.

Tring Reservoirs Four reservoirs with many wildfowl and waterside birds, notably the Black Tern and the Great Crested Grebe. Also abundant marsh and water plants. This is a national nature reserve and public access is permitted along waymarked pathways.

Marsworth A quiet scattered village centred around the Grand Union Canal and the Aylesbury Arm. The Icknield Way, a Roman road, passes the village. Dunstable Downs rise to the southeast, gliders are a common sight and occasionally a hot air balloon may be seen floating along in the sky.

Pitstone and Ivinghoe An attractive although greatly expanded pair of villages, which radiate from the large 13th- and 14th-century church, notable for its crossing tower and Jacobean pulpit. The main street, leading west from the church, contains the old town hall, partly 16th-century. A little south of the village is Pitstone Green Mill, a post mill scheduled as an ancient monument. There is an Iron Age Hill Fort 1 mile northeast of Ivinghoe, on top of Beacon Hill. The triangular hill fort encloses 6 acres: within this area stands a bowl barrow thought to date from the Bronze Age. There is a tumulus to the south and another to the east of Beacon Hill.

Cheddington A residential area spread around the station. The church contains a richly carved Jacobean pulpit. On the hills south of the village are the remains of a medieval field cultivation.

Mentmore House A Tudor-style stone mansion built in the 1850s by Sir Joseph Paxton for the Rothschild family. Large plate glass windows, central heating and fresh air ventilation made the house advanced for its time.

THE NAVIGATION

THE WEST COAST MAIN LINE

From Watford onwards the West Coast Main Line (WCML), resplendent with its Pendolino electric trains, is never far away from the navigation. These nine-coach train sets – some now upgraded to 11 coaches to meet burgeoning demand – costing more than £11 million each, built in Birmingham by Alstom and operating at up to 125 mph, have significantly cut journey times, making the trip from London to Birmingham in under 1½ hours and to Manchester in just over 2 hours. Virgin Train's 56-strong Pendolino (Italian for 'tilting') fleet clocks up 40,000 miles daily on the WCML, with at least 44 units in operation on any one day, which explains why they are an almost permanent part of the scenery. Their rapid progress across the landscape, negotiating the track's quite significant curves, is largely due to their ability to tilt into corners (at up to 11 degrees). The whole process is controlled by a tilt and speed supervisory safety system that transmits information from fixed devices along the track. This prevents conflict between the train and line-side equipment and structures, ensuring that it tilts only as required. Initially conceived for 140 mph operation there is, as yet, no commercially viable signalling system available to cope with this speed so the scope of the whole WCML upgrade programme – extending as far as Glasgow and Edinburgh and completed in 2008 – was scaled down, although a section in the Trent Valley may run at 135 mph in the foreseeable future.

At the junction the main line bears round to the northeast, while the Aylesbury Arm (a narrow beam canal) starts its fall west through the first of eight locks towards Aylesbury. Totally isolated and remote, it is one of the most peaceful stretches of canal in the country, passing through modest farmland with good views of the Chiltern Hills over

Refreshment at Stoke Bruerne

to the east and, in the distance to the west, of tall new buildings in Aylesbury. The locks are 7ft wide, and the bridges too are narrow.

Northwards from Marsworth the canal falls steadily away from Dunstable Downs and the Chilterns, leaving the hills as a backdrop to the west. As the hills give way to open grassland, the canal becomes more remote, a quiet, empty section that terminates in the peace of Grove Church Lock. Villages are set back from the canal, only Slapton being less than a mile away. The main feature of the section is the locks, carrying the canal down from the Chilterns toward Leighton Buzzard and the Ouzel valley; these occur frequently, often in remote and attractive settings. The West Coast Mainline railway and a road run parallel to the canal to the west. To the east the canal now runs parallel to the River Ouzel and, leaving the open fields behind, passes through the joined towns of Linslade and Leighton Buzzard, effectively acting as a boundary between them.

Leaving the twin towns of Linslade and Leighton Buzzard, the canal enters the valley of the Ouzel and meanders sharply, making the navigation itself seem like a river, which is rare on the Grand Union. Steep hills rise to the east and west, thickly wooded to the east. This section contains a good mixture of canal townscape and landscape, Leighton Locks having an attractive and well-kept lock house. Both railway and road continue to follow the canal to the west. As the valley widens, the waterway continues its steady fall towards Bletchley, following the Ouzel closely. Flat meadows reaching to the west precede the approach to Bletchley. All the locks, the Soulbury flight of three, and one at Stoke Hammond, form an attractive canalscape, the double-arched bridges showing where the locks were once twinned. Remains of the supplementary locks can still be seen at Soulbury alongside the small pumping station that returns water back up the flight whenever necessary.

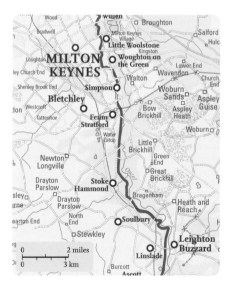

POINTS OF INTEREST

Aylesbury Canal Arm It took 20 years for an arm to be built from the Grand Junction canal at Marsworth, through the 6 miles of remote countryside into the market town of Aylesbury. Negotiation and debate accounted for 17 years, the canal itself taking just 3 years to construct. During that time various proposals were put forward and many objections raised; in essence any scheme that required water from another navigation was strongly resisted. With the town lying in a geographical hollow it was inevitable that every proposal relied on 'borrowed' water for its success; and water was a scarce commodity much sought after by existing navigation authorities and mill owners alike. The most ambitious scheme was to link the Thames at Abingdon with the Grand Junction at Marsworth but this was vehemently resisted by the Thames Commissioners. When the canal actually reached Aylesbury in 1814 it halved the price of coal overnight and went on to be a successful means of transport for coal, agricultural produce and, on one occasion at least, emigrant paupers to the New World via Liverpool Docks. The inevitable railway competition eroded the waterway's profitability throughout the first half of the 20th century and, but for an early hire boat operation in the town basin, together with the Aylesbury Canal Society's concerted efforts, the waterway might well have passed into extinction.

Waddesdon Manor, near Aylesbury Extraordinary French Renaissance-style château with sumptuous internal appointments (including paintings), marvellously landscaped gardens and licensed restaurant and wine shop all in the Rothschild mould, for whom it was created in the 1880s.

Whipsnade White Lion On Dunstable Downs, visible from the canal from around Horton and Slapton. The lion was cut in 1935 and is over 480ft long.

National Waterways Museum, Stoke Bruerne

Grove An attractive group formed by the bridge, lock, lock cottage and the tiny church, a 14th-century chapel with a later bell turret.

Linslade The village is virtually a residential extension of Leighton Buzzard. Traces of the old village can just be found to the north, especially the church, near the canal, easily recognised by its battlements; the front and parts of the structure date from the 12th century. West of the church is a railway tunnel with an extraordinary neo-Gothic portal in grey brick, looking delightfully incongruous.

Ascott House, Linslade Attractive, irregular timber-framed house built in 1606, with extensive additions made in 1874 and 1938, containing a

collection of paintings, French and Chippendale furniture, together with oriental porcelain. There are 12 acres of grounds and gardens containing rare trees.

Leighton Buzzard A picturesque market town with a superlative church. Half-timbered cottages and houses from the 17th and 18th centuries are to be found in the streets leading to the Market Cross, which has stood for some 600 years in the centre of the town. There are also some fine 19th-century buildings; note particularly Barclay's Bank. In North Street stand the almshouses founded by Edward Wilkes in 1633 on condition that the bounds of the parish be beaten every Rogation Monday. The custom is still maintained, and on 23 May a choir boy stands upon his head in front of the almshouses while the appropriate extracts from the donor's will are read.

All Saint's Parish Church, Leighton Buzzard Dates from 1288 and is notable for its 191ft tower and spire and the 15th-century wooden roof. It retains its ancient sanctus bell, 13th-century font, misericords, brasses and a medieval lectern. The medieval graffiti are interesting and include a depiction of Simon and Nellie arguing about whether the Mothering Sunday Simnel cake should be boiled or baked.

Soulbury The church contains a monument in white marble by Grinling Gibbons, 1690. To the south is Liscombe House, a rambling 17th-century brick mansion with a fine Gothic façade of 1774, set in a large landscaped park.

Stoke Hammond Set above the canal to the west, the village overlooks the valley as it spreads untidily along the road. The church, weighted down by its squat central tower, contains a decorative 14th-century font.

THE NAVIGATION

Narrowboat Cetus

BEDFORD & MILTON KEYNES WATERWAY

At bridges 82 and 82A there are signs identifying the site for the proposed starting point of the new Bedford & Milton Keynes Canal, and towards the M1 a waymarked route with interpretation boards has been installed. A scheme to connect these two towns was first mooted by Samuel Whitbread MP in 1810 and today's navigation, costing between £80 and £150 million, would provide a much needed broad beam link between the main waterways system and the Fens. A £50,000 feasibility study has identified the preferred route and demonstrated a positive cost–benefit analysis for a canal approximately 20 miles in length, with a similar number of locks, 6ft deep with a 30ft channel width and 10ft air draught; the lock dimensions would be 100ft x 14ft 6in. Major challenges centre around crossing the M1 motorway, ascending and descending Brogborough Hill (which calls out for a modern, Falkirk Wheel-style structure) and negotiating Bedford's low railway bridges.

The canal runs through open country, but to the south lie the suburbs of the rapidly expanding town of Bletchley, now part of the new city of Milton Keynes. Once north of the town the canal again meanders gently through villages, still following the course of the River Ouzel as far as Woolstone. There is only one lock on this section, but the old arched accommodation bridges abound. The main railway leaves the canal south of Bletchley, but another line, to Bedford, crosses at Fenny Stratford. There is a station close to the canal here.

Continuing northwest, and then at Great Linford turning sharply to the west, the canal runs through attractive, lightly wooded scenery that gradually gives way to hills, following the Ouse valley, as it clings to the south side. Either side, where once there were open fields, the new city of Milton Keynes has been built. There are no locks, but a great variety of bridges. At New Bradwell the canal crosses a dual carriageway on a splendid aqueduct, completed in 1991. The navigation continues westwards past industrial Wolverton, and then turns northwest prior to crossing the Ouse valley by means of an embankment and aqueduct.

A busy scene on the Grand Union Canal

POINTS OF INTEREST

Bletchley This formerly agricultural and lace-making town is now a large, modern place that has swallowed up its neighbour, Fenny Stratford. A small part of the 12th-century St Mary's Church remains; much restoration and alteration has been done.

Fenny Stratford The town is now merged into Bletchley. The building of the red-brick church, 1724–30, was inspired by Browne Willis, the antiquarian; as a result it is an early example of Gothic revival.

Simpson A main road village, much redeveloped as a suburb of Bletchley, but still retaining elements of independence. The church is mainly 14th-century with a notable wooden roof and a monument by John Bacon, 1789. Beyond Woughton Park to the north is Walton Hall, the Open University.

Woughton on the Green The village is attractively scattered round a huge green flanked by the canal to the west. There are houses of all periods, mixed in a random but harmonious manner and presided over by the church built on a mound to the east.

Little Woolstone A tiny hamlet with a pub and a garage. Great Woolstone is even smaller!

Willen A hamlet wholly dominated by the Wren church, which is well worth a visit. All the interior fittings are original, and the plaster work, pews, organ case and font should be seen.

Milton Keynes A typical new town development encompassing Bletchley and the scattered villages to the north. Work on the 22,000-acre area began in the early 1970s and the original population of 40,000 has grown to around 250,000. Strategically placed between Birmingham and the capital, close to the M1 and the main railway line, the

Working boats at rest

Development Corporation has been successful in attracting many companies to the area. Some of the housing schemes are imaginative, and well endowed with green space and trees. Great emphasis is placed on the social and recreational needs of the population and in this respect the new city makes good use of the canal.

Great Linford Great Linford is magnificent: a traditional village street running away from the canal, with a marvellous group formed by church,

manor, farm and almshouses, all in rich golden stone. The 14th-century church right alongside the canal contains Georgian box pews and pulpit, and fine 19th-century stained glass. The almshouses are 17th-century with strong Dutch gables. The manor, symmetrical, dignified and elegant in a totally 18th-century way, completes the picture.

New Bradwell A Victorian railway town, built on a grid of extreme monotony and regularity. The 19th-century Bradwell Windmill has been restored.

THE NAVIGATION

Hills now begin to dominate the landscape to the west as the canal follows the course of the River Tove, an indication of the climb ahead up to Stoke Bruerne. After Wolverton the canal becomes more remote, with only Cosgrove exploiting it. The railway 1 mile to the east provides the only intrusion. There is plenty of canalscape: Wolverton Aqueduct, Cosgrove Lock ending the 11-mile Fenny Stratford Pound, Cosgrove Bridge and the newly restored start of the Buckingham Arm extending west to the A5 dual carriageway – and ultimately into the town of Buckingham itself. After Cosgrove and the old junction, the canal leaves the low hills to the west and passes through open fields to Grafton Regis, where the hills reappear. A quiet, rural stretch, with only the noise of the railway to intrude. The villages lie set back to the west, but are easily approached. Accommodation bridges occur with even regularity, mostly old brick arches.

After Grafton Regis the River Tove joins the canal and then branches away to the west after 3/4 mile.

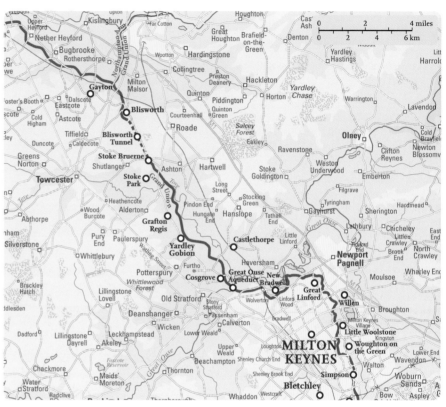

At once the navigation starts the seven-lock climb to Stoke Bruerne, via single wide locks. As the village is approached the hills become more dominant, especially to the west and northwest, anticipating Blisworth Tunnel. After the tunnel and the thickly wooded approach cutting, the hills recede to the west, and the canal, becoming wider but shallow at the edges, reaches Gayton Junction through open fields.

The villages are very much on top of the canal, partly because of the landscape, and partly because of their importance to the canal; Stoke Bruerne is an ideal canal village. Beyond Stoke Bruerne Top Lock the level remains unchanged for several miles, a deep cutting leading to Blisworth Tunnel which is the third longest waterway tunnel in Britain open to navigation. The Canal Museum at Stoke Bruerne makes this altogether an exciting stretch.

POINTS OF INTEREST

Great Ouse Aqueduct North of Old Wolverton the canal crosses the Ouse via an iron trunk aqueduct, a square cast iron trough carried on stone pillars. Built in 1811, it replaced a brick structure that collapsed in 1808. This in turn had replaced nine locks that enabled the Ouse to be crossed on the level, a system abandoned because of the danger of floods.

Cosgrove The village climbs west away from the canal, its spread visually terminated by the wooded church. The best parts are by the canal: a range of warehouses, a curious pedestrian tunnel under the canal, and a splendid stone bridge charmingly decorated in the Gothic style, built in 1800. Its style is unique among canal bridges, and there is no obvious reason for its solitary splendour. The Georgian house that dominates the west bank by the lock is Cosgrove Hall; in 1958 a Roman bathhouse was discovered in front of the hall.

Castlethorpe A quiet village, thatched houses around a green, 1 mile north east of Thrupp Wharf. The main railway running in a cutting below the village is the only disturbance. North of the church is the site of a castle.

Yardley Gobion A small thatch-and-stone village, set on a slope to the west of the canal. The village is bypassed by the busy A508, which has prompted much new development. The church, built in 1864, is now out of reach of the traffic, and is once more serene.

Grafton Regis A quiet stone village that runs gently westwards from the canal, and still preserves a strong manorial feeling. The large church, near the canal, is mostly 13th- and 14th-century.

Stoke Park, Stoke Bruerne The park is 1/2 mile west of the canal. Built 1629–35 by Inigo Jones for

Boat weighing machine

Sir Francis Crane, head of the Mortlake Tapestry Works, the symmetrical façade with its flanking pavilions and colonnade made Stoke Park House (now demolished) one of the earliest Palladian or classical buildings in England. The pavilions and colonnade survived the fire, which virtually destroyed the mansion in 1886.

Stoke Bruerne Perhaps the best example of a canal village in this country. Built mostly of local Blisworth stone, the houses flank the canal, clearly viewing it as a blessing. To the west the hilly landscape warns of the approaching tunnel under Blisworth Hill. The Perpendicular church with its Norman tower overlooks the village, while the warehouses and cottages along the wharf have become a canal centre, greatly encouraged by the presence of the Canal Museum. As a canalscape Stoke Bruerne has everything: a pub, locks, boat scales, a double-arched bridge, museum and canal shops and a nearby tunnel.

National Waterways Museum, Stoke Bruerne Housed in a restored corn mill, a unique collection brings to life the rich history of over 200 years of canals. Exhibits include a traditional narrowboat, boat weighing scales, a reconstructed butty boat cabin, steam and diesel engines, and extensive displays of clothing, cabinware, brasses, signs, models, paintings, photographs, and documents.

Blisworth Tunnel At 3,057yds long, Blisworth is the third longest canal tunnel open to navigation in Britain. The Grand Junction Canal was completed and opened in 1800 with the exception of this tunnel. The first attempt at excavation failed, and so a tramway was built over Blisworth Hill, linking the two termini. Boats arriving at either end had to be unloaded onto horse-drawn wagons, which were then pulled over the hill, and reloaded onto boats. A second attempt at the tunnel was more successful, and it opened on 25 March 1805. Originally boats were legged through (note the leggers' hut at the south end). The then British Waterways' £4.3-million restoration project was completed in 1984. There is no towpath, but the channel is wide enough to allow the passing of two 7ft boats.

Blisworth A large brown-stone village built around the old A43, it climbs up steeply from the canal, which passes through in a cutting shortly after leaving the tunnel. The church, mostly 14th-century, is just to the east of the canal, but appears to sit astride it.

Gayton Set on a hill to the west of the canal junction, the village seems to be composed of large, handsome stone houses, ranging in style from the 16th to the 19th centuries; trees among the houses increase the rural grandeur. The large church with its ornamented tower maintains the unity of the village.

THE NAVIGATION

At Gayton Junction the Northampton Arm of the Grand Union, opened in 1815, branches away to the northeast. The waterway falls steeply through 5 miles of open country to Northampton where it connects with the navigable River Nene and thus with Peterborough, the Fens and ultimately the Wash.

Continuing northwest after Gayton Junction, the canal enters a relatively empty stretch of agricultural land, open fields falling away to the north and steep hills to the south. As it approaches Bugbrooke, the only village on this stretch, it begins to meander as the hills become more dominant. The canal avoids most villages, passing directly only through Weedon Bec, where there is much of interest: aqueducts over a road and the River Nene, an embankment, the old wharf and the elegant Royal Ordnance Depot.

A quiet open stretch follows which gives way to the landscaped woods of Brockhall Park. This peace is short-lived, however, as soon several transport routes merge to produce a strange picture of three totally different means of transport running parallel. The old Roman road, Watling Street (A5), keeping as straight a course as possible through the hills; the canal, its junior by 1,800 years, now looking more outdated than the Roman road; the London–Midland railway line and the 20th-century M1 motorway complete this set of contrasts. Of all the thousands of travellers passing through this area every hour, it must surely be those who travel on the canal who enjoy its potential most as they compare the canal's dignity and quiet progress to the noise and rush of the roads and the railway. For most it will act as a stimulus to head for Whilton and Buckby Locks and the climb up to Norton Junction, accompanied as it is by attractive terraces

of red-brick cottages. All the locks have side ponds, now disused (with some filled in), and ivy-leafed toadflax grows in the lock walls. The system for pumping water back up the flight has been restored, using an electric pump. Above Buckby Locks is Norton Junction, where the Leicester Line branches off to the north while the main line continues west towards Braunston.

From Norton Junction to Braunston the canal runs westward through hills and wooded country, then into a wooded cutting which leads to Braunston Tunnel. A cutting follows the tunnel, and then the landscape opens out although the hills stay present on either side. Long rows of moored craft flank the canal and there are a fine selection of old buildings at Braunston: especially notable are the iron side-bridge and the 18th-century dry dock. The arm in fact was part of the old route of the Oxford Canal before it was shortened by building a large embankment (Braunston Puddle Banks) across the Leam Valley to Braunston Turn. The entrance to this arm was thus the original Braunston Junction. The delightful building alongside, known as the Stop House, was originally the Toll Office between the Oxford Canal (see page 44) and the Grand Junction Canal.

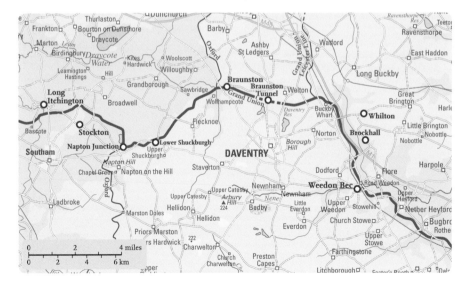

POINTS OF INTEREST

Weedon Bec The heart of the village is close to the aqueduct where a charming sprawl of cottages cluster close to the church, together with most of the facilities, making this a good place to moor.

Brockhall A large, lightly wooded landscaped park climbs gently east away from the canal. In the centre a manorial brown stone village and church are still intact and remote despite the M1 roaring through the west end of the park. The Hall is Tudor in part, with fine 18th-century interiors; large trees screen it from the motorway.

Whilton One mile east of the canal at the end of a road that goes nowhere, Whilton is quiet and unchanged, especially at the east end. There are several fine stone houses, including a pretty Georgian rectory.

Braunston Tunnel Opened in 1796 to bore through the Northamptonshire heights, the tunnel is 2,042yds long. Its construction was hindered by quicksands, and a mistake in direction whilst building has given it a slight S bend.

Braunston Set up on a hill to the north of the canal. The village is really a long main street a little separate from the canal, with houses of all periods. A well-known canal centre, it is no less significant today than when the Oxford and Grand Junction canals were first connected here.

Lower Shuckburgh A tiny village along the main road. The church, built in 1864, is attractive in a Victorian way, with great use of contrasting brickwork inside.

Napton Junction The canal now passes through open countryside with a backdrop of hills, seeming very quiet and empty following all of the waterway activity around Braunston. The land is agricultural, with just a few houses in sight. There are initially no locks, no villages and the bridges are well spaced, making this a very pleasant rural stretch of canal running south west towards Napton Junction, on a length once used by both the Grand Junction Company and the Oxford Canal Company. As the Oxford Canal actually owned this stretch, they charged excessive toll rates in an attempt to get even with their rival, whose more direct route between London and the Midlands had attracted most of the traffic. At Napton Junction the Oxford Canal heads off to the south while the Grand Union Canal strikes off north towards Birmingham. The empty landscape rolls on towards Stockton, broken only by Calcutt Locks. The windmill on top of Napton Hill can just be seen from Napton Junction.

'The Navigation', Stoke Bruerne

THE NAVIGATION

A Dutch barge and traditional narrowboats on the Grand Union Canal

Continuing west, the canal passes to the north of Stockton and descends Stockton Locks, where there are the remains of the old narrow locks beside the newer wide ones. At this point there is a change in landscape, with the hills coming much closer to the canal, broken by old quarries and thick woods along the south bank. The quarries produced blue lias, a local stone and cement which was used in the construction of the Thames Embankment. Huge fossils have been found in the blue lias clay, which is the lowest layer from the Jurassic period. This section contrasts greatly with the open landscape that precedes and follows it. The canal passes Long Itchington, a village notable for its profusion of pubs, including two on the canal, all the while flanked by open arable land backed on both sides by hills. This pleasant emptiness is broken only by further locks continuing the fall to Warwick. Of particular interest are the top two locks at Bascote, just beyond the pretty toll house, which form a staircase. Then the canal is once again in quiet, wooded, countryside.

The waterway makes its descent through the Fosse Locks and continues west through attractive and isolated country to pass to the north of Radford Semele, where there is a fine wooded cutting. Emerging from the cutting, the canal joins a busy road for a short while, then carves a fairly discreet course through Leamington. Midway through the town the navigation enters a deep cutting that hides it from the adjacent main road and railway. Leaving Leamington the waterway swings northwest under a main road and crosses the railway and the River Avon on aqueducts, to immediately enter the outskirts of Warwick.

The canal passes around the north side of central Warwick and, after climbing the two Cape Locks, swings south to Budbrooke Junction, where the old Warwick and Napton Canal joined the Warwick and Birmingham Canal. To the west of the junction, beyond a large road bridge, is the first of the 21 locks of the Hatton flight, with distinctive paddle gear and gates stretching up the hill ahead, a daunting sight for even the most resilient boatman. Consolation is offered by the fine view of the spires of Warwick as you climb the flight. On reaching the top, the canal turns to the northwest, passing the wooded hills that conceal Hatton village and Hatton Park. It then enters the wooded cutting that leads to Shrewley Tunnel.

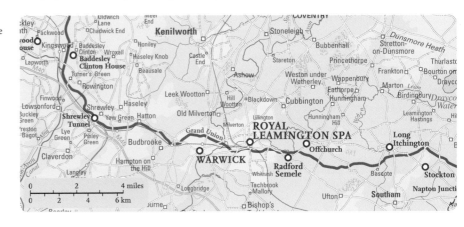

POINTS OF INTEREST

Stockton This is a largely Victorian village in an area which has been dominated by the cement works to the west. St Michael's church is built of blue lias, quarried near Stockton Locks, although the tower is of red sandstone.

Long Itchington A large housing estate flanks the busy A423. The village proper lies a short walk to the northwest, and is very attractive. Apart from the superfluity of pubs there are houses of the 17th and 18th centuries, and impressive poplars around the village pond. St Wulfstan, who later became Bishop of Worcester, was born here in 1012.

Holy Trinity, Long Itchington is a largely 13th-century church whose tall spire was blown down in a gale in 1762, and replaced with a stump. Parts of the south aisle date from the 12th-century, although the 13th-century windows are perhaps the building's best feature.

Offchurch A scattered residential village reflecting the proximity of Leamington. It takes its name from Offa, the Saxon King of Mercia, reputedly buried near here. The church, with its tall grey stone tower, contains some Norman work. To the west lies Offchurch Bury, whose park runs almost to the canal. Originally this was a 17th-century house, but it has since been entirely rebuilt. The façade is now early 19th-century Gothic.

Radford Semele A main road suburb of Leamington, Radford Semele takes no notice of the canal that runs below the village, alongside the River Leam and what was once the railway line to Rugby. Among the bungalows are some fine large houses, including Radford Hall, a reconstructed Jacobean building. The Victorian church of St Nicholas, completely gutted by fire and rebuilt, is set curiously by itself, seeming to be in the middle of a field.

Royal Leamington Spa During the 19th century the population of Leamington increased rapidly, due to the late 18th- and 19th-century fashion for spas in general. As a result the town is largely Regency with later Victorian additions resulting in a most pleasingly spacious layout. Several hotels and churches were designed by J. Cundall, a local architect of some note who also built the brick and stone town hall. The long rows of villas, elegant houses in their own grounds spreading out from the centre, all express the Victorian love of exotic styles – Gothic, Classical, Jacobean, Renaissance, French and Greek are all mixed here with bold abandon. Since the Victorian era, however, much industrialisation has taken place.

All Saints' Church, Leamington Spa Begun in 1843 to the design of J. C. Jackson, who was greatly

influenced by the then vicar, Dr John Craig. It is of Gothic style, apparently not always correct in detail. The north transept has a rose window patterned on Rouen Cathedral; the west window is by Kempe. The scale of the building is impressive, being fully 172ft long and 80ft high.

Jephson Gardens, Leamington Spa Beautiful ornamental gardens named after Dr Jephson (1798–1878), the local practitioner who was largely responsible for the spa's high medical reputation.

Warwick Virtually destroyed by fire in 1694 the town rose again, with Queen Anne styles now mixed with the medieval buildings which survived the blaze.

Warwick Castle Built on the site of a motte and bailey constructed by William the Conqueror in 1068, the present exterior is a famous example of a 14th-century fortification, with the tall Caesar's Tower rising to a height of 147ft. The castle grounds were laid out by Capability Brown.

Collegiate Church of St Mary's, Warwick The most striking feature of the rebuilt church is its pseudo-Gothic tower, built 1698–1704 giving stunning views out over the gently undulating Warwickshire countryside.

Lord Leycester Hospital, Warwick A superbly preserved group of 14th-century timber-framed buildings. Chapel of St James, Great Hall and galleried courtyard. The Museum of the Queen's Own Hussars is also here and the restored gardens are open during the summer.

Shrewley Tunnel 433yds long, the tunnel was opened in 1799 with the completion of the Warwick & Birmingham Canal allowing two 7ft narrowboats to pass.

THE NAVIGATION

THE LEAM LINK

For more than 30 years the Upper Avon Navigation Trust (UANT) has administered, financed, maintained and developed the river for the considerable benefit of the local community. Since 2009 it has been incorporated into the Avon Navigation Trust. It is, arguably, the most popular section of the Avon cruising ring – made up of almost equal lengths of canal and river – and its charms and facilities have been well documented in the Trust's recent *River Avon Navigation Guide and Visitor Guide (2014)*.

To further enhance the value of the Upper Avon, UANT had supported a proposal to construct a navigable link connecting the Grand Union Canal and the River Leam, between Leamington and Warwick. This scheme displayed great sensitivity in enhancing a wide range of wildlife habitats, whilst providing increased opportunities to walkers, fishermen, boaters and cyclists alike. The proposal made imaginative use of natural features and materials to open up a waterway, not only as a potential link between existing river and canal systems but, just as importantly, as a series of environmentally rich, managed and secure sites attracting wildlife to the River Leam. The proposed structures – in the form of locks (four in total), islands, dams and bypass channels – were designed to create adjoining wetlands, complemented by a series of silt banks, reeds and sedges, hardwood copses and hedge planting. Thus birds, fish and mammals would be attracted back to an area which the inevitable urban growth has gradually depleted.

In the initial phase of work, the plan was to connect the Grand Union Canal, east of Leamington Spa, with the River Leam via two locks. A further two locks along the river would be constructed to maintain navigable levels before the Leam meets the River Avon north of Warwick. This would, in turn, enable pleasure craft to access these two historic towns, providing attractive moorings. Longer term plans envisaged a scheme to improve the Upper Avon as a navigation between Warwick and Stratford-upon-Avon, thereby opening up a further wide range of leisure possibilities.

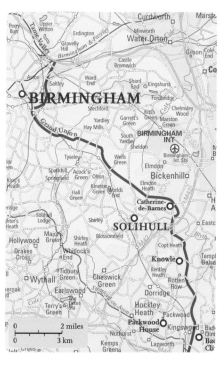

After Shrewley Tunnel, hills surround the canal on all sides as it travels through steep wooded folds. At Turner's Green a beautiful old beamed house stands by the canal; the waterway continues to Kingswood and the junction with the Stratford-on-Avon Canal at Lapworth.

The waterway now continues its northerly route, passing through countryside which is surprisingly peaceful. Knowle Locks introduce more hilly countryside again, and this green and pleasant land continues right through to Solihull, concealing the nearness of Birmingham. The flight of five wide locks at Knowle used to be six narrow ones, until the 1930 improvements; the remains of the old locks can still be seen alongside the new, together with the side ponds (originally built to save water). The locks are comparatively deep, and are very well maintained and pleasantly situated. They are also the northernmost wide locks for many miles now, since all the Birmingham canals have narrow locks. Knowle is set back from the canal, but warrants a visit, especially to see the church. Continuing northwest through wooded country, the canal passes under the M42 motorway and crosses the River Blythe on a small aqueduct.

POINTS OF INTEREST

Baddesley Clinton A very fine example of a late medieval manor house built in a mixture of brick and stone, entered via a small brick bridge over a moat. It is little changed since 1633 when Henry Ferrers, the antiquary, died. He was squire here for almost 70 years. Much of the brickwork dates from the Queen Anne period. The hall has an ornate Elizabethan stone chimney-piece, and 15th-century beams; there is excellent armorial stained glass throughout the building, a tradition started by Henry Ferrers. Pictures painted by Rebecca Dulcibella Orpen, wife of Marmion Ferrers, celebrate the romantic life lived at Baddesley during the late 19th century. The 17th-century stables and parkland complete the feeling of unity.

Packwood House, Lapworth A much-restored timber-framed Tudor house. Cromwell's general, Henry Ireton, slept here before the Battle of Edgehill in 1642. The gardens are noted for their topiary and there are attractive lakeside walks.

Knowle Despite its proximity to Birmingham, Knowle still survives as a village, albeit rather self-consciously. A number of old buildings thankfully remain, some dating from the Middle Ages and including such gems as Chester House (now the library), which illustrate the advances in timber-frame construction from the 13th to the 15th centuries. Around the back there is a splendid knot garden. Half-a-mile north of the village is Grimshaw Hall, a gabled 16th-century house noted for its decorative brickwork. There are good views of it from the canal.

Church of St John the Baptist, St Lawrence and St Anne, Knowle This remarkable church was built as a result of the efforts of Walter Cook, a wealthy man who founded a chapel here in 1396, and completed the present church in 1402. Prior to its building the parishioners of Knowle had to make

Traditional motor and butty

a 6-mile round trip each Sunday to the church at Hampton-in-Arden. This involved crossing the River Blythe, an innocuous brook today, but in medieval times 'a greate and daungerous water' which 'noyther man nor beaste can passe wt. owte daunger of peryshing'. The church is built in the Perpendicular style, with a great deal of intricate stonework. There is much of interest to be seen inside, including the roof timbers, the original font and a medieval dug-out chest. Behind the church is the 3-acre Children's Field, given to the National Trust by the Reverend T. Downing 'to be used for games'.

Catherine-de-Barnes A small village with new housing, which takes its name from the 12th-century Lord 'Ketelberne'. The houses and flats known as Catherine's Court were once a fever hospital, built in 1907.

Solihull A modern commuter development, with fine public buildings. What used to be the town centre, dominated by the tall spire of the parish church, is now a shopping area.

St Alphege Church, Solihull Built of red sandstone, it is almost all late 13th- and early 14th-century. The lofty interior contains work of all periods, including a Jacobean pulpit, a 17th-century communion rail, 19th-century stained glass and a few notable monuments.

Birmingham It is strange to think that the medieval town which centred around a parish church and moated manor originally stood on the site of the present Smithfield market. Industrial and commercial development continued with such speed during the 19th century that Birmingham began to be considered as the trade centre of the Midlands.

THE NAVIGATION

The canal now enters the outskirts of Birmingham, although an attractive screen of trees conceals the expanding built-up areas. Catherine-de-Barnes is the last village recognisable as such before suburbs surround the navigation. There are no locks, the bridges tend to be high above the water and the long, deep cutting creates an illusion of peace. As the waterway continues northwest into Birmingham, the wooded cutting ends and, from this point on, housing estates and disused wharves accompany the canal, brightened with red poppies and ox-eye daisies growing beside the towpath.

The canal curves past the large Energy from Waste plant and the Ackers Trust Basin before reaching Camp Hill Locks. These, and all the succeeding locks, are narrow. After passing through subterranean vaults formed by the criss-crossing of railway viaducts, Bordesley Junction is reached. Ahead, beyond the junction, the canal continues towards the Birmingham Canal Main Line (*see* page 68) joining the Birmingham & Fazeley Canal at Aston Junction, passing a very fine collection of old wharf buildings on the way.

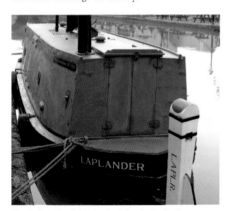

Birmingham Canals Navigation icebreaker Laplander

Welsh Road Lock, Grand Union

Representative of many similar structures, though somewhat grander in both its design and execution, the Lune Aqueduct carries the Lancaster Canal an impressive 664ft over the River Lune. John Rennie was its designer and it was built using traditional bridge building techniques. Five semi-circular arches, each of 70ft span, carry the concrete-lined masonry trough at a height of 61ft above the river, supported on rubble-filled hollow piers, which are themselves founded on timber piles sunk deep beneath the river bed.

The structure once retained its water through the use of puddle clay, 3ft deep, carried on a thick stone lining. Work commenced in 1797 and took three years to complete at a cost of £48,321 – somewhat wide of the budgeted figure of £18,619. Indeed, so much adrift of the original estimate was the final figure that it ensured that a corresponding structure over the River Ribble was never built leaving, until the recent completion of the Ribble Link, the Lancaster Canal as a navigation totally detached from the remainder of the waterway system.

The aqueduct bears two inscriptions – on the upstream face one reads:
'To Public Prosperity'
while on the downstream side the Latin translates as:
'Old needs are served, far distant sites combined.
Rivers by art to bring new wealth are joined.'
This second inscription succinctly embraces so much of what the waterways have come to stand for.

Parapet detail

The Lune Aqueduct, Lancaster Canal

BIRDS

Long-tailed tit A charming resident of woods, heaths and hedgerows. Feeding flocks of these birds resemble animated feather dusters. Outside the breeding season family groups roam widely and often join other families, forming flocks of over 20. At night they roost communally. Their plumage can look black and white, but at close range there is a pinkish wash to the underparts and pinkish buff on the backs. The long-tailed tit has a tiny, stubby bill, a long tail, and an almost spherical body. The beautiful domed nest is built of moss, lichen and spiders' webs. Other adults may assist parents to feed their young, which fly after 14 days.

Long-tailed tit

Mallard A widespread and familiar duck. The colourful male has a yellow bill and green, shiny head and neck separated from a chestnut breast by a white collar. Plumage is otherwise grey-brown except for a black stern and white tail. The female has an orange bill and mottled brown plumage. In flight both sexes have a blue and white speculum (patch on trailing edge of inner wing).

Mallard

Mallard are resident throughout Britain and Ireland on a wide variety of wetlands; often on urban ponds, lakes and canals, where they are usually tame.

Moorhen The Moorhen superficially resembles another widespread and familiar bird, the Coot: told apart by the smaller size, red and yellow bill

Moorhen

and more colourful plumage. They are also easily distinguished by their habit of bobbing while swimming. The sexes appear similar. The adults are dark bluish-brown, with greyer flanks, and a line of pale feathers dividing the upper parts and under parts. Look out for a noticeable pale patch behind the cocked tail. The juvenile is much browner and lacks the colourful bill. Moorhens rarely fly and do not dive. They feed on underwater invertebrates from off or just under the water surface, or from wet grass.

Mute swan

Mute swan A large and distinctive water bird, the commonest swan in Britain. The adult has pure white plumage, black legs and an orange-red bill. The black blob at the base of the bill is smaller in the female than the male. While swimming, the bird usually holds the neck in an elegant curve. In flight the swan has broad wings and shallow but powerful wingbeats that produce a characteristic throbbing whine; the bird is otherwise silent. Mute swans nests beside lakes, rivers and canals; in winter they can also be seen on estuaries and sheltered coasts.

Nuthatch

Nuthatch Recognised by its rounded, short-tailed appearance and its habit of descending tree trunks head-downwards, a trait unique in Britain to this species. The bird has has blue-grey upperparts, a black eyestripe, white cheeks and orange-buff underparts. The chisel-like bill is used to prise insects from tree bark and to hammer open acorns wedged in bark crevices. This woodland species has a falcon-like call. It nests in tree holes, often plastering the entrance with mud to reduce its diameter.

Reed warbler

Reed warbler As the name suggests, these birds are almost always associated with reedbeds around lakes or along rivers. Dense, wet reedbeds may be home to large numbers of reed warblers: a summer visitor, usually seen between May and August. Singing birds clamber up reeds or occasionally use bushes to deliver a grating, chattering song that includes some mimetic elements. The birds have rather nondescript sandy-brown upperparts, paler underparts and dark legs. They construct woven, cup-shaped nests, attached to upright reed stems, usually over water. They feed on insects and spiders. In autumn reed warblers return to central Africa.

Snipe

Snipe These birds are easily recognised, even in silhouette, by their dumpy, rounded body, rather short legs and incredibly long, straight bill. They have a characteristic feeding method: the bird probes vertically downwards with its bill in soft mud, in the manner of a sewing machine. In good light, the snipe has buffish brown plumage, beautifully patterned with black and white lines and bars, and distinctive dark stripes on its head. They are a locally common breeding species on marshy

ground and moors in many parts of Britain and Ireland, although absent from much of southern England in the summer months. More widespread in winter, they can be found in a range of wetland habitats. The snipe utters one or two 'kreech' calls when flushed. In the breeding season they perform a 'drumming' display and make a humming sound, produced by vibrating their tail feathers.

Tree sparrow

Tree sparrow Although distributed widely throughout the country, tree sparrows are decidedly scarce. They are occasionally found on the outskirts of villages but are more usually associated with untidy arable farms, taking advantage of frequent grain spills along with buntings and finches. The sexes are similar and easily distinguished from house sparrows by the chestnut cap and nape, and the black patch on an otherwise white cheek. The plumage is streaked brown on the backs, with pale underparts. The juveniles lack the black cheek patches. Tree sparrows utter house sparrow-like chirps but also a sharp 'tik tik' in flight. They form flocks in winter, sometimes feeding in stubble fields.

THE NORTHWEST

It was in the northwest that Britain can be considered to have seen the birth of the canal system as we know it today. The populist view of history has a penchant for attaching great achievements to great men, especially where the 'great man' originates from humble beginnings. Whether one attributes 'waterway baby' status to the Newry Canal in Ireland – or to the canalization of the Sankey Brook nearer to home, in the vicinity of St Helens – it will always be the partnership between James Brindley and the 3rd Duke of Bridgewater that captures public imagination.

As the rightful subject of the first Milepost in this book, Brindley's role in the development of the canal system of the northwest and indeed, throughout Britain, is thoroughly explored. The impact of his work on the Bridgewater Canal which, in essence, was to unite the source of production with a burgeoning market for its output, was repeated throughout this region as each successive waterway was promoted and constructed. Textile production was synonymous with this whole area, first as a cottage industry, then in the form of huge mills, objects of a great and almost terrible beauty. This transition could not have come about without a reliable transport system and this was never going to be founded on the tortuous, muddy packhorse trails that slithered off the vertiginous Pennine slopes towards an unreliable (in the extreme) river system leading to the coastal ports.

Marple Locks, Peak Forest Canal

The development of the canal system in this region meant that virgin fleece could be spun into wool and cotton boll into yarn on what became a truly epic scale. On the back of these two ingredients came the textile industry which, in turn, produced finished woollen and cotton garments, together with all manner of goods based upon the finished fabrics. While the Midlands saw the manufacture of largely 'hard' products based on metals, the northwest devoted a greater part of its output to softer materials – first from natural sources and then man-made as the chemical industry developed throughout the region. What both regions now shared, in common with the rest of Britain, was the wherewithal to reliably ship in large quantities of raw materials and to export an unlimited quantity of their finished goods.

Whether confronting a packhorse, or a canal engineer out surveying a route for a proposed waterway, the Pennines presented a formidable

The half-timbered Court House and boats at Worsley on the Bridgewater Canal

obstacle and in overcoming their unremitting bulk we have inherited a superb range of canal structures: often totally novel solutions to the engineering challenges at the time of their inception. Civil engineering was in its infancy (as indeed was the profession of the architect) tools were rudimentary with the shovel, pick and wheelbarrow the earthmovers of choice. The JCB was indeed a very long way away! Today, what makes exploration of the northern waterways system truly exciting is to discover and marvel at the plethora of tunnels, locks, bridges, aqueducts and warehouses that were constructed to overcome this demanding terrain and provided the infrastructure that smoothed the passage of waterborne commerce.

Not one, but three canals snake their way tortuously across the Pennine mass: both the Huddersfield Narrow Canal and the Leeds & Liverpool Canal are covered in the following pages while the Rochdale Canal, soaring to a heady 600 feet above sea level and recently rescued from mouldering obscurity, is alluded to in Milepost 24. All make subjects for an exhilarating visit, be it by bike, boat or on foot, and contrast with their more leisurely cousins, the Macclesfield and Lancaster canals. The former is a 'modern' cut and fill waterway, the line originally suggested by Thomas Telford, although eventually engineered by William Crosley. Promoted as late as 1825, it offered a relatively straight link between the Potteries and Manchester: an outlet for the textiles of the silk mills of Macclesfield. The simple, yet ingenious strategy, of grouping all the locks together in a truly charming 12-lock flight at Bosley, otherwise left the boatman an uninterrupted passage.

Albert Dock – adjoining the new terminus of the Leeds & Liverpool Canal

The Lancaster Canal lies very much further to the north of this region and until the recent introduction of a navigable link, via the River Ribble, was not connected into the remainder of the waterways system. This was not the intention of its original promoters, who envisaged it crossing the tidal river via an aqueduct, to connect with the Leeds & Liverpool further south. Unfortunately a shortage of funds meant that this was never realized. However, it was extended as far north as Kendal, in the Lake District, but the construction of the M6 motorway severed this link at Tewitfield some 15$\frac{1}{2}$ miles short of its original destination. As a navigation it is a delight, at places almost finding its way onto the sands of Morecambe Bay, and is notable for having the longest navigable pound – at 42$\frac{1}{2}$ miles – of any waterway in the country. However, six locks do appear on the Glasson

Branch, dropping the navigation 3 miles down to Glasson Docks and its junction with the serpentine estuary of the River Lune, a little to the southwest of Lancaster.

Tunnel End Footbridge, Huddersfield Narrow Canal

BRIDGEWATER CANAL

This is the navigation upon which James Brindley, a hitherto successful and resourceful millwright, cut his true civil engineering teeth and a project upon which the profession itself might consider to have been founded.

As a waterway, its real significance lay in its ability to link the output of the Duke of Bridgewater's coal mines with the burgeoning demand from the rapidly growing population of Manchester. It avoided the difficult, costly and sometimes downright impossible 'road' journey, thereby guaranteeing regular supplies of fuel for the city's inhabitants and industry, together with a substantial and reliable income for the duke.

The Bridgewater Canal near Grappenhall

BACKGROUND

The Bridgewater Canal received Royal Assent on 23 March 1759, four years after the Sankey Brook (or St Helens) Canal and 18 years after the Newry Canal (once known as Black Pig's Dyke), which linked Lough Neagh to the sea below Newry, in Northern Ireland, and was probably the first 'modern' canal in the British Isles. The Bridgewater was built by Francis Egerton, 3rd Duke of Bridgewater, to enable coal from his mines at Worsley to be transported to Manchester and sold cheaply. His agent was John Gilbert and his engineer was James Brindley, who designed a lockless contour canal which crossed the River Irwell on a stone aqueduct – a revolutionary concept and one that was ridiculed by many sceptics. However, the line was open to Castlefield by the end of 1765.

Worsley Delph: entrances to the Duke of Bridgewater's coalmines just visible to the right and the left of the picture

While the canal was under construction, there began the excavation of a remarkable system of underground canals to serve the duke's mines, reached through two entrances at Worsley Delph. Eventually 46 miles of underground canal were built, some on different levels and linked by an ingenious inclined plane built along a fault in the sandstone. The slim craft used in the mines were known as 'starvationers', double-ended tub boats which could carry up to 12 tons of coal. This whole system remained in use until the late 19th century.

In 1762 the duke received sanction to extend his canal to the Liverpool tideway at Runcorn – this was later amended in order to connect with the new Trent & Mersey Canal at Preston Brook (*see page 26*). The route between Liverpool and Manchester was opened in 1776, although Brindley did not live to see its completion. In 1795 the duke, then 60 years old, received the Royal Assent for the final part of the network, which linked Worsley to the Leeds & Liverpool Canal at Leigh.

The coming of the railways did not initially affect the prosperity of the canal. In 1872 the newly formed Bridgewater Navigation Company purchased the canal for £1,120,000, and they in turn sold it to the Manchester Ship Canal Company in 1885. When the building of the new Ship Canal meant that Brindley's original stone aqueduct over the River Irwell was replaced, its successor, the Barton Swing Aqueduct, was no less outstanding than the original, being a steel trough closed by gates at each end, pivoting on an island in the Ship Canal.

The Bridgewater Canal is a tribute to its builders in that it continued to carry commercial traffic until 1974 – indeed its wide gauge, lock-free course and frequent use of aqueducts makes many later canals seem retrograde. It is now an oasis of tranquillity amidst the burgeoning new industry of Manchester.

Over the majesty and grandeur of the Pontcysyllte Aqueduct there can be no absolutely no argument. However in the clear mountain air, between the River Dee and the aqueduct's solid iron trough, dissent hangs like a morning mist stealing in on the dawning of a crisp autumn day. Who should really carry the credit for its conception, for its detailed design and for its final execution?

Easily the most famous and most spectacular feature on the whole canal system, this aqueduct cannot fail to astonish its visitors. Apart from its great height of 126ft above the Dee and its length of 1,007ft, the excitement to be derived from crossing this structure by boat is partly due to the fact that, while the towpath side is fenced off with, albeit widely spaced, iron railings, the offside is completely unprotected from about 12in. above the water level. It is generally considered to have

…crossing the River Dee

Pontcysyllte Aqueduct…

been built by Thomas Telford and, if so, is reckoned to be one of his most brilliant and successful works. The concept of laying a cast iron trough along the top of a row of stone piers was entirely new and, possibly Telford's: he realised that such a high crossing of the Dee valley was inevitable, if time- and water-wasting locks were to be avoided and it was obvious to the canal company that a conventional brick or stone aqueduct would be quite unsuitable.

It appears that this plan for an aqueduct was greeted at first with derision but the work went ahead, was completed in ten years and it opened in 1805 at an estimated cost of £47,018. What becomes less clear, muddied by the passage of time, is at whose door should the true credit for the project be laid. Should it be Thomas Telford, historically acknowledged as its creator, who claimed credit for its construction in his autobiography? Or William Turner, a Whitchurch born architect, who was responsible for the first surveys of the canal and is known to have submitted initial plans for an aqueduct? Then there is William Jessop, a name that appears as

engineer for nearly every major waterway project of the time: Telford's manager and a man far too modest to write an autobiography. The final contender is William Hazeldine, a local iron founder and experienced engineer, with a close involvement in all stages of the project – early design work, final specification for the iron trough and ultimately the manufacturer of the trough and arch sections at his Plas Kynaston and Shropshire foundries.

Standing resolutely aside from this controversy, the aqueduct today remains as built, apart from renewals of balustrading and the towpath structure. The masonry is apparently in prime condition (note the very thin masonry joints, which were bonded by a mortar made from a mixture of lime and ox blood), and the dovetailed joints in the iron trough, sealed with a combination of Welsh flannel and lead dipped in boiling sugar, hardly leak at all. The cast iron side plates of the trough are all wedge shaped, like the stones in a masonry arch. It is, without doubt, a masterpiece and a worthy recipient of its World Heritage Site status.

HUDDERSFIELD NARROW CANAL

One of three trans-Pennine canals, and by far the shortest route, this waterway was conceived in 1793, at the height of 'canal mania' (the bulk of canal construction was concentrated into the 1790s), and encouraged by the success of the Ashton and Huddersfield Broad canals. Benjamin Outram was retained as engineer and he reported in favour of a narrow canal (in the interest of cost saving) following the route of the present navigation.

There was the inevitable conflict with local mill owners over water supply and a total reservoir capacity of 20,000 locks full of water was provided by way of appeasement.

Smudgees Lock on the Huddersfield Narrow Canal

BACKGROUND

As always optimism was in far greater supply than the capital raised from the initial share issue following the enabling Act passed on 4 April 1794. The estimated cost was some £183,000, of which nearly one-third was allocated to the construction of a 3-mile-long tunnel under the Pennines. As work progressed the canal was opened in sections to generate income; the first section opened in March 1797 between Huddersfield and Slaithwaite and two more, linking Slaithwaite to Marsden and Ashton to Greenfield, were completed late in the following year. It was not until 12 years later that the first boat passed through the completed Standedge Tunnel.

From the outset the waterway was dogged by shoddy workmanship and flood damage. In its 436ft rise to the eastern tunnel portal at Marsden, the canal follows the Colne Valley, whilst from the west end of the summit pound – 645ft above sea level – it follows the Tame Valley, dropping 334ft in 8½ miles to Ashton-under-Lyne. Damage extended along 16 miles of canal after flooding during the winter of 1799 and Robert Whitworth, called in to report during Outram's absence through illness, observed that the masonry and earthworks along the navigation 'were the worst executed of any he had seen'.

Benjamin Outram resigned in 1801 and he was not replaced, although subsequently, five years later, Thomas Telford was asked to survey the work to date and advise on its completion. Two further Acts were passed to raise more capital before the navigation was officially opened on 4 April 1811 at a final cost of over £300,000. However, this was only after another disastrous flood occurred after Swellands Reservoir (recommended by Telford as an addition to Outram's design) burst its banks and inundated large areas of the Colne Valley. Six people were drowned and many factories and mills severely damaged.

High tolls, in conjunction with an additional charge levied on boats using the tunnel, suppressed use of the waterway and although individual communities along the route expanded and thrived, within the climate of industrial prosperity brought by the canal, profits were disappointing. With the reduction of dues in the 1830s, trade was greatly stimulated, only to fall in the face of the inevitable railway competition which came with the completion of the Leeds and Manchester Railway in 1841. Three years later the Huddersfield and Manchester Railway Company was formed with the aim of building a line closely following the route of the navigation, which it acquired in 1845. The existing canal tunnel at Standedge was linked at intervals by cross-adits to the infant railway tunnel during construction, thereby greatly reducing time and expense. Subsequent railway tunnels, built as traffic increased, also benefited immensely from the existence of the canal tunnel.

Much trade was surrendered to the railways over the years and by the time of its official abandonment in 1944, regular cargoes were limited to coal and iron ore. The last end-to-end voyage was made by Robert Aickman and fellow IWA members (*see* page 270) in *Ailsa Craig* during 1948.

Huddersfield Narrow Canal at Uppermill

THE NAVIGATION

The canal follows the River Tame east out of Portland Basin, crossing it just over 1 mile later to arrive at the first newly constructed lock in Stalybridge. In 1947 the section from here through the town was culverted and the enthusiasm for the recently exhumed navigation, ascending a series of locks amidst busy streets, is universal. Replacing a forgotten drain, there is now a vibrant waterway, a bustle of activity made colourful with boats: a scene reminiscent of a Dutch town, the canal its central focus, roads subservient. The Pennines beckon over the rooftops of Stalybridge, as the waterway continues on its steady climb towards Scout Tunnel, ducking directly between the legs of an unfortunately sited electricity pylon,

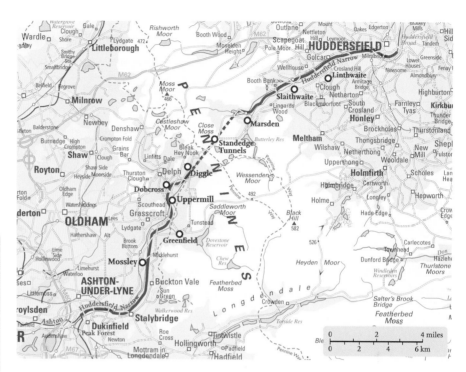

Chief engineer	Benjamin Outram
Assisted by	Robert Whitworth, John Rooth, Nicholas Brown.
Significance	Renown as having the highest, deepest and longest canal tunnel in the country.
Started in	1794
Completed in	1811
Length	19½ miles
Draught	3' 3"
Headroom	6' 2"
Lock size	70' × 6' 10"
Number of locks	74
Tunnels	3
Aqueducts	2
Goods carried	Coal, stone, timber, textiles together with a wide range of raw materials and manufactured goods.
Operating authority	Canal & River Trust
Contact details	enquiries. manchesterpennine @canalrivertrust.org.uk

more recently placed in its path. The climb is unremitting, though largely through leafy glades with just the occasional glimpses of open hill views, punctuated with the dereliction of past industry – largely coal mining. Throughout its ascent, the waterway remains discrete, almost shunning the outside world, winding through woods and passing several attractively sited, waterside picnic areas. Whilst road crossings do briefly intrude, it is the trans-Pennine railway that keeps constant company with the navigation: a not altogether unwelcome diversion bringing a source of well-ordered activity and flashes of colour on a dull day.

The Pennines rear up ahead, although their full impact is softened by the fringe of woodland accompanying the navigation up the valley. To the west the imposingly situated building of Quickwood church, with its needle-like spire, oversees the bustle of road, rail and waterway activity below. Impressive mills, now sadly decaying, line the canal as it winds its tortuous path towards Uppermill, where it is greeted by what appears to be a castle keep, complete with portcullis. Closer inspection reveals a somewhat elaborate stone facing, topped with iron railings and employed to disguise a concrete box culvert, with further embellishment to hide a vertical gas main!

THE NAVIGATION

By now the scale of the textile industry is subdued by the imposing bulk of Saddleworth Moor, while the sprawling conurbation of Manchester gives way to a straggle of attractive villages, constructed in the local gritstone and strewn randomly over the surrounding hillsides. Looking back towards the smoking chimneys, there are wide open views appearing over the high ground that had seemed to pose such a formidable obstacle when viewed from Stalybridge. Beyond the striking Wool Road Transhipment Warehouse the waterway, still climbing, breaks out alongside the railway and together they both pick their way across heathered moorland towards their interlaced passages, the Standedge Tunnels, deep beneath the Pennines.

A CANAL BREWERY

Take an old ice cream cooler, a scrapyard copper, a home-made cask washer and two locally constructed mash tuns; place them in a canalside mill (once a sweet factory) and what have you got? A family-run brewery – whose proprietor (for many years a joiner) is not short of ingenuity. Always fermenting new ideas for the future, his imagination stretches into the often mind-bending task of naming new brews, tapping into local history with names like 'Luddite' and 'Coiners'. When the ailing sweet factory finally called time on its production it was sold, complete with its old manufacturing equipment. Ideas were already brewing as to how it might be pressed into use for ale production. The family are all adept at meeting new challenges, right down to Sooty the brewery cat. Keeping the mouse population in check is a doddle for a four-legged feline; not so easy if you've had the misfortune to lose a leg in a brush with a car.

Clogger Knoll Bridge

It comes as almost something of a relief to leave the activity centred around the tunnel mouth and start the long steady descent into Huddersfield. Lock operation is no less arduous going downhill. In places the hills lining the Colne Valley step back a little, leaving level grazing and fields for hay and silage making. The infant river is never far away and in places is separated only by a narrow band of trees. From time to time the landscape is punctuated by the gaunt remains of a splendid old mill as views open out briefly before the often tree-lined hills close in once again. The railway shadows the canal into Slaithwaite where once again the harmony wrought by its focal position amidst shops and streets is most satisfactory. It is a matter of intense speculation as to why it has taken so long to replace a secret subterranean trickle with this overtly delightful scene.

East of the settlement the waterway settles into a broader valley bottom and the hills become a little more submissive. Attractive tree-lined glades alternate with views of a still bold landscape and everywhere there are the gaunt remains of mills: reminders of this area's supremacy as a textile producer and the canal's real purpose. The descent into Huddersfield is steady and not without contrast – pretty stone bridges vie with an imposing railway viaduct and many of the locks (although still in need of more use) appear in attractive settings.

POINTS OF INTEREST

Mossley A small agricultural hamlet of 1,200 souls in 1821, Mossley had grown into a prosperous cotton town by 1885 with a population of 15,000.

Mossley Industrial Heritage Centre Memories abound and are brought to life in an old cotton spinning mill now owned by Emmaus, a charitable organisation which provides work and a home for people who would otherwise be homeless. The centre now seeks to answer questions about past times in a boom era of cotton and woollen manufacture.

Greenfield Another cotton community attempting to adjust to the demise of a past prosperity.

Uppermill Traditional Pennine village and once the centre of the local cotton and cottage weaving industry, it has become a focus for the tourist trade that has long supplanted all such activity.

Dobcross A delightful village, quintessentially Pennine, every building and winding narrow street a gem, the whole presided over by the charming Saddleworth Bank.

Diggle With its neighbours Dobcross and Delph, Diggle lay at the heart of local hand-weaving until, in the late 18th century, the Industrial Revolution spawned mills as the centres of production, sited further down the valley for easier access.

Marsden Situated at an important trans-Pennine crossing point, Marsden has always been a focus for the weaving industry and is associated with the Luddite riots. Enoch Taylor, pivotal figure in this industrial unrest, is buried beside the fine church and there is a set of stocks nearby. Its popularity as a location for TV soaps now makes a different set of dramatic demands upon its environs.

Marsden Mechanics Institute A striking stone building with a colourful wooden tower (the foundations of the main structure were considered inadequate to bear the weight of anything heavier) erected in 1861 to provide education for the betterment of the working man. Now the library and community hall. Also home to the evergreen Mikron Theatre Company (when not touring the waterways on their boat *Tysley*).

Marsden Moor Estate Over 5,000 acres of moorland in the care of the National Trust and accessible through a series of walks and trails. The exhibition in the Old Goods Yard, beside the towpath at Marsden Railway Station, uses a series of excellent displays to provide a wealth of information about

Wool Road Lock

every aspect of the area, from natural phenomena through to the relatively recent industrial impact of weaving, water, canal and railway.

Slaithwaite Another settlement founded on the woollen and cotton industries with a fine Georgian church and the 16th-century Slaithwaite Hall. The juxtaposition of canal with the village streets is most pleasing.

Linthwaite Although strung out and somewhat detached from the waterway, this village is not without charm and is home to several very striking (and very derelict) mills which tell of its former glory as a textile producer. Happily several of these structures are now undergoing renovation to fit them for their new role as apartments.

Marsden

The Kennet & Avon Canal is one of the most splendid lengths of artificial waterway in Britain, a fitting memorial to the canal age as a whole. It is a broad canal, cutting across southern England from Reading to Bristol. Its generous dimensions and handsome architecture blend well with the rolling downs and open plains that it passes through, and are a solid reminder of the instinctive feeling for scale that characterised most 18th- and early 19th-century civil engineering.

The canal was built in three sections. The first two were river navigations, the Kennet from Reading to Newbury, and the Avon from Bath to Bristol, both being canalised. Among early 18th-century river navigations the Kennet was one of the most ambitious, owing to the steep fall of the river. Between Reading and Newbury 20 locks were necessary in almost as many miles, as the difference in level is 138ft. John Hore was the engineer for the Kennet Navigation, which was built between 1718 and 1723 and included 11 miles of new cut. Subsequently Hore was in charge of

the Bristol Avon Navigation, which he undertook between 1725 and 1727. These river navigations were interesting in many ways, often because of the varied nature of the country they passed through. For instance the steep-sided Avon Gorge meant that a fast-flowing river had to be brought under control. Elsewhere the engineering was unusual: for example the turf-sided locks on the Kennet, now partially replaced with brick structures.

For the third stage, a canal from Newbury to Bath was authorised in 1794. John Rennie was appointed engineer, and after a long struggle the canal was opened in 1810, completing a through route from London to Bristol. This section of the canal is 57 miles long, and included 79 broad locks, a summit level at Savernake 452ft above sea level and one short tunnel, also at Savernake. Rennie was both engineer and architect, anticipating the role played by Brunel in the creation of the Great Western Railway; in some ways his architecture is the more noteworthy aspect of his work.

The architectural quality of the whole canal is exceptional, from the straightforward stone bridges to the magnificent neo-classical aqueducts at Avoncliffe and Limpley Stoke. Rennie's solution to the anticipated water supply problems on the top pound was to build a 4,312yd tunnel, thereby providing a reservoir 15 miles long. The company called in William Jessop to offer a second – and hopefully cheaper solution – and it was he who suggested a shorter tunnel in conjunction with a steam pumping engine. This resulted in a saving of £41,000 and a completion date two years earlier. In some places the canal bed was built over porous rock and so leaked constantly, necessitating further regular pumping. The solution to this problem, which has been adopted today, is to line long sections with a concrete trough, discretely disguised with vegetation wherever possible.

Nevertheless, the canal as a whole was a striking achievement. West of Devizes the waterway descends Caen Hill in a straight flight of 16 locks,

canal in the 1930s, but still it remained open, and the final through passage was made in 1951 by narrowboat *Queen*, with the West Country artist P. Ballance on board.

Subsequently the waterway was closed, and for a long time its future was in jeopardy. However, great interest in the canal had resulted in the formation of a Canal Association shortly after the Second World War, to fight for restoration. In 1962 the Kennet & Avon Canal Trust was formed out of the association, and practical steps towards restoration were under way. Using volunteers to raise funds from all sources, and with steadily increasing inputs from the then British Waterways, the Trust has catalysed the reopening of the entire navigation as a through route from Reading to Bristol. This achievement was commemorated on 8 August 1990, with HM Queen Elizabeth navigating through Lock 43, at the summit of the Caen Hill flight, which now bears her name.

Caen Hill Lock flight...

...approaching Devizes

each with enormous side-pounds. These were designed to hold sufficient water while permitting the locks to be close together in order to follow the slope. In total 29 locks are navigated within 2 miles of Devizes. The many swing bridges were designed to run on ball bearings, one of the first applications of the principle. The bold entry of the canal into Bath, a sweeping descent round the south of the city, is a firm expression of the belief that major engineering works should contribute to the landscape, whether urban or rural, instead of imposing themselves upon it as so often happens nowadays.

Later the Kennet & Avon Canal Company took over the two river navigations, thus gaining control of the whole through route. However traffic was never as heavy as the promoters had expected, and so the canal declined steadily throughout the 19th century. It suffered from early railway competition as the Great Western Railway duplicated its route, and was eventually bought by that railway company. Maintenance standards slipped and this, combined with a rapidly declining traffic, meant that navigation was difficult in places by the end of the First World War. The last regular traffic left the

LEEDS & LIVERPOOL CANAL

With a length of 127¾ miles excluding branches, the Leeds & Liverpool Canal is the longest single canal in Britain built by one company. The canal has its beginnings in the River Douglas, a little river made navigable by 1740 from Wigan to Parbold, Tarleton and the Ribble estuary. Several ambitious trans-Pennine canal schemes had been mooted; one for a canal from Liverpool to Leeds, to connect with the head of the Aire & Calder Navigation which eventually became the 128-mile waterway which we know today.

'The Orwell' with the reconstructed Wigan Pier visible in the background

BACKGROUND

The Leeds & Liverpool Canal was authorised in 1770, and construction began at once, with John Longbotham as engineer. The first (lock-free) section from Bingley to Skipton was opened within three years; by 1777 two long sections were open from the Aire & Calder at Leeds to Gargrave (incorporating many new staircase locks, including the famous Bingley Five-Rise – *see* page 57) and from Wigan to Liverpool.

The Leeds & Liverpool bought out the River Douglas Navigation at an early stage to gain control of its valuable water supply. It was replaced by a proper canal branch to Rufford and Tarleton, where it joined the (tidal) River Douglas. In 1790 work began again, with Robert Whitworth as the company's engineer; but after 1792 and the outbreak of war with France, investment in canals declined steadily. The whole of the main line from Leeds to Liverpool was finally finished by 1816 actually sharing the channel of the Lancaster Canal for 10 miles from Wigan Top Lock to Johnson's Hill Bottom Lock. The Lancaster used to branch off up what became the Walton Summit Branch, now severed by the M61 motorway.

In 1820 a branch was opened to join the Bridgewater Canal (*see* page 138) at Leigh. A short branch (the Springs Branch) was also made to rock

... the Liverpool Canal Link

quarries at Skipton and an important 3-mile-long canal from Shipley to Bradford (now closed). The cut down into the Liverpool Docks was made in 1846. The prosperity of the company after 1820 was not, at first, greatly affected by the advent of railways. The scale of the navigation (the locks were built as broad locks 62ft by 14ft, allowing big payloads to be carried along the canal) contributed to the high dividends paid to shareholders for several years. Water supply was, however, a problem and in spite of the building of copious reservoirs, the canal had to be closed for months on end during dry summers, driving carriers' custom away to the railways. Use of the navigation for freight declined throughout the last century; the hard winter of 1962–3 finished off many traders.

Fresh life has recently been breathed into the navigation with the construction of the Liverpool Canal Link, extending its western terminus into Salthouse Dock, via a series of new cuts and redundant docks. The new waterway now runs between Pier Head and the Royal Liver Building, controversially traversing a World Heritage site. Today this canal offers boaters, walkers and cyclists an exhilarating link between two superb cities.

Princes Dock, forming part of ...

THE NAVIGATION

The Liverpool Canal Link was completed in 2009 and runs from the bottom of the existing Stanley Locks, Stanley Dock to Canning Dock, via the old West Waterloo Dock; Princes Dock and an underground section near Pier Head, in front of the Royal Liver Building. Canning Dock in turn provides a link into the revitalised Albert Dock which will, for the first time in its history, play host to a regular influx of inland waterway craft.

Heading towards Leeds, the navigation runs north from the city centre for about 6 miles, parallel and close to Liverpool Docks, before turning east to Aintree, Wigan and the Pennines. The water is surprisingly clear.

North of Litherland the canal turns east to Aintree, which marks the limit of Liverpool's outskirts and is of course the home of the Grand National. Soon the first of many swing bridges is encountered as the waterway turns north again and emerges into open countryside, although Maghull soon interrupts this with a further flurry of bridges.

Town class short boat Bradford *passing war transport vehicles on the Leeds & Liverpool Canal*

Chief engineer	James Brindley superceded by John Longbotham.
Assisted by	Robert Whitworth
Significance	Longest continuous canal built by a single company.
Started in	1770
Completed in	1811
Length	127³/₄ miles – in addition the Rufford and Leigh branches are both 7¹/₄ miles
Headroom	8'
Lock size	Liverpool–Wigan 72' × 14' 6" Wigan–Leeds 60' × 14' 3"
Number of locks	91
Tunnels	2
Aqueducts	14
Goods carried	Coal, limestone, timber, stone, textiles together with a wide range of raw materials and manufactured goods.
Operating authority	Canal & River Trust
Contact details	enquiries.northwest @canalrivertrust.org.uk

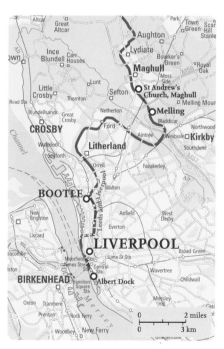

THE NAVIGATION

Butty Eileen

Dry Dock in Wigan

The canal now enters continuous open countryside, which soon establishes itself as extremely flat and intensively cultivated lowlands: indeed it is more akin to Cambridgeshire or Lincolnshire than to the rest of Lancashire. However, it is pleasant enough and the canal forms one of its more important features – a view which is borne out by the large number of people usually to be seen walking and boating upon it, as well as the hundreds of anglers enjoying their sport in this well-stocked length of canal. As if in compensation for the unexciting landscape, the traveller is offered a truly astonishing number (and variety) of pubs on or near the canal, all the way from Lydiate to Wigan. The digging of the canal is reputed to have commenced in the low cutting between bridges 24 and 25, and this clearly provided an excellent source of stone for local bridges.

POINTS OF INTEREST

Liverpool In the first century AD it was *lifrugpool*, a settlement next to a muddy creek; now it is one of Britain's largest ports. Famous worldwide as the place where the Beatles began their march to fame, and equally well-known for the exploits of Liverpool Football Club. There is much to be seen in this ancient port. The Anglican Cathedral, begun in 1904 and finished in 1978, is the largest in the world; the Roman Catholic Cathedral has stained glass by John Piper and Patrick Reyntiens. On the pierhead is a memorial to the engineers lost on the *Titanic*, which sank in 1912. The superb Albert Dock development and Liverpool Tate and the Walker Art Galleries, together with a wide range of theatres and museums, are attracting an ever increasing number of tourists. As a city it has more Georgian buildings than Bath, a UNESCO World Heritage waterfront, and has convincingly re-established itself upon a reputation as a cultural and leisure centre which was recognised with the award of European City of Culture 2008.

Albert Dock, Liverpool The largest grouping of Grade I listed buildings in England – opened in 1846 as warehousing for a range of precious cargo from around the world, these buildings have been transformed into an award-winning tourist destination including shops, cafés, restaurants, galleries and museums.

Liverpool Cathedral The largest Anglican cathedral in Britain, resplendent in red sandstone, built to the design of Sir Giles Gilbert Scott and begun in 1904. The 331-ft tower extends the full width of the building and is home to the heaviest ringing peal of bells in the world – all 30 tons of them. Inside there are soaring gothic arches, a massive organ and together with worship there are regular recitals and concerts.

Metropolitan Cathedral, Liverpool Standing on the site once occupied by the Poor Law Institute, today's striking building, with its interior lantern tower of multi-coloured glass, has had a somewhat chequered career. Of the original design by Sir Edwin Lutyens, dating from 1933, only the Crypt was built and after the war inflation had raised the estimated cost of completion to £27 million. Sir Frederick Gibberd produced a design that met the new brief, namely, that the cathedral should be completed within five years, incorporate the original crypt and cost no more than £1 million. Building recommenced in 1962 and the finished cathedral – known locally as 'Paddy's wigwam' – was consecrated in May 1967.

Museum of Liverpool An opportunity to explore the richness of the city's cultural diversity in a striking new building rearing up over the Liverpool Link on its approach to Mann Island.

Prince's Road Synagogue, Liverpool Arguably Europe's finest example of Saracenic or Moorish revival style of synagogue in a Grade II listed building.

Royal Liverpool Philharmonic, Liverpool Art Deco building opened in 1939 to replace the original which was destroyed by fire and now home to the Royal Liverpool Philharmonic Orchestra. The hall hosts around 60 orchestral concerts a year together with drama, film and other arts.

St George's Hall, Liverpool A stunning reflection of the city's prosperity in the 19th century, built in the neo-classical style to house the law courts and as a music venue. One of the first buildings to greet the visitor arriving at Liverpool Lime Street Station, it has recently undergone a £23-million refurbishment.

Sefton Park Palm House, Liverpool An octagonal, three-tiered, Grade II listed Victorian glasshouse housing Liverpool's botanical collection. Inside and outside the palm house are beds of formal bedding and statues.

Speke Hall, Liverpool Black and white, half-timbered house dating back to 1490 complete with priest hole, fine Jacobean plasterwork, a Great Hall, Victorian kitchen and servants' hall.

Tate Liverpool One of the largest galleries of contemporary and modern art outside London, housed in part of the splendidly converted Grade I listed warehouses surrounding Albert Dock.

Williamson Tunnels Heritage Centre, Liverpool A unique labyrinth of tunnels under Edge Hill created by 19th-century philanthropist Joseph Williamson – 'the Mole of Edge Hill'. The visitor centre offers an insight into the life and underground world of one of Liverpool's most eccentric characters.

Floating exhibit in Albert Dock, Liverpool

THE NAVIGATION

On now past a massive caravan site on one side and attractive woods containing the Victorian Gothic Scarisbrick Hall on the other, then out again into the open flatlands. The Southport–Manchester line converges from the northwest; it runs near the canal all the way into Wigan, and has some wonderfully remote stations. A further flurry of swing bridges brings the canal into Burscough. Just beyond is the junction with the Rufford Branch.

The Rufford Branch leaves the Leeds & Liverpool main line just east of Burscough, through an imposing arched bridge dated 1816. A canal settlement, now a conservation area, surrounds the top lock and the roomy dry dock here. The locks come thick and fast to begin with, as the canal falls through the fertile and gently sloping farmland towards the distant Ribble estuary and a connection

with the Lancaster Canal (*see page 133*). The country is generally quiet, flat and unspectacular. At times the busy A59 intrudes noisily. A line of trees and the spire of Rufford church are followed by the beautiful Rufford Old Hall, on the west bank. Then the waterway leads back out into open, flat and fairly featureless countryside, with the River Douglas never far away but initially out of sight. At Sollom there used to be a lock, but now it is no more. This is where the canal turns into the old course of the River Douglas, and it twists and turns as though to prove it. The 'new' course of the Douglas (which was once navigable from the sea right up to Wigan) comes alongside the canal at the busy road bridge near Bank Hall, a house hidden by trees. From here it is only a short distance to the final swing bridge and Tarleton Lock, where the canal connects with the tidal River Douglas – which

The River Douglas – once the arterial highway linking Wigan to the sea

in turn flows into the River Ribble near Preston forming the recently constructed Ribble Link with the Lancaster Canal.

East of the junction with the Rufford Branch, the canal meanders through the flat countryside to the village of Parbold with its ancient sail-less windmill. Here the canal crosses the River Douglas and then joins the Douglas Valley, a pretty, narrow wooded valley which the canal shares with the railway. Appley Lock is reached: there are two locks alongside, now semi-derelict and therefore only the lock on the main line is in operation. The shallower locks were once used as a navigable side pond for boats passing in opposite directions.

POINTS OF INTEREST

Bootle Now a busy suburb of Liverpool, this settlement was described in early Victorian times as 'containing, with the township of Linacre, 808 inhabitants. The village comprises several good houses and is very much resorted to during summer for the benefit of sea-bathing.'

Melling The village stands on an isolated hillock at a safe distance from the big city. The church is a landmark in the area; it was built in the 15th century with rock from an adjacent quarry.

St Andrew's Church, Maghull Although built in the late 19th century, its style is in imitation of that of the 13th century to accord with the tiny 700-year-old chapel, known as Old St Andrew's, which sits in its grounds.

Haskayne There are just two pretty houses here: the old post office and a thatched cottage opposite. The remainder of the village sprawls away from the navigation but there is no sign of a church.

Halsall There is a handsome tall 14th–15th-century church here (St Cuthbert's), with a fine spire. The choir vestry, erected in 1592, was formerly a grammar school. There is an interesting pair of pulpits/lecterns. One of them is generously illuminated by a solitary overhead window; the other, more sheltered, gives the occupant the unfortunate air of being behind bars.

Burscough Formerly a canal village and a staging post on the one-time Wigan–Liverpool packet boat run, this place attaches more significance nowadays to the benefits of road and rail transport. It still boasts two stations (one is on the Preston–Liverpool line) and suffers from heavy through traffic.

Tarleton Main road village noted for its hall. The church is a small Italianate Victorian building

containing many monuments to the Heskeths who owned Rufford Hall for several centuries; obviously a prolific family, judging by one large sculpture depicting a brood of 11 children, dated *c.*1458. The family now resides in Northamptonshire.

Rufford Old Hall A medieval timber-framed mansion with Jacobean extensions given to the National Trust in 1936. The interior is magnificently decorated and furnished in period style, especially the great hall with its hammerbeam roof and 15th-century intricately carved movable

Canalside bench

screen – one of the few still intact in England. The hall also houses a folk museum and an exhibition.

Parbold Parbold is prettiest near the canal bridge, where the brick tower of the old windmill is complemented by an equally attractive pub. Unfortunately the rest of the village is being engulfed by acres of new housing. Local landmarks are the tall spires of Parbold's two churches, and Ashurst's Beacon high on a hill to the south. The latter was built in 1798 by Sir William Ashurst in anticipation of an invasion by the French. The beacon was intended as a local warning sign.

Douglas Navigation The little River Douglas, or Asland, was made navigable in the first half of the 17th century, well before the great spate of canal construction. It provided the Wigan coalfield with a useful outlet to the tidal River Ribble, from which the cargoes could be shipped over to Preston or along the coast. When the Leeds & Liverpool Canal was built, the old river navigation became superfluous. The new company constructed their own branch to the Ribble estuary (the Rufford Branch). Between Parbold and Gathurst it is possible to find many traces of the old navigation, including several locks.

MARTIN MERE

This was once an area of low lying marshland, much of it below sea level and, consequently, thinly populated. The original course of the River Douglas ran close by, joining the sea near Southport. At some point its course was blocked – possibly by giant sand dunes thrown up by a great storm – and it found a new, northern mouth in the Ribble estuary, leaving behind the area known today as Martin Mere. This once extended to 15 square miles but in 1787 Thomas Eccleston of Scarisbrick Hall, with the help of John Gilbert, set about draining it for agricultural use (it was Gilbert who, as agent to the Duke of Bridgewater, enlisted James Brindley's help in constructing Britain's first major canal). Once drained the mere required vast quantities of manure to raise its fertility for crop production. 'Night soil' was shipped in along the canal from the large conurbations of Liverpool and Wigan and off-loaded at a series of small wharfs, some still visible today. Part of the mere remains undrained, a haven for migrating geese.

THE NAVIGATION

The canal now goes through Appley Bridge and runs up the rural Douglas Valley. Passing three consecutive swing bridges, one soon reaches Dean Locks. East of the locks the valley widens out. Ell Meadow and Pagefield locks lead the canal up towards the centre of Wigan. The Leigh Branch leaves the main line of the Leeds & Liverpool Canal in Wigan, just to the east of the lock and descending through two locks enters the lock-free level, that extends all the way along the Bridgewater Canal (*see* page 138) to Preston Brook and Runcorn, over 40 miles away. The famous Wigan Pier, of music hall fame, is in fact a coal staithe, and has been rebuilt. Wigan is an attractive town running up and down a gentle incline. Many of the older buildings employ a deep red brick and the municipal buildings, particularly the town hall, speak of a past industrial prosperity.

The Leigh Branch passes through a landscape once spoiled by mining but now painstakingly restored as parkland – a wildlife haven. For most of the way, the canal is on an embankment, well above the level of the surrounding landscape; this is a relatively new situation and is due to severe mining subsidence in the area. The canal has had to be built up – appropriately with pit waste – while the land on either side has sunk considerably. It continues eastwards past the Dover Lock Inn, once the site of two locks moved to Wigan as a result of the local subsidence, towards Plank Lane swing bridge (actually a lift bridge and site of

Contrasting modes of transport

another defunct lock) which is self-operated by passing boaters. Beyond the bridge, in Leigh, the canal suddenly becomes the Bridgewater Canal (without the customary stop lock), giving access to Manchester and the Trent & Mersey via Preston Brook (*see* page 26).

Leaving the junction with the Leigh Branch, the main line reaches the Wigan flight of 21 locks. At the top there is a T-junction as the canal meets what used to be the southern end of the Lancaster Canal. Turning left, the traveller is soon aware of the great height climbed as the navigation winds along a hill.

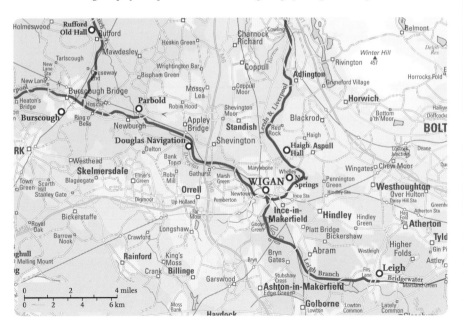

POINTS OF INTEREST

Wigan A large, heavily industrialised town whose skyline is now a mixture of industrial chimneys and towering concrete blocks of offices and flats. There is a covered market hall in the traditional mould, and an Olympic-size swimming pool.

All Saints Church, Wigan A very large and impressive parish church surrounded by beautiful rose gardens. There are several fine stained-glass windows, including a charming William Morris example depicting St Christopher.

Trencherfield Mill The mill, now being converted to offices and apartments, still retains the engine shed – home to probably the largest working steam-powered mill engine in Europe, installed when the mill was built in 1907. At the time of writing the mill is open on Sundays when, occasionally, the engine is steamed, heralded by a loud blast on the steam whistle. The engine is in a beautifully restored condition; its operators are knowledgeable and there is an audio-visual presentation linked to some clever lighting that shows off the engine to its best. There is also a range of working cotton spinning machinery which is used to demonstrate the processes that were once carried out at this mill. This is a marvellous opportunity to get to grips with what made this area such a hub of the industrial revolution: a revolution whose success was, to a large extent, dependent upon the presence of the Leeds & Liverpool Canal.

Leigh Once the archetypal mill town, most of the tall buildings and chimneys have now been demolished. In the market place you can see the fine Edwardian baroque town hall, built 1904–7, facing the battlemented church of St Mary. This church was originally built in 1516 but was extensively rebuilt in the late 19th century and is the burial place of Thomas Tyldesley, killed at the battle of Wigan Lane.

New Springs Once an industrial hub with collieries and ironworks lining the canal as it struggled up the 21 locks to the summit. The acres of partially landscaped waste ground today belie the past activity of Rose Bridge Colliery and Ince Hall Coal and Cannel Company higher up. Hardest of all to imagine is the massive operation of Wigan Coal and Iron Co. who, at the turn of the century, employed 10,000 people at their works beside the top nine locks of the flight. Then one of the largest ironworks in the country, it mined 2 million tons of coal to produce 125,000 tons of iron annually. The skyline here was dominated by ten blast furnaces, 675 coking ovens and a 339ft high chimney. It must have been an impressive sight on the night skyline, viewed from the streets of Wigan.

Haigh Hall, Wigan The pre-Tudor mansion was rebuilt by its owner, the 23rd Earl of Crawford, between 1830 and 1849. The reconstruction was designed and directed by the Earl, and all the stone, timber and iron used on the job came from the estate. The hall is now owned by Wigan Corporation, who allow the citizens to use it for private wedding receptions and the like.

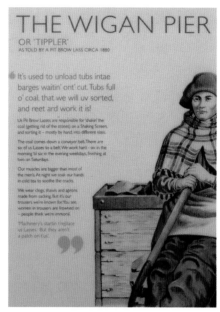

The butt of music hall jokes

FROM PRESTON TO KENDAL, BY WATERBUS

In an age when there is great personal freedom of movement, it is not always easy to imagine that canals, in their time, provided much the same opportunities as buses and trains today. As well as regular water bus services, special excursions were organised. Indeed as early as 1776 boats carried pleasure seekers from Beeston to the Chester Races, on what is now the Shropshire Union Canal.

Such services were scheduled on the Lancaster Canal until 1849. Initially a regular daily service operated between Kendal and Preston, the journey taking 14 hours, with refreshments being provided. In 1833, in order to compete with the stage coaches, an express service was introduced, cutting the journey time to 7 hours 15 minutes, and carrying an incredible 14,000 passengers in the first six months.

'For safety, economy and comfort no other mode of transport could be so eligible.'

THE NAVIGATION

The canal continues to run as a 9-mile lock-free pound – known as the Lancaster Pool – along the side of the valley from which the industries surrounding Wigan can be viewed in the distance. It enjoys a pleasant and quiet isolation in this lightly wooded area. Already the navigation is well over 300ft above the sea, and the bleak hills up to the east give a hint of the Pennines that are soon to be crossed. The conspicuous tower east of Adlington stands on a hill that is over 1,500ft high. Wandering northwards, beyond the village, the waterway remains hemmed in for much of the way by woodland and is undisturbed by the railway and main roads that for a while follow it closely. Soon the greenery gives way to views of Chorley's rows of rooftops across the valley. The canal crosses this valley, but shuns the town.

The canal sidesteps Chorley to the east, passing instead some large and resplendent outlying textile mills as the boater enters a most delightful stretch

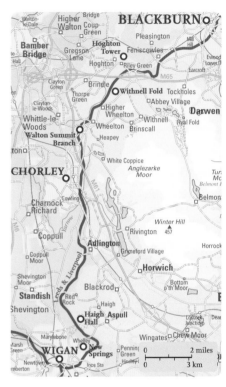

of waterway. The junction with the old Walton Summit Branch features a canal cottage and the bottom lock in the Johnson's Hill flight. A short but energetic spell of windlass-wielding is required here, for the seven locks are very close together. It is rewarding work, for the steep countryside yields good views, and the locks are tidily maintained and painted. Near the middle lock there is an old toll house.

The canal now changes course to northeast and flows along a beautifully secluded and often wooded valley at a height of over 350ft above sea level. Even the old paper mills at Withnell Fold, which once brought a glimpse of industry, have been converted into small, discreet, industrial units. There is an excellent nature reserve developed in the old filter beds and sludge lagoons opposite which, derelict for many years, gradually infilled with silt and reedswamp to provide natural plant and animal habitats.

Launching the mud hopper barge Bingley at Apperley Bridge, December 1955

Passing under the new M65 extension the canal curls round a steep and thickly wooded valley, crossing it on a high embankment before entering the outskirts of Blackburn. It seems to take a long time to get through this large town, as there is a flight of six locks here, raising the canal's level to a height of over 400ft above sea level. The lock keeper maintains a tidy flight – indeed most of the passage through the town is now pleasant – there is little rubbish or graffiti, and the views are excellent.

POINTS OF INTEREST

Salterforth A small village of narrow streets and terraced houses in an upland setting: a decidedly northern settlement.

Barnoldswick Set back from the canal, the mainstay of this town's existence is the Rolls Royce factory, where experimental work is done on aero engines. The centre of the town is compact and dominated by the modern Holy Trinity Church completed in 1960.

Bancroft Mill Engine Trust, Barnoldswick A 600hp steam engine and its two boilers, once powering the looms of Bancroft Mill, saved for preservation and still providing regular steaming and weaving demonstrations.

Pennine Way The Pennine Way is a walking route covering 268 miles of Pennine highland from Edale in the south to Kirk Yetholm in the north. Because of the nature of the route much of the Way is rough, hard walking, but it gives a superb view from the mountains. At East Marton the Pennine Way shares the canal towpath for a short distance – you will notice that the stones here abound with fossils.

Gargrave A very attractive and much-visited village, holding an enviable position near the head of Airedale between the canal and the river, this place is the ideal centre from which to explore the surrounding countryside. The River Aire cuts Gargrave in two, and the bridge over it forms the centre of the village. There is a charming station, and some pretty stone cottages along the green. The church is mostly Victorian, except for the tower, which was built in 1521.

Yorkshire Dales National Park Some of England's finest walking country is contained in this area of fine views, deep valleys, open moorland and rugged hills. Designated as a National Park in 1954 the Dales, covering 680 square miles, are hardly scarred by habitation.

Skipton This is probably the most handsome town along the whole Leeds & Liverpool Canal. It is an excellent place for visiting from the canal, for one can moor snugly and safely about one minute's walk away from the centre. It still maintains its importance as a market town, which is referred to in its name: Saxon *Scip-tun* means sheep-town. The wide High Street is attractive, lined with mostly Georgian houses, and headed at the northern end by the splendid castle and the well-kept graveyard of the parish church. There is an interesting water mill beside the Springs Branch.

Church of the Holy, Skipton Standing opposite the castle, it is a long battlemented church, encircled by large lawns and flourishing gardens. It is in Perpendicular style dating from the 14th century, though it was greatly renovated after suffering serious damage during the Civil War. It has a fine oak roof and a beautifully carved Jacobean font cover.

Springs Branch A short (770yds) but very unusual branch that leaves the Leeds & Liverpool Canal, passes the centre of Skipton and soon finds itself in what is virtually a ravine, overlooked by the castle that towers 100ft above. The branch is navigable by small craft, and makes an interesting diversion by boat or foot. It was built by the Earl of Thanet, the owner of Skipton Castle, to carry limestone away from his nearby quarry. It was extended by 240yds in 1797 from the water mill bridge through the deep rock cutting, and 120ft-chutes were constructed at the new terminus to drop the rock into the boats from the horse tramway that was laid from the quarry to the castle. The quarry still flourishes, but the canal and tramway have not been used since 1946: trains and lorries have replaced them. Now a picturesque backwater the Springs Branch acted for many years as a feeder to the Leeds & Liverpool Canal, taking water from Eller Beck, which runs beside it.

Skipton Castle A magnificent Norman castle, with 17th-century additions, that dominates Skipton High Street. After a three-year siege during the Civil War, Cromwell's men allowed the restoration of the castle, but ensured that the building could never again be used as a stronghold. The six massive round towers have survived from the 14th century and other notable features are the 50ft-long banqueting hall, a dungeon and the Shell Room, the walls of which are decorated with sea shells.

THE SETTLE-CARLISLE RAILWAY

O.S. Nock, the well-known railway writer, described this line (accessible from Skipton station) as 'the only mountain railway in the world built for express trains'. Completed in 1876, at a cost of almost £3.5 million; 72 miles long – including 20 large viaducts, 14 tunnels and no sharp curves and, in common with so many canal projects, some 50 per cent over budget, it was very nearly closed in the 1980s. It was both one of the most awesome feats of Victorian railway engineering and one of the most fiercely contested closure battles. It is, therefore, fortunate that in the light of today's burgeoning rail freight, common sense finally prevailed, saving the line for a rapidly growing commercial traffic – and our wonder and enjoyment. A regular service connecting the isolated communities along the line (swelled by tourist traffic in the summer months) together with ever-increasing pressure on the West Coast Mainline, will undoubtedly ensure the future of this route.

THE NAVIGATION

There is a fine wooded stretch north of Kildwick before the waterway curves sharply round the outcrop on which crouches Farnhill Hall, a mellow stone building. The intriguing village of Kildwick has some well-restored canalside buildings now used as private residences. The main road and the railway cut the valley corner while the canal takes the longer route round to Silsden. Overlooking Airedale, the green hills are very steep and beautifully wooded in places. The distant rows of chimneys, factories and terraced houses across the valley comprise Keighley; most of its industrial and suburban tentacles are quickly passed by the canal, although the constant succession of little swing bridges regularly impedes a boat's progress. This type of swing bridge is prone to intermittent stiffness due to the elements.

The impressive Bingley Five-Rise staircase locks (*see page 57*) mark the end of the long, level pound from Gargrave, and from here to Leeds there are no more views of a sweeping, uncluttered river valley. Just a few hundred yards south of the five locks are the three-rise staircase locks, which bring one steeply down into Bingley. The canal was moved sideways, over a distance of 400yds, in 1994 to allow the construction of a new road. The waterway bisects this town, but one can see little of the place from the water. Leaving Bingley, trees lead to Dowley Gap and the two staircase locks. At the foot of the locks the towpath changes sides and the navigation crosses the River Aire via a massive stone aqueduct. Woods escort the canal along to the single Hirst Lock; from here one moves past the big mills at Saltaire and right through Shipley.

Weather vane on Wigan Dry Dock

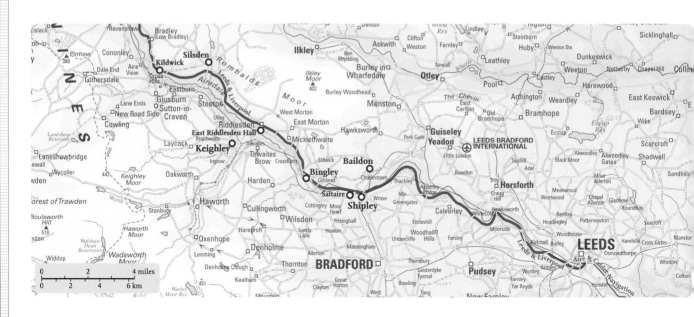

POINTS OF INTEREST

Kildwick An interesting and unusual village spilling down the hillside. The streets are extremely steep; one of them goes under the canal through a narrow skewed aqueduct.

Silsden A well-contained, stone-built industrial town spreading uphill from the canal and close to the Yorkshire Dales National Park. The canalside warehouses are attractive; there is also an old corn mill dated 1677.

Keighley Compared with some other industrial centres in the area, Keighley is a clean and pleasant town. It boasts a large new shopping centre, much modern housing and some handsome older stone terraces. The oldest part is around the parish church of St Andrew, a large Perpendicular building whose main attraction is its shady churchyard.

Keighley & Worth Valley Railway Privately preserved by volunteers of the Keighley & Worth Valley Railway Preservation Society, the line runs for 5 miles from the British Rail station at Keighley up to Haworth, the home of the Brontë family, and Oxenhope. British Railways closed the line in 1961, but the society eventually succeeded in reopening it in 1968 with a regular service of steam trains. In the mornings, the service is operated by diesel railbuses, but in the afternoons magnificent steam engines puff their way along the track. In the goods yard at Haworth the Society has a splendid collection of steam engines and carriages, mostly ancient. The line was made famous by the film *The Railway Children*.

Baildon A very old industrial town huddled on a hilltop on the edge of Baildon Moor. Stretching from Baildon to Bingley is the Glen, a wooded valley that curves below the heights of the moor. A splendid scenic tramway carrying two tramcars connects the coach road to the higher parts of

Baildon Moor – in summer a frequent service operates, but in winter it is arranged only to suit the needs of residents at the upper level.

Shipley A dark-stone town built on a generous scale and based on textile and engineering industries. There are powerful-looking mills to be seen, as well as the town hall and a suitably battlemented Salvation Army citadel. Shipley is lucky enough to be on the edge of Baildon Moor and Shipley Glen. The 3-mile-long Bradford Canal used to join the Leeds & Liverpool in Shipley but this has all been filled in for years.

Saltaire An estate village that owes its existence to the Utopian dream of Sir Titus Salt, a wealthy Victorian mill owner. He was so appalled by the working and living conditions of his workers in Bradford that he decided to build the ideal industrial settlement. This he did in 1850 on the banks of the canal and the River Aire – hence the name Saltaire. He provided every amenity including high standard housing, but no pub – for he was a great opponent of strong drink. The village has

changed little since those days (save the recent addition of a pub!); everything is carefully laid out and the terraced houses are attractive in an orderly sort of way. There is an Italianate church near the canal, and a large park beside the river. Admirers of David Hockney's work will want to visit the art gallery.

Bingley An industrial town now known nationally as a centre for thermal underwear. Standing at the southeast end of the town, amidst several old cottages, is the large parish church of Holy Trinity, with its massive spire conspicuous from the canal.

East Riddlesden Hall, Keighley A 17th-century stone manor house complete with tithe barn. Fine collection of Yorkshire oak furniture, textiles, pewter, paintings and armour. The house is set in mature grounds with beech trees, ducks and a pond and the Starkie Wing provides a striking backdrop to a garden planted with lavender, flowers and a fragrant herb border. Also an orchard garden with wild flowers, bulbs, perennials and, of course, apple blossom.

CHARLESTOWN RAILWAY DISASTER

In 1912, on an adjacent Pennine canal crossing – the Rochdale Canal (*see page 293*) – there was a serious derailment on the Charlestown curve when the 14.25 Manchester to Leeds express left the track, having effectively shattered the alignment of the rails at this point. The accident, involving a 2-4-2 radial tank engine, occurred on the stretch of line just before the railway crosses the canal on Whiteley Arches. The inspector, Colonel Druit, found at the subsequent enquiry that while the 45mph line speed at this point was suitable for normal express running, it was too high for tank engines of this type. Indeed, he went on to question the suitability of tank engines *per se* – with their high centre of gravity and inherent instability – for sustained high-speed traction. The derailed locomotive, together with all its carriages, crashed into the embankment, coming to rest strewn across the grounds of the old Woodman Inn.

THE NAVIGATION

This section sees the end of the wide open moorlands that frame the scenery further upstream: from now on, industry and housing begin to feature more as one approaches the outskirts of Leeds. The navigation, however, is thankfully sequestered from these intrusions into the landscape. Leaving Shipley, the adjacent railway cuts through a 500ft-high hill in two mile-long tunnels. The canal goes all the way round this delightfully wooded hill, tenaciously following the Aire Valley. Halfway round the long curve are Field Locks. Beyond the main railway bridge is a Canal & River Trust maintenance yard at the head of Dobson Locks and housed in a former canal warehouse. Temporarily traversing a built-up area, the navigation emerges yet again onto a wooded hillside overlooking the still rural and charming valley that contains the River Aire.

This is a length of waterway full of contrasts; and it probably represents the most pleasant way of entering the city of Leeds. Although the area becomes more and more built up as one travels eastward, the canal remains unaffected by it, maintaining its privileged position on the wooded south side of the narrowing Aire Valley. Leaving the ruined Kirkstall Abbey on the other side of the river, the navigation passes the old Mackeson brewery, now imaginatively converted to student accommodation, and borders for a while the steeply sloping edges of an extensive park. The site of the old Kirkstall Power Station is reached, with its own private canal lay-by: until the mid 1960s scores of barges used to come up to fuel this establishment every week; now both dock and power station have disappeared.

Appley Deep Lock

At first sight there appears to be an almost indecently large number of tunnels connecting the delightful village of Diggle with its more rugged Pennine cousin, Marsden. The canal tunnel came first, completed in 1809. At 5,698 yards long, Standedge Tunnel is the longest, deepest, highest waterway tunnel in Britain, taking fully 15 years of laborious toil to complete. It was followed by the single bore of the Huddersfield and Manchester Railway dating from 1845. Two years later this railway company was taken over by the LNWR who built a second single – and parallel – track to cope with increasing demand.

In 1894 the present double-track tunnel was constructed to cope with the burgeoning railway traffic. In all instances the canal tunnel, then owned by the railway company and connected to its tunnels by cross-adits, proved invaluable for spoil removal during construction.

Superlatives tend to rain down upon the original canal tunnel in about as great a measure as

The Marsden portal showing the tunnel trip boat (and electric tug)

The Diggle portal of Standedge Tunnel

the Pennine precipitation is driven, often as horizontally as the bore itself, onto the hills above. Most of its length is hewn from solid rock and, in many places, the clearance between cabin roof and tunnel roof is minimal, so much so that boats traversing its watery depths are, today, effectively clothed in the waterway equivalent of bubble wrap.

On re-opening the tunnel, following restoration of the Huddersfield Narrow Canal (*see page 148*) the then British Waterways initially towed boats through, in a snaking convoy, hauled by a battery-powered tug. The trip boat that enters the Marsden portal still employs the same technique. However, girding up their courage in both hands, they have now settled on a strategy of allowing boats through under their own steam (so to speak) albeit under the close scrutiny of a Canal & River Trust pilot.

As mentioned, there are two redundant railway bores running alongside the canal tunnel and interconnected with it. As a boat wends its tortuous way from one end to another, so it is shadowed by a Canal & River Trust 4x4 running in tandem with its progress, so satisfying, we are told, all health and safety requirements.

Plaque commemorating Thomas Telford's input

PEAK FOREST AND ASHTON CANALS

The Peak Forest Canal runs from Whaley Bridge and Buxworth through Marple to the Ashton Canal at Dukinfield Junction. Authorised by Act of Parliament in 1794, it was aimed at providing an outlet for the great limestone deposits at Doveholes, southeast of Whaley Bridge. However, since Doveholes is over 1,000ft above sea level, the canal was terminated at Buxworth, and the line was continued up to the quarries by a 6$\frac{1}{2}$-mile tramway.

Authorised in 1792 and opened shortly afterwards, the Ashton was a strong rival of the Rochdale Canal – with which it connects in Manchester.

The start of the Peak Forest Canal, Ashton-under-Lyne

BACKGROUND

THE PEAK FOREST CANAL

The canal was completed by 1800 except for the flight of locks at Marple, which were not built until 1804. A second, temporary, tramway bridged this gap in the meantime. Bugsworth Basin (*see* page 99) soon became a busy interchange point where the wagons bringing the stone down from Doveholes tipped their load either into canal boats or into limekiln. This traffic, and the boats bringing coal up the canal for firing the kilns, accounted for the greatest proportion of the canal company's revenue.

The Peak Forest was also boosted by the opening of the Macclesfield Canal to Marple Top Lock in 1831, making it part of a new through route from Manchester to the Potteries, via the Trent & Mersey (*see* page 26). The Cromford & High Peak Railway was opened in 1831, joining up Whaley Bridge with the Cromford Canal (*see* page 93) on the far side of the Peak District.

By the early 1840s the Peak Forest Canal was suffering from competition from the Trent & Mersey Canal Company and two new railways. It was leased in perpetuity to the Sheffield, Ashton-under-Lyne & Manchester Railway, later the Great Central. In 1922 the Bugsworth traffic finished, while (through) traffic on the 'lower' Peak Forest Canal had disappeared by the Second World War. Along with the Ashton, full navigation was restored in 1974 and now the splendid Buxworth line is also open.

THE ASHTON CANAL

The interconnecting Ashton and Rochdale canals were constructed almost simultaneously, in part to tap the big coal-producing area around Oldham. The Ashton also opened a new trade route from Manchester to the textile mills of Ashton, while the Rochdale (*see* page 293) served as a broad canal link over the Pennines between the Mersey and the rivers of Yorkshire. In 1831 completion of the narrow Macclesfield Canal made the Ashton part of a through route from Manchester to the Potteries.

The 1830s saw the peak of the Ashton Canal's prosperity. The canal company sold out to the forerunner of the Great Central Railway Company in 1846, who continued to maintain and operate the canal. Traffic declined in the 20th century and by 1962 it was unnavigable. A determined effort by the Peak Forest Canal Society, the IWA (*see* page 270) local councils and the British Waterways Board (as was) resulted in its reopening in 1974.

Portland Basin, Ashton-under-Lyne

THE NAVIGATION

The former Whaley Bridge Branch, now the main line of the Peak Forest Canal, terminates in a small basin at the north end of the town. There is a building here of great interest to industrial archaeologists: it covers a dock and was built in 1832 at this, the junction of the Peak Forest Canal and the Cromford & High Peak Railway. Here transhipment between canal boat and railway wagon could take place under cover. The former railway's Whaley Bridge inclined plane (now a footpath) rises to the south of this historic building. South of the town the canal splits: the original main line turns east across the Goyt on an aqueduct to Buxworth (its name changed from the supposedly

Chief engineer	Benjamin Outram
Assisted by	Thomas Brown
Significance	Provided an outlet for the limestone quarried at Doveholes in the Peak District.
Started in	1794
Completed in	1805
Length	Peak Forest 14½ miles; Ashton 6½ miles.
Headroom	6'
Lock size	70' × 7'
Number of locks	Peak Forest 16; Ashton 18.
Tunnels	2
Aqueducts	5
Goods carried	Limestone, lime, coal, stone, timber, textiles, raw materials and manufactured goods, agricultural produce and manures.
Operating authority	Canal & River Trust
Contact details	enquiries. manchesterpennine @canalrivertrust.org.uk

less desirable Bugsworth) with its fascinating basin complex (*see page 99*) overlooked by a fine pub. The Peak Forest Canal leads off to the northwest; and it rapidly becomes apparent that this is a navigation set in a robust, handsome landscape. Clinging desperately to a wooded hillside overlooking the steep, wide Goyt Valley, it winds its precarious way to New Mills. The trains that traverse the opposite side of the valley look like tiny models on the distant hills. The A6 road and the railway are always close to the navigation, but they detract not at all from its isolation. There are charming stations at New Mills, Furness Vale and Whaley Bridge: from these one may take a magnificent railway trip past two canal-feeding reservoirs and over the hills to the summit, 1,200ft above sea level, then down to

the old Roman town of Buxton, now unfortunately the end of the line. The canal continues northwest along the hillside towards New Mills. It is an enchanting stretch, passing plenty of woods, pastures and grazing horses. As you approach New Mills you will notice the smell of sweets in the air – Matlows, the makers of Swizzels, have their factory here. Near Disley, another railway pops out of the long Disley Tunnel, way below the canal; while yet another line appears above and beside the canal, from High Lane. Thus around New Mills the valley contains three very picturesque railways. One of the pleasant features of this terrain is the easy co-existence of woods, fields and a canal on the one hand, and a certain amount of industry on the other.

THE NAVIGATION

The canal, accompanied by the River Goyt beyond the road to the east, reaches Marple Junction, where the Macclesfield Canal leaves to the southwest by the attractive buildings of Marple Yard. The 16 Marple Locks then carry the Peak Forest Canal down 214ft towards Manchester. The locks themselves, which are spaced out over 1 mile, have

THE VALUE OF RESTORATION

The Ashton Canal is now a part of the Cheshire Ring, a superb 100-mile cruising circuit which can be comfortably completed in a week. Those with extra energy, or a day or two more, can add in a diversion along the Peak Forest Canal, and their efforts will reap just reward. The ability to cruise these waterways is due to those who campaigned between 1959 and 1974 to clear and restore canals that had become both an eyesore and a danger. Extensive lobbying resulted in the formation of the Peak Forest Canal Society, and with the staging of the 1966 IWA National Rally at Marple, restoration gained momentum. Operation Ashton, held over a weekend in September 1968, saw 600 waterway enthusiasts clear more than 2,000 tons of rubbish from the canal (see page 277). Local people were amazed, and began to realise that what had long been regarded as an eyesore and a danger could now become a valuable local amenity. The corner had been turned. Following a rally on the Rochdale Canal at Easter 1971, local authorities and the British Waterways Board decided to proceed with full restoration of the Ashton and Peak Forest Canals. We owe a great debt to all those involved.

Transhipment warehouse at Whaley Bridge Basin – terminus of the Peak Forest Canal

an unrivalled setting in an excellent combination of built-up area, parkland, tall trees and steep hillside; the River Goyt is now hidden down in the wooded valley to the east. Look out for the interesting Possett Bridge, where there is a small tunnel for the towpath (and horse) and an even smaller one for the boatman, leading down to the lock. At the foot of the locks, where the River Goyt is crossed, there is the superb spectacle of a major canal aqueduct with an even bigger railway viaduct alongside. West of here a narrow stretch was once Rose Hill Tunnel, long since opened out. The canal then traverses

a wooded hillside before diving into Hyde Bank Tunnel, 308yds long. The towpath is diverted over the hill, passing a farm. On the other side, a couple of minor aqueducts lead the canal northwards, away from the Goyt Valley and past Romiley, Bredbury and Woodley, where there is a narrow 176yd-long tunnel, this time with the towpath continuing through it.

The canal continues northward through a landscape which becomes less rural, but increasingly interesting. Bridge 6 is a pretty

THE NAVIGATION

roving bridge, grown wider over the years. To the north, beyond the M62 motorway, the industrial tentacles of Hyde – Greater Manchester – ensnare the canal traveller, but the approach to Dukinfield Junction and Portland Basin is still very pleasant. The towpath is tidy, with plenty of grass, trees and seats. A lift bridge, a canal arm, an aqueduct over the River Tame and a stone roving bridge provide plenty of canal interest as you approach the junction, where the Ashton canal heads southwest into Manchester, and the Huddersfield Narrow Canal (*see* page 148) starts its journey east across the Pennines to Huddersfield. Portland Basin was constructed to allow boats to make the sharp turn here, and was nicknamed the 'weavers rest', since so many weavers had reputedly drowned themselves here during hard times, such as the famine of 1860 and the depression of the 1930s. The warehouse which faces you across the junction, built in 1834, has been well restored. The Ashton Canal takes you into Manchester proper: this remains a fine, solid industrial section of waterway, still with a few steaming factories, tall chimneys and a good clear towpath. If you pass Dukinfield Junction in mid-July, you may see the colourful Tameside Canals Festival, which has been running successfully for many years now.

From start to finish, the Ashton Canal passes through a densely built-up area in which the canal is conspicuous as a welcome relief from the townscape which flanks it. Its clear water, excellent towpath, functional but dignified old bridges and the peace that generally surrounds it make it a haven for local school children, anglers, walkers and idlers, indeed for anyone who enjoys an environment that is quite separate from and unrelated to ordinary daily life. The rare pleasure, afforded only by an English canal, of stepping out of a city suburb into the peaceful and unpretentious atmosphere of the 18th century is once again, with continued restoration work, becoming available to all.

POINTS OF INTEREST

Whaley Bridge Built on a steep hill at the end of the canal, with good views across the Goyt valley, this is now a quiet and pleasant place, a new bypass having removed much of the traffic. The beautiful nearby hills are, however, more noteworthy than the town.

Cromford & High Peak Railway In the early 1820s a physical connection was planned between the Peak Forest Canal at Whaley Bridge and the Cromford Canal (*see* page 93) way over to the southeast on the other side of the Peak District, using a junction canal. However a waterway would have been impracticable through such mountainous terrain, and so a railway was constructed. Known as the Cromford & High Peak Railway (C & HPR), it was opened throughout in 1831, and was 33 miles long. With a summit level over 1,200ft above sea level, this standard-gauge goods line was interesting chiefly for its numerous slopes and inclined planes, up which the wagons were hauled by either stationary or tenacious locomotive steam engines (the steepest gradient on the line was 1 in 7). The C & HPR closed in 1967; now much of the route has been turned into a public footpath and bridleway. Around Whaley Bridge one may still see the remains of the short inclined plane which brought the goods down the hill, then through the town to the wharf at the terminus of the Peak Forest Canal.

Buxworth The main feature in Buxworth (Bugsworth as it was once known) is the fascinating old terminal basin system. This used to be a tremendously busy complex, and is of great interest to industrial archaeologists (*see* page 99 for further details).

New Mills A mostly stone-built town on the Cheshire/Derbyshire border; its industries include textile printing, engineering and engraving. A boatyard occupies old canal buildings to the east of the bridge.

Portland Basin Social & Industrial History Museum

THE NAVIGATION

At Fairfield Junction the top lock of the eighteen which climb from Ducie Street Junction is encountered. It is a picturesque canal scene here with traditional buildings, including a shed dated 1833 standing over a canal arm, giving the area a quiet dignity. Descending the locks, you may wish to look out for the remains of several old canal arms: one of the more important was the 5-mile Stockport Branch, leaving from Clayton Junction, just below lock 11. The canal then falls through the remaining locks into Manchester. The surroundings are brightened by the well-cared-for Beswick flight of four locks, standing next to the new stadium, where you can see the wonderful 'B of the Bang' sculpture, an explosion of spikes designed by Thomas Heathwick, to mark the success of the Commonwealth Games held here in 2002. Large-scale redevelopment has been completed at Paradise Wharf and Piccadilly Village, making this final stretch unusually gentrified, with smart flats, basins and a crane. The Rochdale Canal, joined here, stretches from Ducie Street Junction for 33 miles over the Pennines to join the Calder & Hebble Navigation, and is once again open to through navigation after many years of campaigning. The bottom mile or so of the Rochdale Canal remained navigable, from the junction with the Ashton Canal at Ducie Street down to Castlefield and its meeting with the Bridgewater Canal, and provided a vital link between the Bridgewater and Ashton Canals in the 100-mile Cheshire Ring cruising route.

Roving bridge – junction of the Macclesfield Canal with the Peak Forest Canal

THE CHESHIRE RING – THEN AND NOW

This route has remained one of the most popular cruising circuits for many years now – a one-week trip encompassing parts of the Trent & Mersey, the Bridgewater, the Ashton, the Peak Forest and Macclesfield canals, passing through a wide and exciting variety of canalscape. Part of the journey includes a passage through central Manchester, a pleasant experience these days, but it was not always so.

The problem used to be timing your passage through the city so that the 'Rochdale Nine' locks were open, and your subsequent overnight mooring was a safe one! Local children preyed upon you as you tackled the Ancoats, Beswick and Clayton flights, leaping across the locks from one side to the other, begging lifts, and 'picking up' anything you might have left lying around. The lock machinery was stiff, water supply uncertain, and the things which fouled your propeller defied description . . ..

It is, thankfully, VERY different now, and the city passage is extremely attractive, interesting and enjoyable. Just take the usual precautions.

POINTS OF INTEREST

Disley The centre of the village is quite pretty, spoilt slightly by the A6 traffic. The village is up the hill, southwest of the navigation. The attractive church stands among trees above the little village square. It was greatly renovated in the last century, but the ancient tower with the griffin leering down at passers-by dates from the 16th century.

Marple Once a famous hat-making centre, the town is most interesting by the canal.

Marple Locks The 16 locks at Marple were not built until 1804, four years after the rest of the navigation was opened. The 1-mile gap thus left was bridged by a tramway, while the canal company sought the cash to pay for the construction of a flight of locks. This was obviously a most unsatisfactory state of affairs, since the limestone from Doveholes had to be shifted from wagon to boat at Bugsworth Basin, from boat to wagon at Marple Junction, and back into boat again at the bottom of the tramway. Not surprisingly, a container system was developed – using iron boxes with a 2-ton payload – to ease the triple transhipment. However, this was no long-term solution, and when the necessary £27,000 was forthcoming the company authorised construction of the flight of locks. Today they stand comparison with any flight on the network. Note especially Samuel Oldknow's superb warehouse, by lock 9, now tastefully converted to offices.

Marple Aqueduct Deservedly scheduled as an ancient monument, this three-arched aqueduct over the River Goyt is a very fine structure, in an exquisite setting almost 100ft above the river. Designed by Benjamin Outram, its construction utilises circular pierced shoulders above each arch to reduce the weight of the rubble filling whilst providing a decorative feature. Contrast and interest are further added by the use of two different colours of gritstone in the parapets and ledges.

Marple Locks

Ashton-under-Lyne To the northwest of Portland Basin there is the church of St Michael, which was begun by Sir John de Assheton in the early 15th century and completed by his great grandson before 1516. The church has a tall west tower rebuilt by Crowther in 1886–8. Particularly notable is the stained glass, depicting the Life of St Helena and dating from the 15th–16th centuries. The town was granted a market in 1284, but by 1801 the population still numbered only 4,800. It expanded rapidly, due to the growth of cotton weaving in the area, and by 1851 totalled over 30,000.

Portland Basin Social and Industrial History Museum This museum is housed in a superb reconstruction of a canal warehouse dating from 1834, at the junction of the Ashton, Peak Forest and Huddersfield canals. It tells the rich story of Tameside's social, political and industrial history, drawing upon many different facets of local life. The museum features a street of the 1920s, working models, computer interactives, sound and film. The original water wheel is restored to working order on the wharfside. Displays include topics such as glassmaking, textiles, hatting, printing, and canals.

Fairfield Immediately south of Fairfield Junction is a group of neat and tidy buildings around a fine chapel. This is an original Moravian settlement, established in 1785 by Benjamin Latrobe and consisting of tidy rows of cottages built in brick, intended to house the members of a self-contained community.

Velodrome, Manchester This is the National Cycling Centre, where the track is widely regarded as one of the finest and fastest in the world. There is a full programme of exciting cycle races staged in this magnificent stadium, which hosted the track events of the Commonwealth Games 2002.

City of Manchester Stadium A wonderful 48,000 capacity stadium used for the 2002 Commonwealth Games. The foundation stone was laid by Tony Blair on 17 December 1999, and the stadium was built at a cost of £90 million.

Along the border separating Devon and Cornwall, the River Tamar snakes its ponderous course, tucked away deep between soft wooded hills. This sylvan idyll is at times punctuated by a dwelling, built usually of the local granite, perched on a promontory, with views out over any passing craft. For the most part the scene is mellow as time is told only by the gentle rise and fall of each successive tide. Not always was this such a placid picture, however. Time was when the area rang with the sounds of pick, shovel and hammer, echoing to the detonations of gunpowder and to the shouts of men: both copper miners and sailors, the latter often in tongues totally foreign to West Country ears.

At the heart of all this activity was Morwellham Quay, tucked away round a sharp bend in the river, an inland port to rival any built in the country and connected directly to the sea via the Tamar estuary. The Great Dock and its quays were constructed between 1857 and 1858, to provide an outlet for copper from Devon Great Consoles Mine, one of the richest in Europe. Sizeable sailing schooners transported the ore for smelting in Swansea – known as the Copperopolis of the west – returning with coal to fuel the mine's steam pumps and lifting gear. Constructed on former water meadows, the quays were owned by the Duke of Bedford, who also

The Dock at Morwellham Quay

The Tavistock Canal with the viaduct that once carried the LSWR London–Plymouth line in the background

carrying copper from the Duke of Bedford's Wheal Friendship and Wheal Crowndale mines. It was also anticipated that it would drive mining and mill machinery. It crossed the River Lumburn on a sizeable aqueduct and there was a 2-mile spur, opened in 1819, running to slate quarries at Mill Hill. Inclined planes (*see* Milepost 19) were used both in the connection to the quarries and down a 237ft drop to Morwellham Quay. There were no locks and no evidence survives to tell us about the dimensions of the craft used.

The whole course of the navigation is still visible today, even though it was closed by the Duke of Bedford when he purchased it in 1873. Sixty years later it was resurrected for use in a hydroelectric generating scheme, a function that it still faithfully fulfils to this day.

Waterwheel at Morwellham, once powered by the Tavistock Canal

leased the mine and collected dues on every facet of the operation between underground seam and cargo hold.

The peak output of 26,693 tons from the mine was in 1863, representing well over 50 per cent of the total copper production of Devon and Cornwall. A further 19 per cent came from the duke's Tavistock mines, some 4 miles away and connected to the quay by a slender tub boat canal.

Since 1980 much work has been carried out on the site, which had fallen into a state of almost total dereliction. Following a full archaeological survey, the silted up dock was dug out and more recently the timber side walls have been repaired

and strengthened. The raised tramway sidings, which carried the ore down from the mines and from the terminus of the Tavistock Canal, have been recreated as faithfully as possible and where necessary new tiles laid to the dock surface. All this effort has been recognised by UNESCO, with the dock forming part of a World Heritage Site, under the designation of the Cornwell and West Devon Mining Landscape.

The Tavistock Canal was authorised by Act of Parliament in 1803, although it had actually been built a year before. It is a tub boat canal 16ft wide and 3ft deep, passing under Morwelldown in a 2,540yd tunnel. The waterway has a slight flow towards the Tamar, designed to assist laden boats

RIVER WEAVER

This is very much a waterway of contrasts: one minute snaking its way through the woods of Vale Royal, the next a focus for the salt producing town of Northwich. Then on it swirls past the wharfs of a multi-national chemical giant – all gleaming vats and convoluted pipework – before meandering through tranquil pasture with only cows for company. Some 50 miles in length, only twenty of these are navigable between Winsford and the Manchester Ship Canal at Weston Point, where once there were bustling docks: a transhipment point for both imported and exported goods.

The River Weaver in Northwich

NORTHWICH

RUNCORN

WESTON POINT
DOCKS

FRODSHAM

WINSFORD

N

BACKGROUND

The river itself, which rises in the Peckforton Hills and proceeds via Wrenbury, Audlem, Nantwich, Church Minshull and Winsford to Northwich and Frodsham, is just over 50 miles long. Originally a shallow and tidal stream, it was long used for carrying salt away from the Cheshire salt area. The mineral was carried down by men and horses to meet the incoming tide. The sailing barges would load at high water, then depart with the ebbing tide.

In the 17th century the expansion of the salt industry around Northwich, Middlewich and Winsford gave rise to an increasing demand for a navigation right up to Winsford. In 1721, three gentlemen of Cheshire obtained an Act of Parliament to make and maintain the river as a navigation from Frodsham to Winsford, 20 miles upstream. By 1732 the Weaver was fully navigable for 40-ton barges up to Winsford.

When in 1765 the Trent & Mersey Canal (*see* page 26) was planned to pass alongside the River Weaver the trustees of the Weaver were understandably alarmed; but in the event the new canal provided much traffic for the river, for although the two waterways did not join, they were so close at Anderton that in 1793 chutes were constructed on the Trent & Mersey directly above a specially built dock on the River Weaver, 50ft below. Thereafter salt was transhipped in ever increasing quantities by dropping it down the chutes from canal boats into Weaver flats (barges) on the river. This system continued until 1871, when it was decided to construct the great iron boat lift beside the chutes at Anderton (*see* page 231). This remarkable structure is now completely restored and in full operation, thus effecting a proper junction between the two waterways.

The Weaver Navigation did well throughout the 19th century, mainly because continual and vigorous programmes of modernisation kept it thoroughly attractive to carriers, especially when compared to the rapidly dating narrow canals. Eventually coasters were able to navigate the river right up to Winsford.

In spite of this constant improvement of the navigation, the Weaver's traditional salt trade was affected by 19th-century competition from railways and the new pipelines. However, the chemical industry began to sprout around the Northwich area at the same time and, until recently, Brunner Mond's works (now Tata Chemicals) at Winnington supplied virtually all the remaining traffic on the river.

Today, following the restoration of the Anderton Boat Lift, much of the river provides a haven of peace and tranquillity outside – the relatively short, industrialised reaches – and it is beginning to attract boaters more used to the confines of the inland canal system. Sections, especially in the Vale Royal area, are very beautiful, whilst other lengths are remarkably remote, especially for an area so well-known for its extensive chemical manufacture.

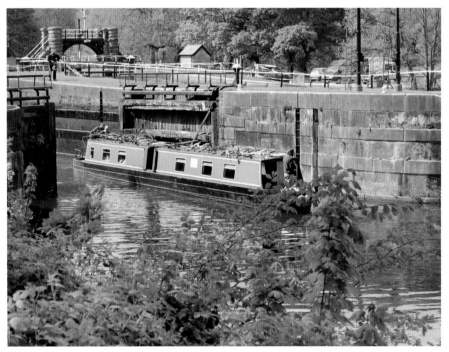

Vale Royal Locks

Holly Blue butterfly

Ladybird The Seven-spot ladybird is the most familiar of ladybirds and the one that is generally thought of as the typical ladybird. When handled, they exude a strong-smelling, acrid yellowish fluid as a defence against predators, reinforced by their bright warning colours. Both adults and larvae are active aphid hunters, scouring a wide range of plants for food, and are very welcome in gardens and amongst crops. The adults hibernate, often in clusters in leaf litter or sheltered hollows close to the ground. Common and widespread throughout most of Britain and Europe, the ladybird migrates widely in high population years. Active March to October.

Ladybird

Large Skipper butterfly This butterfly favours grassy places of all kinds and flies during June and July. The upperwings are dark brown and orange-brown with pale markings. The underwings are buffish orange with paler spots. In common with most other skipper butterflies, at rest the Large Skipper often holds its wings at an angle and can look rather moth-like. The caterpillars feed on grasses.

Large Skipper butterfly

Marsh Fritillary butterfly This butterfly has beautifully marked wings. It flies between May and June but is only active when it is sunny. Favouring damp heaths and moors, but also dry chalk grassland, the larvae feed on Devil's bit scabious and plantains.

Marsh Fritillary butterfly

Orange-tip butterfly

Orange-tip butterfly An attractive spring butterfly, seen flying between April and June. The male has an orange patch on the dark-tipped forewing, which is absent in the female. The hind underwing of both sexes is marbled green and white. The larvae feed mainly on the Cuckoo flower.

Speckled Wood butterfly

Speckled Wood butterfly A double-brooded butterfly, flying April to June and again July to September. It favours clearings and is fond of sunbathing. The upperwings are dark brown with pale markings; the underwings are rufous brown. The caterpillars feed on grasses.

THE NORTHEAST

There is a danger that each region represented in this book will find itself vying for a place in history as the founder of the man-made, waterway transport system that we see today. A more rewarding approach might well be to view the significance of the contribution made to the overall picture of inland navigation and the northeast's primary impact lies both in its past and present success in commercial carrying.

True, the Romans did build the Fossdyke in around AD 120 and it is seen as the oldest artificially constructed waterway in the country which is still navigable. It was designed to connect the River Witham (also made navigable by the Romans) to the Trent and thence to the Humber. The two waterways were subsequently used by the Danes when they invaded England and later by the Normans to carry stone used in the building of Lincoln Cathedral. In his concept for the Grand Cross scheme of inland navigations, Brindley also recognized the significance of the River Trent and its confluence with the Yorkshire Ouse to form the Humber providing, as it does, access to the North Sea port of Hull.

Today it is really only the waterways in this region that offer the opportunity to carry realistically economic loads. In the early 1980s, the waterways comprising the South Yorkshire Navigations (essentially Goole to Rotherham) together with the Aire & Calder were upgraded to the then Euro-barge standard of 700 tonnes, with either new or lengthened locks. In many ways this was too little too late as today's standard, prevailing throughout the Continent, is represented by vessels of up to 3,000 tonnes. However, those barge owners operating the smaller craft in this country have demonstrated that, given the right

John and Jonathan Branford, father and son

cargoes, in conjunction with suitable facilities, it is possible to make waterborne transport financially viable.

John Branford, the last but one in a long family line of barge owners – dating back more than 200 years – is typical of a breed of boatmen determined to keep carrying alive on the waterways of the Northeast. Now well past retirement and ready to hand on the business to his son Jonathan, he has been carrying cargoes of gravel and sand on the Trent and the canals of Yorkshire since leaving school. At one point he was even forced to put a small fleet of lorries on the road to fulfill a contract to transport specialist glass-making sand, when the riverside pit that he had hitherto serviced by barge became worked out, with operations moved further inland. This was a less than enjoyable interlude and he was glad to get back to carrying by water, only too well aware that one 600 tonne barge, with a 450 tonne payload, can carry the equivalent of 15 juggernauts, causing a fraction of the environmental impact.

Ingenuity is his stock in trade and with the help of an EU grant he has converted ex-tanker barges into bulk transporters, through the simple expedient of cutting open two-thirds of the tanks, retaining the ability to flood the remainder as ballast, to enable him to duck under the low bridges on the Aire & Calder when coming down empty. When he first contemplated taking a 600 tonne vessel through the tortuous bends of the River Trent, with a view to loading sand at a riverside pit at Besthorpe (just north of Newark) his fellow skippers thought he had gone one step too far but his consummate skill, based on years

of experience, proved them wrong and, until this contract finally came to an end in 2014, he regularly repeated the trip on a twice-weekly basis. However, the excitement of sitting in the wheelbox of his 200-foot barge, pivoting around the hairpin bend of Stoney Bight – between Gainsborough Arches and Gainsborough Railway Bridge – is a memory that will never fade!

His perspective on life's rich pattern, gained from long hours spent at the wheel of a barge, is probably unique and might be described as 'mid-river'. The Trent is tidal below Besthorpe and there is very little likelihood (save in times of flood) that there will be sufficient water beneath the keel of a loaded sand barge, to float her out onto the Humber – and thence back to Goole – in one go. Therefore, still more time elapses, sitting on the bottom, within the confines of a reach such as Destructor, Potteries or Ewsters: time to eat, to patch up the paintwork, time for further contemplation or to catch up on some sleep. (But woe betides the skipper that sleeps through his alarm, allowing the incoming tide to pluck his boat off the bottom and whip her round into contact with the adjoining banks!)

The time for contemplation is one of the key spin-offs from boating, be it leisure or commercial. Those tasked with shaping our transport policy for the future – ultimately, those who can be instrumental in saving us from the catastrophic effects of global warming – could do far worse than listen to the thoughts of someone who knows as much about the most environmentally friendly method of transport as anybody. Sitting beside

John Branford loading cargo at Besthorpe

John Branford, in the snug of the wheelbox, watching the green water meadows of the Trent valley unfold interminably slowly beside us, it is not unusual for his mobile to chirrup and for him to take a call from a potential customer, enquiring whether he would be interested in taking on a contract to move some bulk commodity or another. His response is nearly always that, in principle, he'd be delighted to explore the project further, only, is it possible, he asks tentatively, to identify somewhere to load and unload: nothing fancy, just a place to stand a mobile crane and space to manoeuvre a lorry or the like.

You see, while on the one hand all the powers that be (and have been … and no doubt ever will be) are extorting us to think 'green' in examining our transport solutions, when it comes to the everyday practicalities – such as the provision of basic wharfage and manning locks to match a schedule dictated by tides – there is suddenly a glaring lack of interest. This is an approach that John, in his wisdom, has for a long time now, labelled 'kidology'.

CHESTERFIELD CANAL

The Chesterfield Canal was initially surveyed in 1768 by John Varley to follow a line between Chesterfield and Bawtry, on the River Idle, as an improvement upon the existing trade route. However, both Worksop and Retford were anxious to benefit from the proposed waterway, so Varley undertook a second survey a year later along a route to West Stockwith, on the River Trent, that bypassed the Idle altogether.

The following year James Brindley who had, due to pressure of other work, delegated the initial survey to Varley, called a public meeting at the Red Lion in Worksop endorsing his colleague's proposal.

Retford on the Chesterfield Canal

BACKGROUND

Work started on the canal in October 1771 with John Varley as resident engineer, Brindley being still too busy with other schemes to be permanently on site. Most of the work, including digging the 2,893yds long Norwood Tunnel, constructing the summit level reservoir and building the lock flights, was let as separate contracts and carried out by individual contractors. Brindley's method was to make each section of the canal navigable as soon as it was completed to enable the company to benefit from the carriage of the heavy construction materials.

Brindley's death in September 1772 was a sad blow to the undertaking and led to Varley being placed in overall charge of this, his first large project. Ultimately Hugh Henshall, Brindley's brother-in-law, was made inspector of works, later to become chief engineer with a salary of £250 per annum. In the following year he discovered work, carried out by John Varley's father and two brothers, in the construction of Norwood Tunnel, to be unsatisfactory. Soon other examples of dubious contractual arrangements and slack management came to light, all reflecting badly on the Varley family. The extent of John Varley's complicity in these matters remains to this day a matter for debate.

On 4 June 1777 the canal was officially opened from West Stockwith to Chesterfield. Norwood Tunnel caused problems from the outset, as did the shortage of water to the summit pound. Boats travelling less than 12 miles empty, or lightly laden, were penalised when using a lock. Over the next 25 years a more satisfactory solution was provided by the building of three large reservoirs at Killamarsh, Woodhall and Harthill.

Early in 1841 a cargo of Anston stone, bound for the construction of the new Houses of Parliament, was carried for transhipment at West Stockwith, the

The canal approaching West Stockwith

first of approximately 250,000 tons despatched over a period of four years. As always, amalgamation with a railway company, in this case the Manchester & Lincoln Union Railway, led to a steady decline in the canal's fortunes and a reduction in maintenance. By 1904 it was reported that the minimum headroom in Norwood Tunnel was reduced to 4ft 10ins, owing to subsidence, while a roof collapse on 18th October 1907 led to its final closure.

Between the wars the canal was reasonably maintained, while the tidal lock into the Trent was enlarged and repaired in 1923–5. The navigation was temporarily resuscitated by the transport of munitions during the Second World War but traffic virtually came to an end in 1955 when the small trade from Walkeringham brickworks (near Gringley) to the Trent finished. One cargo that did linger on into the early 1960s was that of warp: a fine natural silt dredged from the Trent at Idle Mouth and used as a metal polishing material in the Sheffield cutlery trade. To the end all boats – known as Cuckoos – remained horse-drawn.

THE NAVIGATION

The canal itself begins at Tapton Mill Bridge, where it leaves the River Rother above a weir. The original intention was to cross over the river at this point and continue the waterway into Chesterfield. However, a shortage of funds dictated that the cheaper option, provided by a short section of river navigation, was chosen, hence the present terminus south of Wharf Lane Changeover Bridge. This in fact superseded the original terminal basin and warehouse (slightly further north) that were severed from the river by the building of the Manchester, Sheffield and Lincolnshire Railway in the late 19th century – which has, in turn, been replaced by the Inner Relief Road. A single floodgate protects the canal at its junction with the Rother and before long the navigation becomes embroiled in a group of road crossings, bracketing the first lock and the excellent Tapton Lock Visitor Centre. Beyond are two further bridges – this time carrying the main line railway junction – as the waterway turns northeast and heads for open countryside. There is little to remind the one of the proximity of town and industry as the canal enters a side cutting overhung with the trees of Bluebank Wood. Dixon's Lock was newly reconstructed in a position some 200yds below the original to avoid the ravages of open-cast mining, and newly planted spoil tips are still very much in evidence as the waterway enters a shallow cutting.

Chief engineer	James Brindley
Assisted by	John Varley, Hugh Henshall.
Significance	Early Brindley canal with superb examples of staircase locks.
Started in	1771
Completed in	1777
Length	45½ miles
Draught	2' 6"
Headroom	7' 1"
Lock size	72' × 6' 10"
Number of locks	65 (numbers 6–19 derelict).
Tunnels	2 (1 abandoned)
Aqueducts	3
Goods carried	Coal, stone, corn, lime, timber, iron, pottery, ale, munitions, warp.
Peak tonnage carried	200,000+ tons in 1848.
Operating authority	Canal & River Trust
Contact details	enquiries.eastmidlands @canalrivertrust.org.uk

The basin at West Stockwith – looking east with the lock down into the Trent visible in the background

THE NAVIGATION

Hollingwood and Staveley (once the home of a vast canalside iron foundry) maintain a discrete distance from the navigation, separated by a tract of gently rising pastureland, and it is a matter of wonder how rapidly nature (with a little assistance from the bulldozer) regains control. Just to the east of Eckington Road Bridge, waterway and Trans Pennine Trail diverge: the trail heads north along an abandoned railway line, while the largely infilled course of the canal wanders off across the fields towards Mastin Moor.

When the Great Central Railway built their line from Sheffield to Nottingham in 1890, its straight-as-a-die route between Staveley and Killamarsh conflicted on a very regular basis with the contoured course of the Chesterfield Canal. Rather than incur the substantial cost of building a succession of bridges, the Railway Company straightened the line of the canal, excavating cuttings as required, and it is for this reason that both canal and the now-disused railway run in tandem north and west of Renishaw. Here the navigation makes a second sweep to the east, passing through what was once a vast foundry complex, now demolished and built upon. Moulding sand had, over the years, been tipped into the canal bed and the waterway has only recently been re-excavated.

At Forge Bridge and almost doubling back on itself, the navigation finally settles on a more easterly course, picking its way through the houses of Killamarsh. Vociferous protest in the 1970s failed to prevent a part of the canal being built upon and now, in places, the original line is difficult to follow. However, alternative routes are under investigation to link in with future plans at Norwood, where 13 locks await restoration. Here a superb flight of staircase locks – three groups of three and one of four – lift the canal to the

Retford Town Lock

bricked-up western portal of Norwood Tunnel. The building at the bottom of the flight was once the Boatman Inn; the large decorative 'lakes' were side pounds: storage for the considerable quantity of water needed to operate the locks, and in turn connected to reservoirs in the hills

above. Between the top two staircase lock groups a dwelling has been converted from an old sawmill. This very early example of waterway construction dates, in the main, from 1775 and within $1/3$ mile encapsulates some of the very best in canal engineering, all within an idyllic setting.

POINTS OF INTEREST

Chesterfield Probably best known as the town with the crooked spire, Chesterfield prospered well before the relatively recent wealth introduced by local metalworking industries and coal mining. It was known as *Cestrefeld* by the Anglo-Saxons, the 'Cestre' prefix indicating that the Romans were active here well before them. In this important market town many street names are of ancient origin and hint at a range of medieval trades that were once dominated by industries linked to the plentiful supply of wool produced on the surrounding hills. George Stevenson lived at Tapton for more than a decade, moving to the area whilst surveying a route for the North Midland Railway between Derby and Leeds. While digging the Mile Long tunnel at Clay Cross, just south of

Chesterfield Canal paddle gear

Chesterfield, extensive iron and coal deposits were discovered in 1837, which Stevenson went on to exploit, launching the Clay Cross Company. Today Chesterfield is a prosperous market town, retaining excellent railway connections but with little of its former industry.

Barrow Hill Roundhouse, Chesterfield Built in 1870, this is in fact a square building constructed to house, maintain, coal and water and, in many cases, to turn steam locomotives. With the demise of steam haulage, most roundhouses were demolished, but, thanks to its continuing use for diesel traction and the dedication of the Barrow Hill Engine Society, this example survives and now houses one of the largest collections of electric, diesel and steam engines in the country.

Revolution House High Street, Chesterfield Once an alehouse, known as the Cock & Pynot (magpie), this cottage was the meeting place for three local noblemen intent on overthrowing King James II in favour of William and Mary of Orange.

St Mary and All Saints Church, Chesterfield Whether viewed from near or far, most attention is focused on the spire rather than upon the church itself. Standing 228ft from ground to weathervane, leaning 9½ft out of plumb and grotesquely twisted, the whole edifice is constructed from 150 tons of wood and 32 tons of lead; and nothing secures it to the tower save its own mass. Legends abound as to the cause of its twist, involving wizards, devils, blacksmiths and virgins, though not necessarily all at once. More reasonably, the nature of the green oak from which it was constructed over 600 years ago, shrinking as it seasoned in situ, is the most likely culprit, aided and abetted by a design that eschews cross-bracing and allowed the bottom timbers to gradually decay over the years. A holy building in one form or another has stood on the

East Stockwith – viewed from West Stockwith Lock

site since the middle of the 7th century; the present building was dedicated in 1234 and completed in 1360, when the spire was added. The Norman font was dug up in the vicarage garden in 1848, although the cause of its migration remains a mystery. The spire almost fell prey to a serious fire in December 1961 and was within minutes of total destruction.

Well Dressing, Derbyshire While its origins remain something of a mystery, but undoubtedly pre-dating Christianity, this decorative art thrives in the area throughout the summer in a variety of forms.

Staveley Mentioned in the Domesday Book, part of the Frecheville family estates in the 16th century and more recently owned by the Dukes of Devonshire, Staveley has, post Industrial Revolution, been the focus for the iron and coal industries in the area, with large foundries beside the canal at Hollingwood.

THE NAVIGATION

Leaving the eastern tunnel portal, the waterway settles into an open cutting before gliding through woodland coppice to emerge beside the Anston stone quarries, the source of the stone used in the construction of the Houses of Parliament. Nothing can prepare the boater for the magic of the next few miles: it is pure waterway witchcraft as beyond, against rolling farmland to the north, the canal heads for the first of the treble locks, followed immediately by three single locks and another treble. So begins a truly awesome length of waterway and an amazing feat of early canal engineering. Two double and two single locks take the navigation down into Turnerwood Basin, ringed by a charming collection of waterside cottages. Thence by seven locks, following in quick succession, the waterway tunnels into a delightful ribbon of woodland on its approach to Ryton Aqueduct and Boundary Lock, newly constructed to accommodate mining subsidence in the area. At Shireoaks the navigation ducks under the rebuilt road bridge sitting beside the local cricket field – a perfect replica of a county ground in miniature.

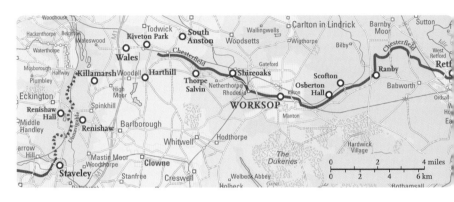

The basin at West Stockwith – looking north

Once below Worksop Town Lock, the boater will have descended one of the most splendid flights of locks anywhere on the waterways system: 31 in all, over a distance of just four miles. Representing hard work for today's navigator, it also presented an amazing challenge to the canal's original builders and acts as a tantalising preview to the eventual

resurrection of the spectacular (and currently derelict) 13 lock flight immediately to the west of Norwood Tunnel.

On leaving the town, the waterway heads out into open countryside and passes the attractive farm buildings of Osberton Hall. Beyond here it wanders eastward, passing beyond the hubbub of the A1 at Ranby, on its approach to the contrasting peace and isolation of Forest Locks.

The straight road crossing the canal at Barnby Wharf Bridge was a Roman highway. It was, in fact, the original course of the Great North Road but 200 years ago the citizens of Retford got the road diverted to pass through their town, thereby increasing its importance and prosperity. They must now be equally relieved to have rid themselves of it again. In the open countryside around here are the four Forest Locks while below the locks the outskirts of Retford are clearly visible as the waterway winds its way towards the town, passing through West Retford Lock and over three minute aqueducts, arriving close to the town centre. Here is the last of the narrow locks with a large canal warehouse beside it.

POINTS OF INTEREST

Renishaw Another foundry town once producing a vast array of complex castings for a wide range of industries.

Renishaw Hall, near Sheffield The 300-year-old home of the Sitwell family who established themselves as coal magnates and iron founders long before displaying their literary credentials.

Killamarsh Known as *Chinewoldemaresc* at the time of the Domesday survey, with a manor held by the tenure of providing a horse to the value of five shillings, with a sack and a spur, for the King's army in Wales. More recently and much more prosaically, a coal-mining centre, its deposits now exhausted.

Wales A mining community that now sits above the M1. The older area is set around the church. It was here that the body of Sir Thomas Hewitt, the somewhat eccentric owner of Hewitt Hall at Shireoaks, was eventually laid to rest. A confirmed atheist, Sir Thomas had begun to build an elaborate mausoleum at his home but died before it was completed. His servants tried to outwit the family's wishes to bury him at the church in Wales and one night filled the coffin with stones and set off with his body through the local woods at dead of night. Rumour has it that a strong wind blew out their torches and the servants were so frightened that they returned hastily to the hall with the body, which was then buried according to the family's plan. Scratta Wood was eventually felled and burned following reputed hauntings!

Kiveton Park A cluster of houses and industrial units where once there were major stone quarries.

Harthill Mentioned in the Domesday Book, the first church was established here in 1078 by the son-in-law of William the Conqueror. Its successor

houses some fine wooden carvings and an imposing timber roof. It is here that the body of John Varley was buried in 1809.

South Anston A sprawling settlement overlooked by the pretty church of St James with its elegant spire.

Thorpe Salvin A tiny village which has several times been winner of Britain in Bloom and had the onerous task of representing England in the European competition. The small nucleus of attractive stone houses is dominated by the now-ruined Elizabethan Thorpe Hall and the church. A very fine Norman doorway, a chained bible and a font depicting the four seasons are some of the treasures which can be seen within.

Shireoaks It is worth taking the time to explore this village whose splendid terrace of miners' cottages leads down the hill to the church. The village takes its name from a giant oak tree which cast its shade into Yorkshire, Derbyshire and Nottinghamshire and which was said to have measured 94ft in circumference. The money for both the church and the cottages was given by the 5th Duke of Newcastle following the sinking of the pit. The presence of coal in the area brought work for up to 600 men and it is easy to imagine the impression that the newly-built colliers' cottages of Shireoaks Row must have made on the village. It is still possible to identify some of the original window casements and doors with their elaborate strap hinges, although many of the dwellings have cast history aside for more comfortable 20th-century fitments. The foundation stone of the church was laid in 1861 by Edward VII, then Prince of Wales. The quill pen which he used at the ceremony can still be seen in the church. Dedicated to St Luke, the building housesa beautiful altar, commemorating the Duke of Newcastle, and a painted ceiling.

In 1975 the spire of the church had to be removed following subsidence caused by the mining in the area. A miner's lamp hangs above the pulpit as a poignant reminder of the industry which was the lifeblood of the village until the closure of the pit in 1990. The village has twice won the best-kept village award. Just beyond Shireoaks Row stands the impressive half-ruined Jacobean Hall, built in 1612, whose coach-house has been sensitively converted into a pub. The 45 acres of land behind the hall were laid out as a water garden to include a lake, cascade and ornamental canal.

PARLIAMENTARY LINKS

Above John Varley's remarkable flights of locks near Shireoaks are woods and stone quarries. Anston Quarries not only offered a ready source of stone for the locks and bridges along the canal, but were also the source of almost 250,000 tons of stone used to rebuild the Houses of Parliament after they burnt down in 1834.

However, the traffic has not been entirely one way. The small community of Shireoaks lost 24 young men in the First World War (who are commemorated by a Calvary Cross) and exactly half that number in the Second World War. In their memory a clock was installed in the turret of St Luke's parish church with a double, three-legged gravity escapement. The significance of this mechanism is that not only will it resist outside influences – such as wind pressure on the hands – but also that it is a direct copy of Edmund Becket Denison's design for Big Ben.

THE NAVIGATION

There are visitor moorings immediately north of Hayton Low Bridge tucked under rising ground in pleasant contrast to the wide open arable vistas to the north and west. Beyond, the navigation circles around the village of Clayworth, passing the boat club now based in the white building beside Clayworth Bridge, once the White Hart public house. The straight road that crosses the canal at Gray's Bridge is of Roman origin.

Again the waterway curls around the next habitation, skirting an attractive courtyard housing development built on the site of Wiseton Park's old walled kitchen garden. The brick from the enclosing walls has been put to good use in the construction of many of the houses. Heading towards Drakeholes, the canal passes the stern features of a bearded man on the parapet of Old Man Bridge and, accompanied by woods, reaches the attractive moorings nestling beside the tunnel entrance. Drakeholes Tunnel (154 yds) is cut through rock and is mostly unlined. The navigation to the north is a thoroughly delightful stretch, heavily overhung with trees from Gringley to Drakeholes, running along the bottom of a ridge of hills. Wildlife near the water's edge includes coots, moorhens, water rats and bats. It is very secluded but the intimate feeling of the thickly wooded cutting beyond the tunnel has been ruined by the construction of a large road bridge.

The course of the navigation is entirely rural and pleasant, passing well-established but often decaying farm buildings and two disused brickworks, one now the repository for canal dredgings. At Misterton there are two locks close together and between them there once stood the Albion Flour Mill, powered by canal water from a small reservoir beside the top lock. The church spire of East Stockwith stands opposite the point where the Chesterfield Canal enters the Trent.

Rope grooves worn in an iron bridge-protector

Quarry Lock, Turnerwood Basin

POINTS OF INTEREST

Worksop Old buildings of note in Worksop are the Priory and its gatehouse.

Mr Straw's House, Worksop When William and Walter Straw's father died in 1932, the brothers kept his house as a shrine and altered nothing. In 1991 William died and left the property, with a legacy of £1.5 million, to the National Trust. They have preserved this time capsule and opened it to visitors.

The Priory, Workshop The church dates from the 12th century. Much rebuilding has taken place since then: in fact from 1970–2 the superstructure was added to, incorporating a new spire. Interesting paintings and monuments are inside the church and a gruesome relic from Sherwood Forest – a skull with the tip of an arrow embedded in it.

Within a few miles of the town there are some interesting places and beautiful countryside to visit. All around are the surviving woods of Sherwood Forest, while to the south of the town is the area called the Dukeries, each of the adjacent estates of Thoresby, Clumber and Welbeck having been owned by a duke. Welbeck is now an army college, Thoresby Park is open to the public. Clumber House was demolished in 1938 but the park, owned by the National Trust, is one of its most visited properties. Three miles west of Worksop is an outstanding building well worth visiting – the tiny Steetley Chapel – described as 'the most perfect and elaborate specimen of Norman architecture to be found anywhere in Europe'. The quiet villages of north Nottinghamshire were home to the Pilgrim Fathers. The full story is told in Worksop Museum which acts as a starting point for the Mayflower Trail leading out into the villages themselves.

Osberton Hall Built in 1806 by James Wyatt and enlarged and altered in 1853.

Scofton This is the tiny estate village for Osberton Hall. The old stable block is impressive and is surmounted by a clock tower.

Ranby A small rambling village with a pub on the canal, the only one for miles in either direction.

Retford A market town with good railway connections. There are funfairs held on the last weekend in March and first weekend in October.

West Retford Church Mainly 13th-century with a crocketed spire, said by the great architect Pugin to be a 'poem in stone'.

Hayton In nearby Bolham, where the local inhabitants once lived in caves hewn in the rock, there are the remains of an ancient chapel.

Drakeholes Tunnel

POINTS OF INTEREST

Clayworth A quiet and pleasant village extending along a single main street. The houses are of all periods, the new blending well with the old. In the old days a passenger boat used to run every Saturday from this pub to Retford, so that the villagers of Clayworth, Hayton and Clarborough could take their produce to Retford Market. The goods were loaded into the 'packet' boat on the Friday night, then the people would return early on Saturday morning, leaving at 06.30 to reach Retford by 08.30. The boat used to return in the evening when the market closed. A handsome sundial sits over the porch of the pretty village church, inscribed with the words 'Our days on earth are as a shadow'. Inside there is a series of beautiful wall paintings.

Wiseton A superbly elegant estate village set in a landscaped park, still clearly fulfilling its original manorial function. Trees and grass separate the various buildings, of which the large stable with its handsome clock tower is the most significant.

Secluded mooring on the Chesterfield

Turnerwood Basin

The hall, a modern red brick building, which replaced the original in 1962, is well hidden behind high walls.

Gringley on the Hill The village is about a mile's walk up from the canal. A small rise on a level with the church tower gives a good view. On a clear day the pinnacles of Lincoln Cathedral can sometimes be seen, nearly 20 miles to the southeast.

Misterton The village has a thriving Methodist church, as do most of the places in this area. John Wesley came from nearby Epworth.

West Stockwith At the junction not only of the Chesterfield Canal with the Trent, but also of the River Idle with the Trent. East Stockwith is just across the river, tantalisingly out of reach. The two communities used to be connected by a ferry. In a way, the total lack of communication with the other village, only 50yds away, serves to enhance the magical sense of remoteness that Stockwith possesses – especially when one sees big barges appearing round the bend, churning past the two villages and then as quickly disappearing again.

No account of the waterways of Britain would be complete without a mention of Thomas Telford. Born in 1757 in Dumfriesshire, he cut his teeth on roads and upon the bridges that carried them over the rivers and streams they encountered. As a trained mason, stone was the material of his choice and many of his bridges are still doing sterling service on our highways today. Most famous of his roads is probably the A5, connecting London to the Irish Sea port of Holyhead in Anglesey.

Prior to Telford, canal engineering had developed firmly within the 'contour mould'. James Brindley demonstrated a marked reluctance to ascend or descend a hillside whilst any chance of following a contour, however sinuous, remained a possibility. He also avoided high embankments and deep cuttings wherever he could, if only because there

was little in the way of machinery available to him beyond pick, shovel, wheelbarrow and the sheer muscle power of his Navigators (or Navvies).

Running side-by-side, the Wolverhampton (a Brindley construction) and the Birmingham (a later Telford addition) Levels of the Birmingham Mainline (*see* page 68) ably demonstrate these two approaches. In building what we now call the Shropshire Union Canal – affectionately known as the Shroppie amongst its many devotees – Telford in many cases chose the shortest line between two points, whether this involved deep cuttings or high embankments. Both gave him considerable headaches during the construction of this navigation, especially the embankments, one of which – Shelmore – was to haunt him to his grave. Indeed so often did it slip in the course of its construction, it was not finished until a year

The Shropshire Union Canal at Audlem

after the remainder of the navigation opened: a full 5½ years after it was started. In Shropshire, his canal and his A5 road intersect, the road squeezing under the delightful Stretton Aqueduct: a later construction of Telford's and therefore executed in cast iron.

Immediately to the west of Gloucester, at Over where the Herefordshire and Gloucestershire Canal is once again to join the River Severn, is another Telford bridge – one that once carried the main A40 over the river. Replaced by a modern concrete construction, carrying a relatively new dual carriageway alongside, it is possible to see that the great man did not always get things right. Clearly visible, now that the motorist does not sit atop the bridge, is a 10in. sag at the centre of its single arching span: evidence that the supporting centring was removed too soon and proving that, as mere mortals, we are all fallible.

'The Shroppie Fly' and crane

AIRE & CALDER CANAL

The River Aire was first made navigable to Leeds in 1700 and rapidly became a great commercial success, taking coal out of the Yorkshire coalfield and bringing back raw wool, corn and agricultural produce; Selby and later Goole becoming Yorkshire's principal inland port. The opening of the New Junction Canal in 1905 further secured its suitability for commercial traffic, which until recently amounted to some 2 million tons.

However, the current cessation of coal carrying to Ferrybridge Power Stations has transferred 1^{1}/$_{2}$ million tons from the navigation onto road and rail annually, together with the associated environmental cost.

For the boater it is a good idea to moor at Stanley Ferry Marina and walk to the road bridge for a full view of this fine structure – Stanley Ferry Aqueduct, a trough suspended from a two-pin cast iron arch – built on the same principle as the Sydney Harbour Bridge, which it predates by 100 years. Nearly 7,000 tons of Bramley Fall stone and 1,000 tons of cast iron were used in its construction. The first boat to pass across it was the *James*, a schooner of 160 tons drawn by three grey horses, on 8 August 1839. The 700 men who worked on it were fed at the nearby public houses, one of which, The Ship, still stands.

Designed by George Leather, the strength of the structure was severely tested when, soon after opening, the largest flood for 20 years caused the river below actually to flow into the trough. The towpath is carried on a separate steel girder structure designed to protect both aqueducts during such floods. The newer aqueduct alongside was built in 1981, to accommodate large barges, although the original is still in water. Boats heading west use the old structure, those travelling east the new one.

Set beside the original structure, the contemporary concrete design is a singularly boring construction, totally without adornment, unremittingly functional. Its bedfellow, however

Stanley Ferry Aqueducts

is a riot of decoration in the classical mould displaying wrought-iron columns and pilasters, complete with decorative hoods and pediments. Such unashamed flamboyance rarely has an equal in today's utilitarian world, more's the pity. Just imagine for a moment the sheer joy and bravissimo driving such an exuberant design. What a set of challenges for the iron founder, what rewards reaped upon the successful conclusion of the project – more aesthetic than monetary.

By way of contrast, on the adjacent bank, are two large buildings of almost factory proportions and enough timber – much of it of massive section – to float a battleship. This is one of the centres of Canal & River Trust's lock gate building operations from which replacement gates are dispatched all over the waterways system, though few by boat. Even a single gate for a narrow canal lock is a substantial beast, although made to a

precision not always appreciated by the casual onlooker. One of a pair of gates for a lock on a wide canal weighs in at well over a ton and, fitting them so that they are watertight, is a highly skilled operation.

Lock gate manufacture

Approaching the aqueducts

RIVER TRENT

As with many of this county's rivers, improvements to benefit navigation gradually unfolded over the centuries giving rise to the waterway we see today. Some 50 years before James Brindley started work on the Bridgewater Canal, Lord Paget, owner of coal mines in the Nottingham area, obtained an Act of Parliament permitting him to build locks, wharfs and artificial cuts at his own expense. At Newark, an Act, granted in 1772, improved the navigation into the town with two locks; while spurred on by these beginnings, other interests agitated for improvements, which gradually followed on the back of William Jessop's 1782 survey.

Trent Bridge, Newark-on-Trent

BACKGROUND

The River Trent is a historic highway running for about 100 miles from the Midlands to the Humber ports and the North Sea. It is thought that as long ago as the Bronze Age the Trent was part of the trade route from the Continent to the metal-working industry in Ireland.

The Romans also recognised the value of the river as a route to the centre of England from the sea. Around AD 120 they built the Foss Dyke canal to link the Trent valley with *Lindum Colonia* (now Lincoln), the River Witham and the Wash. The Trent later acted as an easy route for the Danish invaders, who penetrated as far as Nottingham. Around AD 924 Edward the Elder expelled the Danes from Nottingham and built the first bridge there. The second bridge at Nottingham was built in 1156 and lasted 714 years. The third bridge was built in 1871 and forms the basic structure of today's Trent Bridge.

The first Act of Parliament to improve the Trent as a navigation was passed in 1699. In 1783 an Act authorised the construction of a towpath, thus allowing for the first time the passage of sail-less barges. Ten years later the Trent Navigation Company's engineer drew up a comprehensive scheme to build locks and weirs, to increase the depth in certain reaches and build a number of training walls to narrow and thus deepen the channel. In 1906, the Royal Commission on Inland Waterways adopted it as the official future plan, authorising locks at Stoke Bardolph, Gunthorpe, Hazleford and Cromwell. The works were completed in 1926.

Trade soon increased fourfold. At its peak in the 19th and early 20th century, the Trent formed the main artery of trade for the East Midlands, connecting with the South Yorkshire Navigations, the Chesterfield Canal, the Fossdyke, the Grantham Canal, the Erewash Canal, the River Soar Navigation

The conveyor at Besthorpe

and the Trent & Mersey Canal. Although it remains connected today to all but the Grantham Canal, the large trade between these waterways dwindled away with railway competition. Today the sand and gravel traffic from riverside pits at Girton and Besthorpe – just below Cromwell Lock – is no more, with the material now brought by road to Whitwood from a quarry near Ripon.

The Trent remains a useful through route for pleasure craft, easy to navigate and with many interesting connections. It is the only way to access the Chesterfield Canal and the Fossdyke & Witham navigations and provides a useful link into the South Yorkshire Navigations, and to the River Ouse for the intrepid.

CLEANING UP THE RIVER SOAR IN LEICESTER

For nearly two decades the appearance of the combined River Soar and canal skirting Aylestone, on the outskirts of Leicester – and along the Mile Straight, bordering the city itself – was of an inky, opaque blackness far removed from the image of a burbling, infant stream. This off-putting and unnatural phenomenon served only to reinforce the perception that Leicester was not a city to linger in and it was better to make a beeline for the relative safety of the nearby River Trent. In reality the cause was trade effluent from several long-established dye works passing straight through the local sewerage treatment works. New legislation, however, imposed colour conditions on discharges amounting to full colour removal: a real challenge for the Environment Agency's hard-pressed chemists.

Yet what remained was the puzzle of the problem's relatively recent origins. One plausible explanation lay in the changing nature of the fashion industry. Once, ostensibly, buyer-led (we responded to the length of a skirt or the cut of a suit) our sartorial whims became firmly orchestrated by the industry itself, colour consistently being its key device. In unison went a definite movement towards man-made fibres and their reactive dye processes; bright colours predominated in wardrobes, their turgid residues lingered in rivers.

THE NAVIGATION

Downstream from Derwent Mouth (*see* Trent & Mersey Canal on page 26) the navigation passes through Sawley Cut ending in a pair of locks, followed by a large railway bridge over the river. To the east the cooling towers of the huge Ratcliffe Power Station are clearly visible, but they are discreetly tucked away behind Red Hill and their intrusion into the landscape is thus minimised.

Chief engineers	William Jessop (1783), W. E. Hopkin (1869), Henry Rofe (1881), Frank Rayner (1896).
Surveyed by	William Jessop, Thomas Dadford Senior and Junior, John Smith, Robert Whitworth.
Significance	Arterial waterway connecting central England to the North Sea forming the northeastern leg of the Grand Cross.
Started in	1699–
Completed in	–continuing until after the First World War.
Length	93½ miles
Draught	Variable
Headroom	Shardlow to Nottingham: 8' Nottingham to Gainsborough: 13'
Lock size	Shardlow to Nottingham: 81' × 14' 6" Nottingham to Gainsborough: 165' × 18' 6"
Number of locks	12
Goods carried	Sand, gravel, petroleum products, raw materials and manufactured goods.
Operating authority	Canal & River Trust
Contact details	enquiries.eastmidlands@canalrivertrust.org.uk

Trent Lock marks the junction of the Erewash Canal with the River Trent, while at the foot of the wooded Red Hill is the mouth of the River Soar. A pair of protective flood gates lead the navigation into an artificial cut and under an attractive white accommodation bridge. At the end of the cut is Cranfleet Lock; from here one may enjoy a view of the woods hiding Thrumpton Park.

The river winds on towards Nottingham passing the picturesque Barton Island, old gravel pits of the Attenborough Nature Reserve and many sailing boats; this is clearly a popular stretch of the river. To the south runs a ridge of hills on which stands Clifton Hall.

Beeston Lock introduces the Beeston Canal which bypasses an unnavigable section of the River Trent. The navigation passes first a housing estate and then Boots Estate, followed by Lenton Chain. This marks the end of the short Beeston Canal for at this point the Nottingham Canal used to flow in

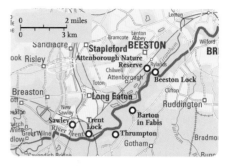

from the north. The junction was called Lenton Chain because the Trent Navigation Company used to lock their Beeston Canal (with a chain across it) from Saturday evening until Monday – without fail. The major part of the Nottingham Canal, from Lenton to the Erewash Canal at Langley Mill is now closed, but the rest of it forms the main line of through navigation from the Beeston Canal back to the River Trent at Meadow Lane Lock.

Gunthorpe Weir and Lock

THE NAVIGATION

East of Lenton Chain, the Nottingham Canal continues towards Nottingham Castle which is clearly visible on its rocky cliff near the centre of the city. Here is the shallow Castle Lock, bounded by an area of vibrant new building and centrally placed for the railway station and access to the city. Approaching a sharp, right angle corner, once hemmed in by massive stone viaducts (a memorial to the Great Central Railway) the waterway opens out and, rounding the bend at what was once a junction, progresses in a cutting towards Meadow Lane Lock and the River Trent.

Traffic on the Trent

Downstream from the railway bridge, the wide river soon leaves Nottingham behind and enters pleasant countryside. This section serves to establish the Trent's attractive rural character as it continues to sweep along through Nottinghamshire. Passing under a railway bridge, one sees a very steep escarpment of tree-covered hills, effectively cliffs, rising out of the water: Radcliffe on Trent is concealed in the woods above. Further downstream is the delightfully secluded Stoke Lock – the lock island covered with trees. Below the lock, the river bends northwards and crosses over to the other side of the valley, leaving behind the woods and cliffs. At Burton Joyce the river rebounds from the side of the valley and turns east again. The water meadows that accompany the river serve to keep at bay any inroads by modern housing.

POINTS OF INTEREST

Sawley The tall church spire attracts one across the river to Sawley, and in this respect the promise is fulfilled, for the medieval church is beautiful and is approached by a formal avenue of lime trees leading to the 600-year-old doorway. Otherwise Sawley is an uninteresting main road village on the outskirts of Long Eaton.

Trent Lock A busy and unusual boating centre at the southern terminus of the Erewash Canal. There are both pubs and boatyards here, together with a steady stream of gongoozlers.

Thrumpton This little village beside the Trent is, like so many other places on the river, a dead end. Motorists only go there if they have good reason to. Hence Thrumpton is a quiet and unspoilt farming village, with new development only up at the far end. Although the impressive hall is hidden away at the west end of the village, its large uncompromising gateway serves to remind the villagers what they are there for. The tiny church, with its narrow nave and a tower, was built in the 13th century but restored in 1872 by the well-known architect G. E. Street, at the expense of Lady Byron. The single street winds past it down to the river – there used to be a ferry here.

Thrumpton Hall Basically a James I mansion built around a much older manor house. The hall is famous for its oak staircase, which dates from the time of Charles II. The ground-floor rooms are well-used, and elegantly decorated; the grounds are delightful, encompassing a backwater off the River Trent.

Barton in Fabis A small and isolated village, composed mainly of modern housing and set well back from the river. The 14th-century church seems unbalanced in several respects; it has a great variety of styles. The building has, however,

considerable charm, being light, and attractively irregular. It contains several monuments to the Sacheverell family.

Attenborough Nature Reserve, Nottingham Worked out gravel pits, once derelict and unsightly, are now providing an interesting habitat for plant and animal life. There are comprehensive nature trails and a wooden observation hide. Designated an SSSI.

Beeston Lock, Nottingham This is a splendidly kept lock in an attractive setting. The pretty cottages and the little backwater off the canal are a hint of its past importance; until some years ago there used to be a lock down into the river here, at right angles to the present lock. The river channel used to be navigable – by shallow-draught vessels – from here down to Trent Bridge.

Nottingham The city's prosperity derives largely from the coal field to the north, and the long-established lace industry. John Player & Son made all their cigarettes here and Raleigh turned out bicycles for the world. The city centre is busy and not unattractive – there is an imposing town hall in Slab Square – but little of the architecture is of note. Modern developments are encouraging, however, notably the superb Playhouse Theatre and the appearance of a variety of theme festivals spread throughout the year.

Nottingham Castle William the Conqueror's castle, which was notorious as the base of Robin Hood's unfortunate enemies while King Richard I was away crusading, has been destroyed and rebuilt many times during its tumultuous history. It was a Yorkist stronghold in the Wars of the Roses and it was here that Charles I raised his standard in 1642, starting the Civil War. Though the original secret caves beneath the castle still exist, the present building dates only from 1674.

Nottingham Goose Fair The Goose Fair is now a conventional funfair but on a gigantic scale. It still features traditional entertainments like boxing bouts (challengers invited to fight the house champ) as well as the usual mechanical fairground delights.

Grantham Canal A long-disused but delightful canal running from Trent Bridge, Nottingham, to Grantham. The canal was built purely to serve the agricultural communities of eastern Nottinghamshire, so it pursues a remarkably circuitous course through pleasant farmland, including the Vale of Belvoir (pronounced 'beever'). Belvoir Castle, seat of the Duke of Rutland, is only about a mile from the canal at one point. A tramway was constructed to connect canal and castle, in order to carry coal up to the castle using wagons drawn by horses. Traces can still be seen of this, one of Nottinghamshire's earliest railways. The Grantham Canal still feeds water down from secluded reservoirs at Knipton and Denton to the Trent and large sections of the towpath are available for walking and cycling. There are well-advanced plans for its complete restoration and re-connection to the River Trent.

Tugs in Newark

THE NAVIGATION

Passing Shelford Manor, one arrives at the sleek arches of Gunthorpe Bridge – the only road bridge over the river in the 24 miles between Nottingham and Newark. To the east of the bridge are the grand houses up on the hills of East Bridgford.

The next 5 or 6 miles below Gunthorpe are probably the most beautiful and certainly the most dramatic on the whole river. On the east side, the wooded cliffs rise almost sheer from the flat valley floor to a height of 200ft, allowing here or there the presence of a strip of fertile land on which cattle graze. Only at two places does a track manage to creep down the perilous slope to the river; otherwise, access is impossible. On the west side, by contrast, the ground is flat for miles, across to the other side of the valley.

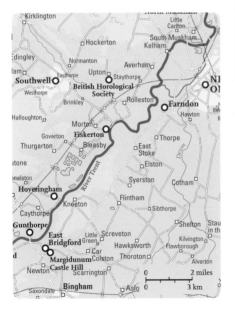

Messing about on the river, Trent Lock

The river continues along its superb isolated course, with the forested cliffs of the Trent Hills striding along the river's east bank, while on the other side the flat plain of the valley rolls away through green fields and quiet Nottinghamshire villages. The old Hazelford Ferry Hotel, now a retirement home, is on the left bank near an island in the river while below the old hotel a ferryman plies across the river for fishermen.

Beyond Hazelford Lock the steep Trent Hills dwindle away and the river leaves the woods (near the battlefield of East Stoke) for Fiskerton. Downstream of Fiskerton, the river sweeps round past the parkland at Stoke Hall. The site of a 4-acre Roman fort is on the nearby Fosse Way.

On the way into Newark, the navigation passes an old windmill, a boatyard at the mouth of the River Devon (pronounced 'Deevon'), some extensive old maltings, and a restored warehouse with the words Trent Navigation Company in faded lettering on the side. The townscape at this point is dominated by the northwest wall of the ruined Newark Castle. Nearby is a splendid old seven-arched stone bridge. The size of the arches limit the width of boats which can use the navigation but this bridge is listed as an ancient monument and so cannot be altered to accommodate bigger vessels.

POINTS OF INTEREST

Holme Pierrepont An isolated village east of Holme Locks, this is an ancient, strange place, with few surfaced public roads. The hall is an extensive stuccoed building with the little 17th-century church next to it gently decaying. Well to the west of the village is the international rowing course. This award-winning recreational centre was built from a string of worked-out gravel pits. A lot of wild birds frequent this area, including yellow wagtails, sand martins, little winged plover, common terns and great-crested grebes. There is also an internationally acclaimed canoe slalom course beside Holme Lock.

Stoke Bardolph The focal point is the riverside pub. This is one of several on the river in Nottingham-shire which, by their very presence (invariably on the site of a ferry), have caused the development of a tiny isolated colony of houses. They are a magnet for thirsty day-trippers and anglers.

Shelford A flood bank protects this quiet and isolated village from the Trent. The old church has a wide Perpendicular tower which commands the Trent valley.

Shelford Manor The old manor was burnt down in 1645 after 2,000 Roundheads attacked this Royalist stronghold. They massacred 140 of the 200 men inside. The manor was rebuilt in 1676. Horse trials are held here today.

Gunthorpe Gunthorpe has been an important river crossing point for over 2,000 years. The bridge built in 1875 was replaced by the present one in 1927. Prior to this there was a ferry here.

East Bridgford The village is accessed via a shady lane up hill from the river. The church is pleasantly light. Rector Oglethorpe, one-time incumbent of this parish, crowned Queen Elizabeth I.

Margidunum Castle Hill, East Bridgeford One-and-a-half-miles southeast of East Bridgford is the site of *Margidunum*, a Roman town on the Fosse Way (the straightest road in England). *Margidunum* was probably located here to guard the ford at East Bridgford.

Hoveringham A village intimately linked with the gravel extraction industry.

Fiskerton Charming riverside village with excellent access for boats. Although the normal river level is well below the wharf, all the buildings along the splendid front are carefully protected from possible flood by stone walling or a bank of earth.

Southwell Three miles north west of Fiskerton, this very attractive country town is well worth visiting in order to see its minster. The minster was founded at the beginning of the 12th century by the Archbishop of York, and is held by many to be one of the most beautiful Norman ecclesiastical buildings in England. Its scale is vast for Southwell, but it is set well back from the houses and is in a slight dip so it does not overawe the town centre, in spite of the two western towers and the massive central tower. Chief among the treasures inside the building are the naturalistic stone carvings in the late 13th-century chapter house, and the wooden carvings of the choir stalls.

Farndon A local ferry still transports the fishermen to the far side of the river in this attractive village. The pub makes it a popular spot in summer as do the sailing boats. Extensive renovation of the 14th-century church in 1891 revealed a stone coffin containing a Saxon bronze sword.

West and East Stockwith silently regard one another across the Trent

THE NAVIGATION

Beyond Town Wharf the navigation passes the oldest and most interesting industrial buildings in Newark – an old ironworks, more redundant maltings, a brewery (now only a distribution centre) and a glueworks giving off a smell of old leather. Gradually these buildings, or their sites, are undergoing renovation and wholesale redevelopment. North of the town the navigation rejoins the main channel of the River Trent.

From Newark, the Trent follows a generally northerly course towards the Humber, which is still over 50 miles away owing to the very sweeping and tortuous line of the river. The villages of North Muskham and Holme face each other across the water and used to be connected by ferry. St Wilfrid's in North Muskham dates from the 11th century and is Grade I listed. A mile or more below Holme is Cromwell Lock and Weir. On 28 September 1975 ten volunteers of the 131 independent parachute squadron of the Royal Engineers lost their lives here whilst taking part in Expedition Trent Chase. Cromwell has always been a significant place on the river; in the 8th century a bridge was built at this point; the lock here now marks the beginning of the tidal section of the Trent

This is a typical stretch of the upper section of the tidal Trent. The river meanders along its northward course, flanked by flood banks and with no bridges. The land is largely grazed as permanent pasture nurtured by the high summer water table maintained by the winter flood (now of course contained). Evidence of an ancient landscape is glimpsed, often on the inside of a sweeping bend, in the form of isolated stretches of hedgerow. These are rich in an abundance of species including ash, willow, wild roses and hawthorn – a picture of white blossom in springtime. Apart from these tantalising views there is little to see save for the occasional sand barge.

Elsewhere the land yields a vast quantity of glacial gravel quarried for building and road construction. On the east bank is Besthorpe Wharf, which was used for feeding gravel from the adjacent pits into the river barges.

The river wriggles around Plum Bank and Short Corners on its approach to High Marnham, passing the course of the Old Trent River. High Marnham was at one time two hamlets: Ferry Marnham and Church Marnham.

The remains of Newark Castle

POINTS OF INTEREST

British Horological Institute, Upton A library, training and educational centre for all those interested in matters horological together with a fascinating museum open to the public. Housed in Upton Hall, built in 1828, the museum displays the original 'Six Pip' generator and the actual watch worn by Captain Scott on his final, disastrous expedition, amongst many other gems.

Newark-on-Trent Newark is magnificent, easily the most interesting and attractive town on the Trent, and it is very appealing from the navigation. Situated at the junction of two old highways, the Great North Road and the Fosse Way, the town is of great historical significance. During the Civil War it was a Royalist stronghold which was besieged three times by the Roundheads between March 1645 and May 1646. The defensive earthworks or sconces constructed by the Royalists are still visible. Today Newark, like everywhere else, is large, busy and surrounded by industry and modern housing. But the town centre is intact and still full of charm.

Church of St Mary Magdalene, Newark The enormous spire is all that one can see of this elegant church from the market place, for the buildings on one side of the square hide the body of the structure. Inside, the church is made light and spacious by soaring columns and a magnificent 15th-century east window in the chancel. The building was begun in 1160 and completed about 1500. It is rich in carving, but one of the church's most interesting features is a brass made in Flanders to commemorate Alan Fleming, a merchant who died in 1375. The monument is made up of 16 pieces of metal and measures 9ft 4ins by 5ft 7ins – one of the biggest of its type in England.

Market Place, Newark It is worth making a point of visiting Newark on market day to view the scene in the colourful old market. In opposite corners

of the square once stood two ancient pubs: one of them, the White Hart, now re-sited elsewhere in the town, was built in the 15th century and is the oldest example of domestic architecture in the town; the other is the Clinton Arms where W. E. Gladstone made his first speech in 1832. He later became Prime Minister.

Newark Castle, Newark Only a shell remains, the one intact wall overlooking the river. The first known castle on this site was constructed c.1129, probably for Alexander, Bishop of Lincoln. The present building was started in 1173, with various additions and alterations in the 14th, 15th and 16th centuries – notably the fine oriel windows. King John died here in October 1216, soon after his traumatic experience in the Wash. The castle was naturally a great bastion during the Civil War sieges and battles that focused on Newark. When the Roundheads eventually took the town in 1646, they dismantled the castle.

Holme Separated from the river by a flood bank and a line of trees. Holme is really more of a large farming hamlet than a village. The church is a delightfully irregular shape.

North Muskham A small, quiet village right on the river bank. The church was built mainly in the 15th century, and has large clerestory windows.

Sutton on Trent This pretty village is close to Carlton Wharf. The almost oriental white cap of a converted windmill, typical of this area, can be seen from the river.

Laneham The church of St Peter is well worth a visit. Its wonderful Norman doorway, heavily decorated with chevron, herringbone and sunflower patterns, still contains the original Norman door, hanging on the very hinges on which it was

QUAY STRATEGY

Navigating the tidal Trent, the boater is constantly aware of the potential – both past and present – to move large bulk loads effortlessly. Evidence of the river's past glory as a waterways highway can be found at every tortuous twist and turn in the form of decaying wharves and abandoned jetties. The waterfront at Gainsborough, once heaving with barge traffic – often as many as three deep – jostling for position to load or unload, is now moribund, locked in by concrete flood defences. This apparent shame at a past prosperity, one that was largely water-generated, is a telling indictment on the importance now attached to what was arguably the original form of green transport. Logic, it would appear, is lacking in a system that eschews the economies of scale of water transport in favour of diesel-powered lorries. But, on reflection, is it? It has been argued that the more diesel consumed, the more revenue for the government, and so, the greater the number of lorries on the roads, the greater the income from the road fund licence. Could it be that in promoting the benefits of water transport the Chancellor would be shooting himself in the foot by encouraging low tax-contributing traffic.

mounted in the 11th century. The tower was once used as a watch tower over the Trent ferry. The ringing chamber of the tower contains 25 wedding rings or cheeses. These date back to the period between 1813 and 1840 when it became the custom for couples married at the church to pay the ringers a sage cheese or five shillings each for the privilege of having their initials placed in a ring.

THE NAVIGATION

Near the railway viaduct is the isolated church of St George, situated equidistant between North and South Clifton in order to serve both parishes. North Clifton once had the use of a ferry which was free to its inhabitants. One-and-a-half-miles further, the river describes a sharp S-bend as it passes a welcome little ridge of hills, pleasantly wooded. But the ridge fades away as one reaches Dunham Toll Bridge (the present structure replacing one built in 1832) and the iron aqueduct that precedes it. Once a market town, Dunham was notorious for its flooding. The Trent frequently caused buildings to be awash with up to 10ft of water. As a consequence most of the inhabitants were boat owners in order to maintain communications during the floods. Recent flood protection measures have, hopefully, made such events a thing of the past.

At Laneham the traveller will enjoy a little relief from the Trent's isolation. Here there is a church and a few houses on a slight rise near the river. A farmhouse on the river bank was built on the site of the old manor. The cellars in the building are reputed to date back even further than this to the time when the land belonged to the palace of the Archbishops of York. To the north of the village, yet another power station – Cottam – appears as the river turns back on itself to the south before swinging northwards again at the junction with the Fossdyke Navigation at Torksey. Nearing the railway viaduct at Torksey, one sees the gaunt ruin of Torksey Castle standing beside the river. As at Newark, the façade that faces the Trent is the most complete part of the building – the rest has vanished. (The castle has been abandoned since the 16th century.) For the first 15ft or so from the ground, the castle is built of stone – above this it is dark-red brick.

From Cottam, the river continues to wind northwards towards Gainsborough. This is not as dull a stretch as those further south. A windmill marks the exaggeratedly named Trent Port, which is in fact the wharf for the small village of Marton, while the next place of interest is Littleborough, a tiny riverside settlement.

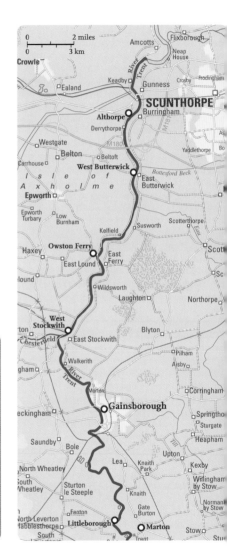

HISTORY IN THE TRENT

Viewed from the wheelbox of a sand-carrying barge, the Romans and their ilk were untidy fellows. Clearly they thought nothing of tossing their rubbish into the river – to make a ford or empty a failed kiln – and might be considered the forerunners of the contemporary litter lout. A heavily laden barge lumbers down the Trent with difficulty, banging the bottom on even the most generous ebb, unsure where she'll finally come to rest to await the next flood tide. History's cast-offs do nothing to help the situation and invariably result in an unscheduled halt, mid-river. Piling stones on the river bed, to form a ford at Littleborough, might have seemed a good idea to the Romans at the time. It is not, however, an opinion widely shared amongst barge skippers of today. Littleborough doubtless offers plenty to excite the archaeologist with its wealth of antiquity, whilst a short distance upstream, connoisseurs of porcelain can wax lyrical about the decorative output from the 19th-century Torksey Pottery. The common thread lies in the debris thrown into the tideway (commemorated in the naming of this reach, Potteries), making it a frequent resting place for loaded barges and a regular bed and breakfast stop for their crew.

POINTS OF INTEREST

Marton Marton was important in Saxon times because of its position near the ford where a Roman road (now the A1500) crossed the Trent. This ford marked the western boundary of the ancient kingdom of Lindsay. Many historians believe that Saint Paulinus baptised some of the first Saxon Christians here in AD627. The church of St Margaret has evolved around an early Saxon church, side aisles being added to the original structure. The tapering Anglo-Saxon tower still reveals some fine herringbone masonry. In 1904 it was discovered that the entire structure was unsafe as it had been built on foundations only two feet deep made of sand and pebbles.

Littleborough The little church stands on a slight rise; it is a delightfully simple Norman structure and incorporates much herringbone masonry. It is assumed from various finds, that this was the site of the Roman camp *Segelocum*. The paved ford dating from the time of Emperor Hadrian became visible during a drought in 1933. King Harold's army crossed this ford on its way to Hastings in 1066.

Gainsborough Gainsborough is best seen from the river, where the old wharves and warehouses

Cog boat (beside a bargeman's tools)

> ## VICTOR WADDINGTON
>
> The wharf at Burton-upon-Stather, downstream of Keadby, was built and operated by the late Victor Waddington whose barges, once moored on the Aire & Calder Canal, clustered around the western outskirts of Goole Docks (*see page 193*) awaiting incoming shipments of steel. Similarly his boats were to be found tied up several deep at Waddington Lock, on the South Yorkshire Navigations, and were a testimony to his great commitment to waterways transport. His enthusiasm, often in the face of a less than co-operative bureaucracy, was only matched by the immense carrying capacity of his total barge fleet. He is alleged to have observed, about the perilous state of his home navigation, that 'The top's too near the bottom, the bottom's too near the top and there's nowt in between.'

serve as a reminder of the town's significance as a port in the 18th and 19th centuries. Once qualifying as Britain's furthest inland port, there is now no evidence of the boats (of up to 850 tonnes deadweight) that used to carry animal feedstuffs, grain, fertilisers and scrap metals. Gainsborough was a frequent battleground during the Civil War and George Eliot described it as St Ogg's in *The Mill on the Floss*.

West Stockwith From the river, West Stockwith, now a conservation area, presents a closed-in, almost intimate, aspect with its many tall three-storey buildings. It is possible to catch the occasional tantalising glimpse into the village up tiny passages, or ginnels, running between the houses. Once a thriving boat building community – there were five boatyards only 100 years ago – West Stockwith had a population of 5,000 in the 1880s; it is now reduced to 240. The brick-built church, looking more like a chapel capped with a squat bell tower, is one of only three of its kind and was completed in 1722. Inside, the plasterwork is classic Adam.

Owston Ferry The conical tower of an old windmill on the left bank has been restored as part of a spacious new dwelling on a fairly grand scale – even to the point of having a helipad sited on an adjacent

field. This feature, very much of the 21st century, contrasts strongly with the mellow buildings of Owston Ferry directly ahead. As the channel swings to the right, the pleasing scale of the riverside houses becomes apparent. Skilfully constructed using local brick and tile, they are both solid and graceful in appearance. There is something reminiscent of a Dutch painting in the views over the river seen from the lower part of the village. At Robin Hood's Well to the northwest, Roman coins have been found, indicating that this is a settlement of some antiquity.

West Butterwick This is another village with a strong Dutch influence evident in the local buildings. It has an attractive church built in 1841 from creamy white brick, deceptively stone-like from a distance. It follows the Gothic style, and has a small octagonal spire together with period interior fittings. In contrast, East Butterwick is a plain place with a small church built in 1884 at a cost of £500. It was once described as being 'surrounded by root crops and often by fog'.

Althorpe The church nestles in amongst the houses. Dedicated to St Oswald, it owes its origins to Sir John Nevill whose 1483 tower and chancel are incorporated into a larger structure.

THE NAVIGATION

Below Littleborough is a beautiful reach with steep wooded hills rising from the water's edge on the Lincolnshire side. The attractive brick and stone building set in the parkland is Burton Château. Heading towards Gainsborough, the cooling towers of West Burton Power Station stand out prominently in the flat landscape on the west side of the river.

The river moves away from the wooded slopes, passes the power station (the northernmost on the river) and heads for Gainsborough, which is clearly indicated by a group of tall flour mills. Below the railway bridge, the river bends sharply before reaching these mills, the bridge at Gainsborough and the desolate wharfs. With the completion of the new flood defences, much of this area has been changed into an attractive riverside walk with an imaginatively landscaped area just below Gainsborough Arches. The town is set entirely on one side of the river and was once a centre for heavy engineering and home to Marshall Tractors, manufacturers of the famous traction engines and the firm where L. T. C. Rolt (see page 270) carried out his apprenticeship.

On leaving Gainsborough the navigation bends sharply to the left, passing Morton Wharf with its Flemish gables, and winds its way past the hamlet of Walkerith towards West Stockwith. Immediately after the sharp right-hand bend in the river the entrance lock into the Chesterfield Canal (see page 198) is visible on the left. While just downstream from the basin the River Idle, barricaded in by steel flood doors, joins the Trent beside West Stockwith's unusual 18th-century Georgian church. This was once the main highway from the industrial areas of South Yorkshire, terminating at a large wharf in Bawtry. Goods travelled to and from the town by horse and cart and, before the development of the River Don as a reliable navigation, were dependent upon the River Idle for onward transport. In draining the Isle of

Axholme in the 17th century, Cornelius Vermuyden modified the course of the Idle and drastically reduced its effectiveness as a navigable waterway.

On leaving West Stockwith, the Trent follows a comparatively straight course passing the isolated hamlets of Gunthorpe and Wildsworth, barely visible to the boater hidden as they are below the river's flood banks. All this area bordering the river was, in AD 886, part of the Danelaw, and place names with 'by' and 'thorpe' endings are of Viking derivation. A sense of isolation and independence persists into the 21st century from a time when the Wash, the Trent and the Humber effectively cut this area off from the remainder of the country. In those times the inhabitants identified more with Denmark, Holland and the sea than with the rest of England.

Flowing northwards the river regains its isolation amidst the flat, fertile countryside behind the flood banks. Throughout history this area has been known as the Isle of Axholme – a remote yet fertile area of land.

The twin villages of East and West Butterwick now come into view, facing each other across the river. As seems so often to be the case on the lower part of the Trent, the village to the west is larger than its eastern counterpart.

Now the river begins to broaden out, passing under the M180 viaduct, built in 1978, and rising out of the flat countryside to clear the navigation. To the north two further villages sit opposite one another – hiding behind flood embankments – before Keadby is reached. These are Burringham to the east, with its early Victorian brick and slate church squatting beside the river, and Althorpe to the west.

Less than a mile downstream of these villages is the combined road and rail bridge, built in 1916, which

was the only bridge into the Isle of Axholme before the construction of the motorway viaduct. A further half mile below this bridge, on the left, is Keadby Lock leading into the Stainforth & Keadby section of the South Yorkshire Navigations.

The final section of the river plays host to serious continental shipping and is punctuated by a series of bustling wharves. Coasters come and go with the tides carrying steel, coal and fertilisers while the constant activity of cranes on the busy jetties warms the heart of the true waterways enthusiast. It is perhaps not insignificant that the wharves are all in private ownership and, although relatively modest, they are nonetheless efficient and clearly most cost-effective enterprises.

Now the steep wooded hills that have followed close to the east bank of the river start to peel away as the mouth of the Trent and its junction with the Ouse (to form the Humber) is approached. Large areas of low-lying ground – part mud flat, part rough grazing – accompany the waterway to its conclusion, only to be dwarfed by the vast acreage of water that is the confluence of these two great rivers. There is a lonely eeriness about so much water with only the village of Alkborough in the distance to suggest human habitation.

Warehouse in Newark

The Anderton Boat Lift in Cheshire is one of the most fascinating individual features of the canal system. This amazing and enormous piece of machinery built in 1875 by Edward Leader Williams (later becoming engineer for the Manchester Ship Canal) to connect the Trent & Mersey with the flourishing Weaver Navigation, 50ft below. As built, the lift consisted of two water-filled tanks counter-balancing each other in a vertical slide, resting on massive hydraulic rams. It worked on the very straightforward principle that making the ascending tank slightly lighter – by pumping a little water out – would assist the hydraulic rams (which were operated by a steam engine and pump) in moving both tanks, with boats in them, up or down their respective slide.

In 1908 the lift had to have major repairs, so it was modernised at the same time. The troublesome hydraulic rams were done away with; from then on each tank – which contained 250 tons of water – had its own counterweights and was independent of the other tank. Electricity replaced steam as the motive power.

However, neglect as the waterways system declined and the ravages of time took their toll, meant that by the end of the 1980s the structure was once again deemed to be unsafe. For many years it seemed that it would quietly be forgotten, so great was the size of the estimate given for return to safe working order. However, times change and the value of our heritage gradually became apparent. What was once considered to be a liability and not worth repair, was suddenly perceived to be a tourist attraction, something to draw curious onlookers, something that will make money.

It draws thousands of sightseers every year now that the restoration to full working order has been completed, following the original 1875 hydraulic design, using oil as the motive force rather than the chemically contaminated water that was the cause of the 1908 failure. The more

The Anderton Boat Lift viewed from the River Weaver

recent counter-balance weights, together with their ungainly supporting structure, have been retained, alongside, in order to demonstrate the engineering development of the lift.

The concept of raising craft vertically, from one level of the waterway to another, is by no means new and there are several well-known boat lifts earning their keep on the European waterways.

The Anderton Boat Lift viewed from the Trent & Mersey Canal

MAMMALS

Badger Badgers are easily recognised by their black-and-white facial stripes. They are common, but unobtrusive and their largely nocturnal habits make them easy to overlook. With care, badgers can be easily watched emerging from their underground setts at dusk. Badgers are very fond of peanuts but slugs and earthworms are important in their natural diet.

Badger

Brown hare The Brown Hare was formerly widespread and common, but has declined in many areas, in part due to persecution but also because of changes in land use. They are larger and longer legged, with longer, black-tipped ears than a rabbit. The males chase and box one another in spring.

Brown hare

Daubenton's bat

tunnel entrances. In winter, they hibernate in caves, mines and cellars. Widespread and fairly common in Britain.

Fox Common but previously wary of man given the history of persecution of this species. Many people, particularly urban-dwellers are finding

Daubenton's bat A medium-sized bat with comparatively short ears. It is frequently associated with water and seen flying low over lakes, ponds and canals just as dusk is falling. Daubenton's bat also feeds along woodland rides. The chirps can be heard by those with good hearing. In summer, they roost, sometimes in colonies, in hollow trees and

Fox

them increasingly bold. Foxes have colonised towns and cities in recent years, as their natural habitats are built upon and we leave take-away offerings and other food detritus on the streets. Foxes are easily recognised by their dog-like appearance, the orange-red fur and bushy, white-tipped tail. They give birth and spend much of the daytime in underground 'earths'.

Harvest mouse This mouse is Britain's smallest rodent. It has orange-brown fur and is mainly nocturnal. Its presence is usually indicated by tennis ball-sized nests of woven grasses constructed among plant stems. The prehensile tail is almost as long as its body and is used when climbing among plant stems.

Harvest mouse

Mink American Mink are an unwelcome alien which have become established after escaping from fur farms during the past few decades and are now established throughout the UK. The dark brown fur makes confusion with the otter possible, but the mink's smaller size, slimmer build and proportionally shorter tail help distinguish it. The American mink usually has white patches on its chin and throat, and small amounts of white fur may be present on the upper lip. It is invariably associated with water, particularly rivers, canals and lakes, where it feeds on water birds, fish and waterside small mammals – it poses significant threat to water vole populations.

Mink

Otter Superbly adapted to an amphibious lifestyle, their dives may last for several minutes. Otters feed mainly on fish. Persecution from fishing interests, hunting and habitat destruction have caused a serious decline in numbers, but otters are increasingly seen.

Otter

Water vole A charming waterside mammal, now rather scarce, in part due to habitat loss and predation by mink. Often rather confiding but will dive into the water if danger threatens. These voles swim well, both on the surface and underwater. Their burrow complex usually has at least one submerged entrance.

Water vole

WALES

The topography of Wales does little to lend itself to the building of artificial navigations or, indeed, to the canalization of existing waterways. However, those same hills that produce such gushing torrents of fluvial excess, at the merest hint of a drop of rain, also cloak a rich range of minerals upon which the fruits of the Principality's contribution to the Industrial Revolution were largely founded. Working from north to south, a look at what is today known as the Llangollen Canal will show (from its uncharacteristic west–east current) that it fulfils the dual role of water supply – both for the thirsty inhabitants of Cheshire and to top up the Shropshire Union Canal – and of a navigation, which once conveyed the output from Welsh coalfields and ironworks. Today it is a magnet for boaters and walkers and attracts more craft than any other waterway, leading to motorway-style tailbacks and a concomitantly slow passage. Nevertheless it traverses some stunning terrain, with unrivalled views and launches itself into space on aqueducts that have no waterway equal.

In mid-Wales there is a particular dearth of navigable waterways which somewhat belies the number of schemes, all stillborn, for their promotion and intended construction. Milestone 9 hints at one such project that partially saw the light of day. Much of the problem lies in the lack of realistic cargoes to carry and an overall shortage of markets to transport them to! Many truly rural waterways failed to make a profit or pay a dividend to their shareholders due, in greater or lesser part, to the impracticalities of transporting light, bulky loads of agricultural produce such as hay and straw: contemporary engravings depict narrowboat steerers, elevated on all manner of contraptions, in an attempt to see over what amounted to a floating hay stack.

Ellesmere on the Llangollen Canal

The south of the Principality contained large deposits of valuable minerals including lead, iron ore and of course coal. However, canal construction now pitted the ingenuity of man against the terrain and brought into play the equation of expenditure versus return on capital. As in other hilly, mineral terrain a compromise was soon arrived at

White Hart Bridge, Talybont-on-Usk

With the expansion of the collieries in the Tawe Valley, the growth of the Ynysgedwyn Iron works, increased copper smelting, improvements to Swansea harbour and the lack of a turnpike road, the demand for a canal in this area became irresistible and work commenced in 1794. Completed some 50 years before railways invaded the Welsh valleys, the Swansea Canal was another comparatively short-lived navigation which but for its role as a water channel, might have totally faded into oblivion. Today some 5½ miles are navigable, winding its way through some splendid scenery.

with waterways constructed wherever possible in valley bottoms fed by tramways leading down from the higher ground. Under this configuration, gravity – and the tendency of any mass, be it water or minerals, to head for the lowest point – became a positive help rather than a lock-constructing hindrance and the best of both worlds was achieved. The Mons & Brecs Canal (to use common canal parlance) which is in fact a combination of the Brecon & Abergavenny Canal and the more southerly Monmouthshire Canal system, was met along its route at several transhipment points by tramways, descending from hillside mines and quarries. Branches of the latter canal lead directly into the South Wales coalfield and the cargoes of both waterways found their way into the docks at Newport for onward shipment, largely via coasters plying to ports around the British coastline. As was often the case before our joined up

waterway system was constructed (and to some extent the subsequent rail system) it was often quicker and cheaper to transport cargoes such as coal several hundred miles by sea, rather than a few dozen miles by land. A classic example, prevalent before the completion of the Grand Cross, was of London's coal supplies coming almost exclusively by sea from Newcastle, rather from more local pits in, say, neighbouring Kent.

The Welsh Valleys, joined in the north and open to the sea in the south, invite access by water: albeit water that is making serious attempts to find the sea, owing to the overall topography of the area. However, the Neath & Tennant Canals – fed by numerous branches and tramways – both make successful attempts to overthrow this general pattern and once provided a way out for the vast reserves of coal mined in this region.

Lower Lock, Cwmcrawnon

MONMOUTHSHIRE & BRECON CANAL

Able only to accommodate a diminutive 55ft craft – rather than the more usual 72ft narrowboat – the Mons & Brecs (as it is affectionately known) appears as little more than an oversized ditch, clinging precariously to one hillside after another: but oh, what a spectacular ditch it turns out to be! In its relatively short length it embraces eleven significant aqueducts, two tunnels, a plethora of locks and charming stone bridges, together with spectacular mountain scenery to rival its Scottish and North Wales cousins.

Theatre Basin, Brecon

ABERGAVENNY

CWMBRAN

PONTYPOOL

NEWPORT

ABERCARN

BRECON

RISCA

N

BACKGROUND

In 1792 the Act of Authorisation for the Monmouthshire Canal was passed. This gave permission for a canal to be cut from the estuary of the River Usk at Newport to Pontnewynydd, north of Pontypool. In addition to this Main Line, there was to be an 11-mile branch from Malpas to Crumlin. Thomas Dadford Junior was appointed engineer, and the canal was opened in 1796. When the Act for the Brecknock & Abergavenny Canal was passed in 1793, the canal was planned to connect Brecon with the River Usk near Caerleon, but the directors of the Monmouthshire Canal persuaded the promoters to alter their plans to include a junction with their own canal. And so the Brecknock & Abergavenny Canal, with Thomas

Goytre Wharf Heritage, Activity & Study Centre

CRUMLIN RAILWAY VIADUCT

The Crumlin Arm of the Monmouthshire section of the canal appears in substance at Pontywaun. With steep wooded hills rising to the north, and the conurbation of Crosskeys to the south, in the valley of the Afon Ebwy, its setting is quite dramatic. Not as dramatic, however, as the Crumlin Railway Viaduct which, until 1966, crossed the valley, at a height of 208ft and with a span of 1,658ft. Designed by T.W. Kennard, it was the longest and highest railway bridge in Britain and the third highest in the world. An exciting scene from the film *Arabesque*, starring Sophia Loren and Gregory Peck, was shot on the viaduct in 1965, a year after the last scheduled passenger train had crossed. But although the Ministry of Housing and Local Government recognised its international significance, British Railways did not and, after having stood for 109 years, it was demolished and sold as scrap.

Dadford Junior again as engineer, was cut from Brecon to Pontymoile Basin, where it joined the Monmouthshire Canal. The Brecknock & Abergavenny Canal was fully opened in 1799. For a while the two canals were profitable, because the iron and coal cargoes justified the use of both canal and tramway. However, the greater speed and efficiency of the railways soon became apparent, and by the 1850s there were several schemes to abandon the canal. In 1865 the Monmouthshire bought the Brecknock & Abergavenny Canal

Company, but already it was too late for this to be effective. Bit by bit the original Monmouthshire Canal was closed, but the Brecon line was kept open as a water channel. In 1962 the network was formally abandoned, and parts were filled in. In 1964 the slow task of restoration was begun, and boats were once more able to cruise from Pontymoile to Talybont. The present limit of navigation is Five Locks, although plans to extend south to Newport and Pontywaun to reclaim the Monmouthshire Canal are now coming to fruition.

View looking up the flight of Foxton Locks from below, Herbert Dunkley's motorboat Prince *can be seen (1974)*

it was closed completely and the machinery sold for scrap. Today it is the subject of a vigorous restoration campaign, although with the locks at Watford Gap still only able to accommodate a narrowboat, there remains no inland waterways link between the north and south of the country for wide beamed boats.

The Foxton lock flight, built in 1810 on what was later to become known as the Leicester Arm of the Grand Union Canal, is comprised of ten chambers, in two groups of five staircase locks (*see* Milepost 4) with a passing pound in the middle. The locks, which negotiate a steep escarpment, have side pounds (sometimes called 'ponds') to help conserve the water which is in such short supply on the 20-mile summit pound of this navigation.

it off the other, thereby either raising or lowering the tanks. Each caisson was full of water and, with or without a boat, weighed in at 230 tons. The total rise of the lift was 75ft 2in and it was constructed on a gradient of 1 in 4.

In use, boats were simply floated into the upper or lower tank which was then sealed with a guillotine gate. The operator signalled the engine room, with the equivalent of a ship's telegraph and drive from the steam engine was engaged. On arrival at the bottom, the descending tank sunk gracefully into the lower section of the canal, the gate was raised and the boat(s) sailed out. To compensate for the reduction in weight of the lower tank, as it became immersed in water at the end of its travel, the upper tank simultaneously met a reduction in the gradient and, by an ingenious set of devices, matched up to the iron channel at the top of the lift, whilst still remaining horizontal.

The waterway's engineer at this time was Gordon Cale Thomas and the inclined plane was his idea and his design. It was built by W. H. Gwynne of Hammersmith, London and was opened on

10 June 1900. As with the Falkirk Wheel today (*see* Milepost 23) it immediately became a tourist attraction and a focus for boat trips: a popular draw for Sunday school outings and their ilk.

However, the promised extra FMC traffic never really materialized, largely due to the one bottleneck that remained on the navigation, namely Watford Gap Locks (at the other end of the summit pound) which were never widened. This meant that all through traffic was confined to narrowboats, even when FMC moved from horse to steam power, allowing 24 hour, non-stop 'fly' operation. The lift was not generally used at night so the lock flight crept back into use and the inclined plane was mothballed in 1911 to save money. This would, in part, have been motivated by the structure's heavy maintenance costs and the need, after more than ten years continuous operation, for substantial overhaul. It also required at least three operators.

The inclined plane was maintained for a few years but allowed to sink into decline as the locks gradually returned to full use. Eventually, in 1928,

WORKING FOXTON LOCKS

As with all locks, water flow to and from the lock chamber is controlled by paddles, which are in effect large taps, letting water in and out as required (*see* diagrams in the Glossary). Water moves from the waterway above the lock into the chamber for it to fill, or from the chamber into the waterway below when it is emptied, via culverts, which are in effect large pipes, usually built of masonry. A past lock keeper on the Foxton Flight chose to paint the paddles used to fill these locks red, and the ones to empty them white, in order that he could better describe lock operation to the boaters he was assisting. He was, therefore, able to explain things thus: 'Red afore white and you'll be alright, white afore red and you'll wish you were dead!' Get the sequence wrong and you risk making yourself very unpopular by flooding the pub below!

LLANGOLLEN CANAL

Fulfilling the dual roles of drinking water supply (to the good people of Cheshire) and navigable waterway, the Llangollen Canal winds its way through some spectacular scenery. Ranged along its 46 mile length are two notable aqueducts (both now contained within the boundaries of a World Heritage Site) a staircase lock flight and as much peace and quiet as even the most solitary individual could desire. No major towns are encountered, yet this is undoubtedly one of – if not the – most popular waterways in the country, drawing a host of walkers, boaters and gongoozlers throughout the year.

Boats outside Beech House, Ellesmere

LLANGOLLEN   CEFN-MAWR   HURLESTON JUNCTION   NANTWICH   WHITCHURCH

N

BACKGROUND

In 1791 a plan was published for a canal from the Mersey to the Severn, to pass through Chester, and the iron and coal fields around Ruabon, Ellesmere and Shrewsbury. There were to be branches to the limestone quarries at Llanymynech, and to the Chester Canal via Whitchurch. The new terminus on the Mersey was to be at the little fishing village of Netherpool, known after 1796 as Ellesmere Port.

After extensive arguments about routes, the company received its Act in 1793. William Jessop was appointed engineer and work began.

By 1796 the Wirral line from Chester to Ellesmere Port was open, and was immediately successful, carrying goods and passengers (in express fly boats) to Liverpool. The same year, the Llanymynech

Branch was completed. The company continued to expand and build inwards, but failed to make the vital connections with the Dee and the Severn; the line south to Shrewsbury never got further than Weston, and the line northwards to Chester stopped at Pontcysyllte.

By 1806 the Ellesmere Company had opened 68 miles of canal, which included lines from Hurleston on the Chester Canal to Plas Kynaston via Frankton, and from Chester to Ellesmere Port; there were branches to Llanymynech, Whitchurch, Prees and Ellesmere, and a navigable feeder to Llangollen; the two great aqueducts at Chirk and Pontcysyllte were complete. However, it was a totally self-contained system, its only outlet being via the old Chester Canal at Hurleston. Despite this, the Ellesmere Canal was profitable; it serviced a widespread local network, and gave an outlet to Liverpool (via the River Mersey) for the ironworks and the coalfields that were grouped at the centre of the system. This profitability was dependent upon good relations with the Chester Canal Company. An attempted take over in 1804 failed, but in 1813 the inevitable merger took place, and the Ellesmere & Chester Canal Company was formed.

Today the Llangollen Canal – the name that now embraces the network detailed above – is quite justly one of the most popular canals in the country, with fascinating architecture, spectacular aqueducts and splendid scenery. It is a magnet to boaters and walkers alike and the Pontcysyllte Aqueduct has been declared a World Heritage Site. Many sections of the waterway are formed as side cuttings, following a contour across sloping ground. As such the canal is vulnerable to breaching, especially at times of high rainfall and spectacular (and very expensive) inundations of the local countryside do occur from time to time.

Lift Bridge at Wrenbury

THE NAVIGATION

The Llangollen Canal rapidly establishes its character as one of the most popular cruising waterways in the country. It is generally remote and pretty, with spectacular scenery further west. Leaving Hurleston Junction, the canal immediately climbs the four tidy Hurleston Locks before running through a very shallow valley to reach Swanley Locks. A few houses, some with attractive canalside gardens, are passed before the canal enters flat, rich farmland. The next three locks encountered are at Baddiley, within sight of Baddiley Hall – a tall Georgian house surrounded by trees.

The canal passes Wrenbury Hall and soon the first of many delightful lift bridges is encountered. Their scale seems entirely sympathetic with that of

the canal and, whilst most are generally left open, those that require operation provide added interest for the boater. Wrenbury Wharf is a splendid place where there is a fine restored warehouse converted into a pub, a former mill now occupied by a boatyard, and another pub, all grouped around the push-button lift bridge.

Beyond the wharf, the soft green Cheshire countryside leads to Marbury Lock: the village is a short walk to the south, along School Lane, and is well worth visiting. The tall obelisk visible to the southeast is in distant Combermere Park. Leaving Marbury the waterway again enters remote and peaceful countryside before reaching Quoisley Lock, where the road briefly intrudes, and then continues towards Willeymoor Lock.

The canal continues to rise through a series of isolated locks as the valley begins to close in. At the end of a straight stretch a massive railway embankment precedes a sharp bend to the bottom of the six locks at Grindley Brook: the first three locks are followed at the A41 bridge by three staircase locks. The canal now approaches Whitchurch where a lift bridge marks the entrance to the Whitchurch Arm. After passing

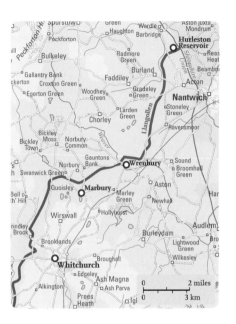

under the busy road bridge, and by the boatyard, the canal once again enters typically quiet and pretty countryside.

Chief engineer	William Jessop
Assisted by	Thomas Telford (Pontcysyllte Aqueduct)
Significance	Linked industries of North Wales and Cheshire with markets.
Started in	1793
Completed in	1805 (with the completion of Pontcysyllte Aqueduct)
Length	46 miles
Draught	2' 3"
Headroom	7'
Lock size	70' × 6' 10"
Number of locks	21
Tunnels	3
Aqueducts	3
Goods carried	Iron and coal. Also passenger fly boats.
Operating authority	Canal & River Trust
Contact details	enquiries. northwalesborders @canalrivertrust.org.uk

THE QUAY TO THE MARCHES

Prior to the building of the Montgomery Canal (see page 250) the River Severn was a natural artery for trade with the Welsh Marches, navigated above Shrewsbury as far as Pool Quay. Of course such river transport was unreliable, and low water levels would result in long delays. The beams in the Powis Arms (at Pool Quay) were marked for each day the boatmen were stranded for lack of water.

It was from Swan Wharf, opposite the pub, that Montgomeryshire oak was shipped downstream to the naval dockyards at Bristol. In 1712 the *Duchess*, owned by George Bradley, was transporting 40-ton loads to Bristol and back. Until the Montgomery & Ellesmere Canal linked with the main inland waterways network in 1833, Pool Quay remained an important transhipment point.

THE NAVIGATION

The canal now begins to traverse a very remote and underpopulated area, passing no villages for miles. At Platt Lane the navigation straightens out and is carried on an embankment across the uncharacteristically flat area of Whixall Moss. A solitary lift bridge interrupts the long straight followed by the junction with the Prees Branch, which leads to a marina and a nature reserve. The first bridge on the branch is a Grade II listed structure and has been restored.

The main line veers off to the north west along another straight embankment, this time accompanied by woodlands, crossing the border between England and Wales. While leaving Whixall Moss, the canal passes Bettisfield and begins to wind this way and that, passing into Wales and then out again.

Soon the open countryside gives way to the hilly wooded landscape that lies to the east of Ellesmere and contains several beautiful meres. The canal skirts first Cole Mere, which is below and mostly hidden from it by tall trees; there is a delightful

Detail of staircase locks at Grindley Brook

THE MONTGOMERY CANAL

The Montgomery Canal – which leaves the Llangollen Canal 3 miles west of Ellesmere – has much to offer walkers and boaters alike, with its rural charm and peacefulness. It is both rich in wildlife and in reminders of its industrial past. The villages dotted along the canal are mostly quiet and picturesque self-contained communities with pleasant country pubs, in which boaters and walkers can relax and explore.

The initial development of this canal was sparked by the publication of the plans for the Ellesmere Canal, which inspired a separate company to plan a canal from Newtown northwards to join the Llanymynech branch of the Ellesmere Canal at Carreghofa. The canal was authorised in 1793, and by 1797 the line was open from Carreghofa to Garthmyl. The Montgomery Canal was mainly agricultural; apart from transporting limestone, it existed to serve the farms and villages through which it passed, and so was never really profitable. The lack of capital and income greatly delayed the completion of the western extension to the River Severn at Newtown, which was not finally opened until 1821, having been financed by a separate company. So what eventually became known as the Montgomery Canal was in fact built by three separate companies over a period of 30 years.

The downfall of the canal became inevitable with the First World War when a pattern of regular and heavy losses started, from which the company was never able to recover. In 1921 the company gave up canal carrying and sold most of its boats to private operators. Locks began to close at weekends and standards of maintenance began to slip. The situation remained this way for many years, and with many road bridges lowered, it was thought that the waterway would fade away gracefully. But today the canal is dotted with restoration works, and considerable lengths are once again open to navigation.

timbered cottage at the west end. Then the navigation runs right beside Blake Mere: this is a charming little lake, surrounded by steep and thickly wooded hills. The canal enters the 87yd Ellesmere Tunnel and emerges into open parkland beyond. There are many oak trees alongside the canal around here – this is said to be the legacy of the Shropshire Union's policy of planting trees to provide the raw materials to replace their carrying fleet.

Leaving Blake Mere and the tunnel, Ellesmere is soon reached, and access is via a short arm. A fine old warehouse and a small canalside crane testify to the canal trading that used to be carried on from

here. The main line of the canal to Llangollen bears round sharply to the south west at the junction: the buildings here house the Canal & River Trust office and maintenance yard, with facilities for pleasure boats. Beech House was once the canal company's office.

Beyond the yard, the country once again becomes quiet and entirely rural, while the canal's course becomes very winding. At Frankton Junction the Montgomery Canal branches south towards Newtown: it is currently navigable to Gronwyn Wharf, just beyond Maesbry Marsh, and further restoration continues.

POINTS OF INTEREST

Hurleston Reservoir With a capacity of 85,000,000 gallons, Hurleston Reservoir receives its supply, via the Llangollen Canal, from the River Dee at Llantysilio. It is used both as drinking water, and as a supply for the Shropshire Union Canal.

Wrenbury A quiet village recorded in the Domesday Book as *Warenberie*. Two miles to the southeast are the remains of Combermere Abbey, established by Cistercian monks in 1133 who, in 1180, took the village church as a daughter chapel. By the church gates is the schoolmaster's cottage: this stood next door to one of the earliest parish schools in Cheshire, founded in 1605. There are some thatched magpie cottages around the green and, remarkably, the railway station still operates.

St Margaret's Church, Wrenbury Overlooking the village green, this large, battlemented 14th-century church is built from red Cheshire sandstone, with a late 15th-century west tower and an early 17th-century chancel and pulpit. The interior is very light and airy and contains a number of fine monuments. You will also notice the visible manifestation of an enduring dispute between two important local families: the Cottons of Combermere Abbey, and the Starkeys of Wrenbury Hall. They challenged each other's ownership of land and rights to church pews for over 400 years, to such an extent that an arbitrator, in 1748, allocated the south side of the church to the Cottons and the north to the Starkeys, in an effort to resolve matters. Next to the door is 'the dog-whipper's pew'. The job of the dog-whipper, later known as Beadle, was to throw out unruly dogs, and to keep dozing parishioners awake during particularly tedious sermons. The last holder of this esteemed position, Thomas Vaughan, died in 1879 and is buried by the door. Visible in the churchyard are some most unusual cast iron grave plaques, dating from the early 1800s. These were an example, in their time, of the very latest technology.

Decorative shelter beside the canal at Ellesmere

Marbury Centred on an ancient farm, this enchanting village boasts several other fine old and timbered buildings. Marbury Merry Days are held in May, and the village wakes (holidays) once featured dancing bears, and puddings.

St Michael's Church, Marbury This is a gem, and its setting is unrivalled: it stands on top of a small hill overlooking the beautiful Little Mere. The church was first mentioned in 1299: what remains today dates from the 15th century. When you walk around the building look out for the many gargoyles: monkeys and grotesque faces expressing both pleasure and pain. The pulpit is the second oldest in Cheshire and, dating from the 15th century, is in excellent condition. The grounds contain not just a graveyard but a charming garden: from here you will be able to see that the tower has developed an alarming tilt.

Whitchurch This is a fine town with some beautiful old houses of all periods in the centre. The streets are narrow and there is much to discover. It has its origins in Roman times as *Mediolanum*, 'the place in the middle of the plain', a stop on the route from Chester to Wroxeter. It was recorded in the Domesday Book as *Westune*, but was later to become White Church, or Whitchurch, for obvious reasons. There are lots of splendid pubs in the town, but unfortunately none near the canal. J. B. Joyce & Co was established here in 1690, and continued to make very fine tower clocks until final closure in 2012. Sir Edward German was born in St Mary's Street in 1862 – he composed *Tom Jones* and *Merrie England*.

St Alkmund's Church, Whitchurch This striking church on the hill was built in 1713 by William and Richard Smith as the replacement for a late 14th-century building which 'fell ye 31 of July 1711'. This in turn had been built to succeed the Norman White Church which was attributed to William de Warren, one of William the Conqueror's lieutenants, who died in 1089. In 1862 the old pews were removed, and many human bones were found beneath them. These were re-buried and a new floor was laid. Under the porch is buried the heart of John Talbot, who was killed in 1453 at the Battle of Castille, the last of the Hundred Years Wars. He was Earl of Shrewsbury and a principal character in Shakespeare's *Henry VI*. The rector here in 1779 was Francis Henry Egerton, 8th and last Earl of Bridgewater and a successor to the 3rd Duke, who built the Bridgewater Canal. Those who know the Oxford Canal will recognise the present church's similarity to the magnificent church of the same vintage at Banbury. It has very large windows and a stunning interior. Indeed the whole church is on a grand scale and is well worth a visit.

THE NAVIGATION

The navigation continues to run west and north through quiet, green countryside, although there is a brief flurry of activity when a main road crosses at Maestermyn Bridge. Beyond Hindford Bridge the canal climbs through the two New Marton Locks – the last locks to be encountered on the way to Llangollen – which are set amidst open and wonderfully peaceful countryside, still with small fields. Gradually the land becomes hillier as Wat's Dyke and Henlle Park are passed. The hills and mountains of Wales are now approaching, set to replace the gentler scenery passed so far.

As Chirk Bank is reached, the approaching Welsh mountains drive the navigation into a side cutting half-way up the flank of a hill. The canal then rounds a corner and suddenly Chirk Aqueduct

Monks Bridge, Chirk Bank

appears – an impressive structure by any waterway enthusiast's standards, and accompanied by a very fine railway viaduct alongside. At the end of the aqueduct the canal immediately enters a tunnel.

A long wooded cutting follows, and then the railway reappears alongside. Another, shorter, tunnel at Whitehouses is negotiated before the canal meets the valley of the River Dee. Here the railway charges off to the north on a magnificent viaduct, while the canal clings to the hillside.

Now the scenery really is superb and the views over and along the valley of the River Dee are excellent. Passing the village of Froncysyllte, the canal launches out into this deep valley on a massive embankment, then crosses the River Dee on the breathtaking Pontcysyllte Aqueduct (see Milepost 11 page 147). At the north end of the aqueduct there is a fascinating short arm with a boatyard straight ahead, but to continue to Llangollen it is necessary to take the tricky left turn. The short arm towards Ruabon was originally projected as the canal's main line towards Chester and the Mersey, and the dry dock at Trevor Junction dates from this time. The line from Trevor to Llantysilio was envisaged purely as a navigable feeder. However the idea of a direct line to Chester was soon dropped and a connection made instead with the Chester Canal at Hurleston Junction. The canal, now generally quite narrow, continues in a westerly direction towards Llangollen, clinging spectacularly to the side of the valley above the Dee.

POINTS OF INTEREST

Whixall Moss A raised bog rich in flora and insect fauna – including mosquitoes! Like other meres and bogs in the area, Whixall Moss came into existence at the end of the Ice Age, as huge blocks of ice were left behind when the remainder of the ice cap melted and drained off into what is now the Severn valley. The peat surface remains, in spite of the past cutting of the peat for garden use, and is now a SSSI, and an important site for rare insect and plant life which survive on this delicate habitat.

Prees Branch Sometimes also known as the Edstaston Branch, this arm curved round to Quina Brook – it never did reach Prees. Its principal value in recent years lay in the clay pits just over a mile from the junction: the clay from here was used until a few years ago for repairing the 'puddle' in local canals. The arm had been disused for some years, but now the first 1/2 mile gives access to a marina constructed in the old pit. It is all very pleasant, and the canal arm has two lift bridges – one of which is a rare skewed example – and interesting plant communities exist along the unrestored section of the branch.

Ellesmere This handsome and busy 18th-century market town, with its narrow winding streets, is an attractive place to visit, with good access from the canal basin. There are many tall red-brick houses and several terraces of old cottages. It takes its name from the large and beautiful mere beside it.

St Mary's Church, Ellesmere Standing on a hill overlooking the mere, the general appearance of this large red-stone church is Victorian, belying its medieval origins. It contains a medieval chest hewn out of a solid block of oak, many fine effigies and a beautiful 15th-century font.

Chirk Aqueduct Opened in 1801, this is a splendidly massive brick and stone aqueduct

Chirk Aqueduct

carrying the canal in a narrow cast iron trough from England into Wales. The River Ceiriog flows 70ft below, and the great railway viaduct is beside and a little higher than the aqueduct.

Chirk Once a mining village, Chirk is now a residential area for Wrexham. Set on the top of a hill overlooking the border between England and Wales, the town has many buildings of historical interest. The town became a staging post on the London to Holyhead mail road, but now the building of the bypass has thankfully removed the traffic which once clogged the main street.

Chirk Castle An excellent example of a Marcher castle of Edward I's reign, completed in 1310, and inhabited by Roger Mortimer who had a hand in the demise of the last native Prince of Wales, Llywelyn. In 1595 the estate was bought by Sir Thomas Myddelton. The family apartments, state rooms, servants' quarters and dungeons can all be visited. There are also beautiful gardens, and a picturesque hawk house.

Chirk and Whitehouses Tunnels Neither of these tunnels is wide enough for two boats to pass, although each tunnel has a towpath running through it. Chirk Tunnel is 459yds long. Whitehouses Tunnel is 191yds long.

THE NAVIGATION

Boats clustered at Ellesmere

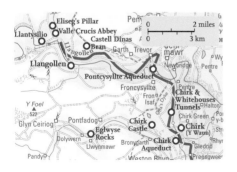

This is another stretch of very great beauty, with the waterway's route through Llangollen being made in an often very narrow channel on the side of tree-covered mountains, with views down into the Vale of Llangollen. The canal passes high above the town, flowing through picturesque white bridges and passing the backs of charming and modestly eccentric houses. But it doesn't stop there: the tiny channel continues beyond the new mooring basin as a feeder to weave up the valley to Llantysilio, passing a country hotel and a chain bridge over the nearby River Dee, while steam trains on the restored railway complete an utterly charming scene. At Horseshoe Falls a large semicircular weir across the Dee, built by Telford, provides the water which is constantly passed into the canal. Then it flows past Llangollen and the aqueducts, right back down to Hurleston Reservoir – to the tune of 12 million gallons a day.

POINTS OF INTEREST

Llangollen Founded in the 7th century by St Collen, the town has become established as one of North Wales' major tourist venues, especially during July, when the International Musical Eisteddfod attracts performers and visitors from across the world. Its superb setting in the upper Dee Valley has made it a great centre for outdoor pursuits, including pony trekking, climbing, walking and canoeing. For the less energetic there are canal trips, steam railway rides, the wonderful house of Plas Newydd, and museums. Visitors to the surrounding hills can explore Castell Dinas Bran, Valle Crucius Abbey and Elisegs Pillar, as well as enjoying superb walks. It was the construction of Telford's A5 road from London to Holyhead in 1815 which firmly placed Llangollen on the tourist map, but another 60 years were to pass before the streets of the town were to exchange their earthen surface for stone, quarried from Trevor Rocks. The town was a staging post on a drover's road, the routes used to move livestock to the distant markets of eastern England. In 1854 George Borrow recorded a meeting with a massive pig being driven along the road near Llangollen in his book *Wild Wales*. He noted that it weighed 'eighteen score of pounds' and 'walked with considerable difficulty'. At this time a pig would change hands at between 18 and 20 shillings – 'dire was the screaming of the porkers, yet the purchaser invariably seemed to know how to manage his bargain'.

At the centre of the town is the parish church of St Collen, who was thought to be the first abbot of Valle Crucius Abbey. The 15th-century carved oak roof and stained glass window of St Collen are well worth seeing.

International Musical Eisteddfod, Llangollen
For one week every July the town attracts singers, dancers and musicians from all over the world, who perform both in organised concerts, and impromptu street events.

Church of St Collen, Llangollen This church was probably founded by St Collen, who was the first abbot of nearby Vale Crucis Abbey. The present building is of Norman origin, with many later additions and alterations. It has a beautifully carved oak roof, dating from the 15th century, and the stained glass window dedicated to St Collen

Boats near Wrenbury

The Canal & River Trust yard at Ellesmere

is worth locating. In the churchyard is the tomb of the Ladies of Llangollen (*see* Plas Newydd) and Mary Carryll, their maid.

Plas Newydd, Llangollen On the southern outskirts of town. From 1779–1831 it was the home of the eccentric Lady Eleanor Butler and Miss Sarah Ponsonby, 'the two most celebrated virgins in Europe'. Their visitors, who included Browning, Tennyson, Walter Scott and Wordsworth, presented them with antique curios, which are now on display in the elaborately panelled rooms.

POINTS OF INTEREST

THE LLANGOLLEN RAILWAY

The original Llangollen station was called Whitehurst Halt, and was situated close to Froncysyllte – the village at the foot of Pontcysyllte Aqueduct (*see* page 147) – from where the hotels in the town ran a taxi service to fetch the visitors. The building of the line was completed in 1862 after many delays, since the work, supervised by the chief engineer Henry Robertson, took much longer than anticipated. Vast numbers of navvies were employed, but in spite of them working on Sundays (to the disgust of the locals), the bad winter of 1860–1 brought their work to a halt. The first passenger train finally arrived on 2 June 1862. The line was later extended to Corwen, when the present station was opened in 1865, and subsequently as far as Dolgellau. Soon trips to the coast at Barmouth were to become very popular amongst the locals. The line closed to passenger traffic in 1965, and to goods in 1968, and the station and tracks were left to fall into a ruinous state. Fortunately local enthusiasts came to its rescue, and they now operate steam and heritage diesel trains to Carrog on over 8 miles of track in the direction of Corwen. They also operate a canal/rail service, special dining trains and a vintage bus service.

Castell Dinas Bran, Llangollen 'Crow City' in English but usually known as Crow Castle, the ruins of the castle built for Eliseg, Prince of Powys, can be seen from the waterway while approaching the town, and stand on a 1,100ft mountain accessible to energetic walkers from various points along the canal, including bridge 45. A prince known as Bran is thought to have built the original fortification on this site, following a dispute with his brother Beli. Their mother was Corwena, who lived near what is now Corwen. The castle is thought to have had links with the legendary Holy Grail. The visible remains date from the late 13th century, and were built by the Princes of Powys.

Eliseg's Pillar, Llangollen Erected in the 18th century to commemorate Eliseg, who built the fortress on the top of Dinas Bran.

Eglwyseg Rocks, Llangollen To the northeast of the town, this is an impressive and brilliantly white escarpment of carboniferous limestone laid down some 400 million years ago, when this area was covered by the sea. It is now very popular with fossil hunters.

Valle Crucis Abbey, Llangollen Finely preserved ruins of the Cistercian abbey founded in 1201 by Madoc, Prince of Powys, and rebuilt in more lavish style after a fire in 1250. The abbey fell into neglect following the dissolution of the monasteries in 1539. Its finest feature is the vaulted chapter house and screened library cupboard. There is also the only surviving monastic fish pond to be seen in Wales.

Llantysilio The village overlooks Horseshoe Falls. Parts of the interior of the church are taken from the nearby Valle Crucis Abbey.

Horseshoe Falls on the River Dee

The Macclesfield Canal, on its course between the Trent & Mersey and the Peak Forest Canal, adheres to a mainly level course, with all the locks (aside from the stop lock at Hall Green) in a single, delightful group at Bosley. Had the visionary scheme proposed by J. F. Pownall, in his work *The Projected Grand Contour Canal to Connect with Estuaries and Canals in England* (1942), come to fruition, the Macclesfield would have formed a part of his grand plan.

He observed that: 'Through the heart of England there runs a natural canal line, as I shall term it. This is a line so naturally favourable for canal construction that a canal can follow it easily for miles at a time whilst remaining throughout at the same level. The old canal surveyors saw this line. . .. A canal following this contour would therefore proceed right through the country solely on one level. . . it [also] proceeds in direct reaches for long-distances at a time. . .. The natural canal line creates the remarkable possibility, never before known, of having a canal go through the length of the country and serve the great industrial areas without any variation from one level.

'[There] are very great advantages. The Grand Contour Canal [would be] uniformly level at 310ft above sea level to serve London, Bristol, Southampton, Birmingham, Manchester, Leeds and Newcastle. All the existing canals would be branches from it. The waterway would be large enough to accommodate coastal vessels of a fair size. The Grand Contour Canal would become the primary water distributor of the country. Along the canal there will be formed a special layer in the bed. . . in this layer pipelines for the transport of commercial liquids and gases would be embedded.

'Precisely because it expresses a natural feature, the Contour Canal will lie unobtrusively on the land and will have a characteristic scenery of its own.'

Precisely.

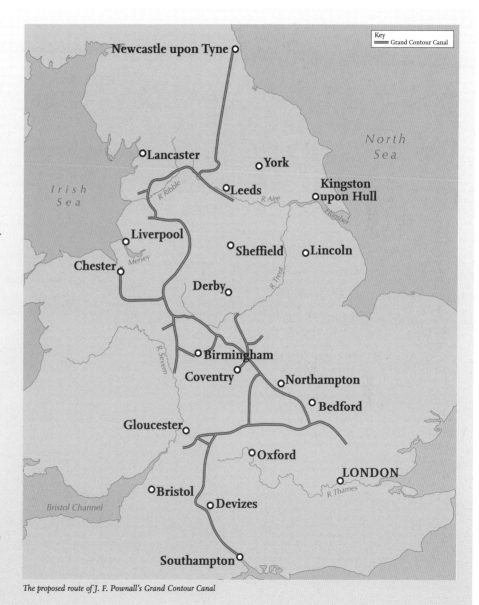

The proposed route of J. F. Pownall's Grand Contour Canal

PLANTS

Bluebell

Cross-leaved heath

Cross-leaved heath A widespread downy, grey-green undershrub. It favours damp, acid soils, typical of boggy margins on heaths and moors. The narrow leaves are in whorls of four along the stems. Pink flowers are borne in terminal clusters between June and October.

Bluebell A familiar bulbous perennial, often carpeting whole woodland floors if the situation suits its requirements. The leaves are narrow and all basal. Bell-shaped flowers in one-sided spikes appear from April to June.

Buddleia This is a plant beloved by butterflies and bees, a common garden shrub and also widely naturalised on wasteground and around the coast. It has long, narrow leaves which are darker above than below. The showy, often drooping spikes of purple flowers appear from June to September.

Buddleia

Devil's-bit scabious

Devil's-bit scabious An erect perennial of damp grassland, woodland rides and marshes. The short, thick rhizome has an abruptly cut-off end – bitten off by the devil! The basal leaves are spoon shaped, in a rosette; the narrow stem leaves in opposite pairs, the upper ones narrow. Blue-purple flowers (rarely pink or white) are borne in rounded heads, and appear June to October. This plant is the food plant of the declining Marsh Fritillary butterfly. The word 'scabious' derives from the former herbal use of this and related plants to cure scabies and other unpleasant skin complaints. The look alike Field and Small Scabious have lilac flowers.

Early Marsh-orchid Found in damp meadows, often on calcareous soils but also acid conditions. The leaves are unmarked, yellowish green and narrow-lanceolate. The flowers are usually flesh-pink but can range from almost white to purple. The three-lobed flower lip is strongly reflexed along the mid-line. Flowers are borne on open spikes, May to June.

Floating pennywort

Floating pennywort A highly invasive North American plant introduced to this country via aquatic nurseries. After accidental 'escape' from garden ponds its existence has been reported in many sites in southern England and Wales. The potential of this plant to wreak havoc should not be underestimated. Floating pennywort roots in shallow slow-flowing water and forms dense mats of vegetation on the water's surface. Allowed to establish it will take over, out-competing most native aquatic plants, causing deoxygenation of the water and harming fish and invertebrates. It will choke drainage systems and sluices, and sometimes cause flooding. It is difficult to control because of its rapid growth rate – up to 8 inches in a day – and because it re-grows from the smallest fragment.

Grey willow Also know as Grey sallow, this tree is named for the ash-coloured hairs which densely cover the young twigs and the underside of the broad oval leaves. The leaves develop inrolled margins with age. It is common to wet habitats and forms a broad crown in mature specimens. The catkins appear before the leaves, in March and April.

Grey willow

Guelder rose A large shrub, or small tree. Found in hedgerows and fairly common except in the north. The leaves are divided into five, irregularly-toothed lobes. Flowers appear between June and July in flat topped heads, the inner ones much smaller than the outer ones. The berries are red.

Guelder rose

Early Marsh-orchid

SCOTLAND

The country of Scotland is blessed with large tracts of spectacular mountain country and some of the most scenic waterways in Britain. Scotland is divided between Lowlands and Highlands. The Highland Boundary Fault runs roughly from Isle of Arran in the southwest to Stonehaven in the northeast. To its north lie the Highlands, including the Grampian and Cairngorm Mountains, and all the land and islands north and west of Inverness, The Highlands itself is split in two by the valley of the Great Glen and its bodies of freshwater, Loch Lochy, Loch Oich and Loch Ness, that separate the Grampians from the Northwest Highlands.

If the topography of the relatively compact principality of Wales provided the canal builder with significant obstacles to his progress, then Scotland is surely in a different league altogether! So too were its needs when it came to an analysis of the reasoning underpinning any development of a waterway system as it is, after all, a relatively long, thin country surrounded on three sides by less than benign seas. However, it was also those very same seas that provided much of its wealth in the form of fish – and a fishing fleet needed to be able to move swiftly if it was to keep pace with the migratory drive of its prey.

So Scottish navigations developed as much to connect the east and west coasts for deep drafted fishing boats, as to provide a conduit for the export of manufactured goods, or the import of raw materials. Exceptions to this loose rule are largely centred around Glasgow in the form of the Monkland Canal and the Glasgow, Paisley & Johnstone Canal, both now long defunct. The former navigation ran 12$\frac{1}{4}$ miles due west from a rich coal seam at Woodhall joining the Forth & Clyde Canal at Port Dundas, immediately to the north of Glasgow city centre. As well as carrying heavy and sustained coal traffic well into the 1930s – even in the face of the usual, stiff railway competition – it acted as a feeder, supplying water to the Forth & Clyde Canal. Today some evidence of this once important navigation can still be found, although much of its length disappeared under the M8 motorway.

The Glasgow, Paisley & Johnstone Canal is of a somewhat different ilk: it was constructed with a view to providing the port of Glasgow with a reliable connection to the sea, in an era when the River Clyde was shallow and prone to regular silting. This was at a time before regular dredging and the building of dykes and training walls had taken place. The promoters envisaged a navigation along the river's south bank from Port Eglinton, in Glasgow, to a new harbour at Ardrossan on the Scottish west coast. An initial 11 miles were built – including two tunnels but with no locks – connecting Paisley with Port Eglinton but by then the Clyde Port Authority had set in train a comprehensive programme of measures to increase the draught throughout the river's navigable length.

The outcome of this increased depth is legend as there can be very few inhabitants of these isles who are not aware of the Clyde's rich legacy of shipbuilding; of heavy engineering and as a major port, shipping the fruits of the area's immense endeavour to all corners of the globe. As the regeneration of Glasgow has been implemented, what little that remained of this heavy industry has moved away from the banks of the Clyde. Now the empty quays are being populated with luxury apartments, shopping centres and light industry.

To the east of the country lie the Firth of Forth and the River Tay together with an intriguing clutch of short, artificial cuts long since faded into obscurity, some never fully completed. The Forth provides a navigable inlet for large tankers as far as the oil refinery at Grangemouth, 43 miles inland from its wide mouth between Bass Rock and the Isle of May, while Alloa – a further six miles inland – is accessible to small craft. Beyond this, on its approach to Stirling, the river becomes somewhat tortuous, strewn with sand banks and unmarked shallows, requiring local knowledge to ensure safe passage. Best known as a salmon river, the River Tay is navigable to Perth with care while, higher up, becomes the preserve of white water canoe enthusiasts.

Scotland's waterway *pièce de résistance* surely lies in the Great Glen, in the form of the Caledonian Canal running from the Beauly Firth to Loch Linnhe. Surveyed by Thomas Telford, in 1801, this is a stupendous feat of engineering taking in some of the country's most stunning scenery and presenting a series of formidable challenges to its builders. Some 380 million years ago tectonic plates, moving against one another, tore open a rift that became home to lochs Ness, Oich, Lochy and Linnhe. Even today minor earthquakes emphasise that the geology of the area is still far from stable.

The navigation as built by Telford and his assistants Matthew Davidson, John Telford and Alexander Easton, is 60 miles in length and approximately one-third is a series of man-made cuts, linking the aforementioned lochs via some quite stunning lock flights: the appropriately named Neptune's Staircase being the most westerly. Completed in 1822 – and in common with most canals, well outside the original time and budget estimates – the waterway proved to be an immense success way beyond the contemporary account given of its opening celebrations:

'The reverberation of the firing, repeated and prolonged by a thousand echoes from the surrounding hills, glens and rocks, the martial music, the shouts of the Highlanders and the answering cheers of the party on board, produced an effect which will not soon be forgotten by those present ... a plentiful supply of whisky, given by the gentlemen of Fort William, did not in the least tend to damp the ardour of the populace.'

Loch Crinan

EDINBURGH & GLASGOW UNION CANAL

The Edinburgh & Glasgow Union Canal, to give the navigation its full name, was a waterway born out of indecision. Indeed, so great were the squabbles, accusations, counter accusations, vested interests and general all round bickering that it was very nearly stillborn. It was conceived in an early form in 1791 and finally opened in 1822, a long and drawn-out gestation period by any standards. Few inland waterways completed at, or after, this time provided much by way of a return for their shareholders, and the Union Canal was no exception.

Manse Road Basin, Linlithgow

FALKIRK

LINLITHGOW

BROXBURN

EDINBURGH

N

BACKGROUND

Initially the four routes surveyed for the Union Canal ran from Edinburgh's neighbouring port of Leith to the Clyde in the Broomielaw district of Glasgow, driven by a strong desire, on the part of the inhabitants of Edinburgh, to tap into the cheap and plentiful coal supplies from the Monklands pits. Dissension was immediately rife, stemming from conflicting interests amongst manufacturers, proprietors of coal mines and the landed gentry.

War put an end to further debate and it was not until 1813, a year of inflated coal prices in Edinburgh, that new plans surfaced. Hugh Baird, engineer on the Forth & Clyde Canal, proposed a line connecting with his waterway at Falkirk and running into the Fountainbridge district of Edinburgh. Strong opposition to this scheme alluded to vested interests, whilst some of the most vociferous criticism revolved around the omission of both Leith and the Broomielaw from the plans.

Against this background of claim and counterclaim, both Robert Stevenson and Thomas Telford were asked to report on suitable routes for the new canal, with the former proposing a level line from Edinburgh to Port Dundas, in Glasgow, entailing a 3-mile tunnel through Winchburgh Hill. Work finally commenced on the navigation in March 1818 with Hugh Baird as engineer.

From the outset proposals for this waterway were not without merit, over and above its ability to attract the opinions of such a large clutch of eminent canal engineers. There was a real need for cheap coal in Edinburgh: stagecoach links through the Lowlands were slow and uncomfortable, and the millers in the Avon and Almond valleys would benefit greatly from improved transport links with their main markets. As Edinburgh expanded, so the

Moorings at the Bridge Inn, Ratho

demand for limestone and sandstone – so readily available in the central belt – increased likewise.

The impoverished farm land to the west of the city consumed large quantities of agricultural lime (also required for building) and construction materials generally were also in great demand. Water was in short supply in Edinburgh and the canal's enabling Act of 1817 allowed any surplus 'waste water' – above the navigation's depth of 5 feet – to be drawn off. Only rubbish and manure, both human and equine, were considered as potential 'exports' and a cargo for west-bound boats.

With three superb aqueducts and a 696 yd-long tunnel, this contour canal embraces some spectacular engineering achievements. It is ironic that Falkirk Tunnel owes its existence to the dictates of William Forbes, a local landowner, and reassuring that Telford's advice was sought during the building of the aqueducts, which were closely modelled on his example at Chirk, on the Llangollen Canal (*see* page 246). They are, nonetheless, striking constructions in their own right and, together with the bridges, wharves, warehouses, stabling, cellars and two inns, add up to a rich legacy of finely crafted structures.

THE NAVIGATION

Atop the Falkirk Wheel the views are splendid and the superlatives come thick and fast as, leaving this unique structure, the boater sets out along a slender trough towards the security and solidarity of the newly constructed Rough Castle Tunnel. Once up the two staircase locks, the recently excavated section of waterway accompanies the railway into trees and a meeting with the old line of the original contour canal at Greenbank, where 11 locks once descended to Port Downie Basin and a junction with the Forth & Clyde Navigation. Beyond is Falkirk Tunnel, part lined and part rough-hewn and all very wet! There is a profusion of colour visible in the rock strata with a dipping coal seam

and impressive calcium deposits. Glen Bridge sits close to the eastern portal with its smiling and miserable faces incised into the arch's keystones. Known as the Laughin' and Greetin' Bridge, the carvings are thought to represent the two canal builders: one happy with the task of digging the relatively easy contour navigation, the other faced with building 11 locks and excavating a lengthy tunnel. Leaving the cutting, the waterway slips into more open country, stretching away on the offside, whilst to the north the housing of Falkirk and Redding maintains a discrete distance. By way of stark contrast, the security fencing and surveillance cameras of the Young Offenders Institution loom up and for a while remain very dominant.

Of the 62 fixed bridges along the canal, many are the original construction and a delight to behold. They employ contrasting stone, often arches in whinstone and trainings in local stone, and again there is contrast between stone and the decorative ironwork that is introduced on a few examples. They are pleasingly solid affairs with, in some instances, skilful restoration to the masonry. East of Polmont, the canal approaches the impressive 12-arched Avon Aqueduct through a secluded, intimate section hemmed in by mature trees, giving little hint of the wonder to come. The water in the iron trough appears as black as the iron railings fringing the towpaths each side, separating the boater from the 85ft drop through the distant tree tops into the diminutive river far below. Ahead is gently rising ground and a pastoral scene to contrast with the excitement of the retreating aqueduct, while from each side of Kettlestoun Bridge there are glimpses of the equally impressive railway viaduct in the distance. The navigation enters Linlithgow in a side cut and from its elevated position there are good views out over the town and of its striking church spire.

Chief engineer	Hugh Baird
Additional advice	John Rennie, Robert Stevenson, Thomas Telford.
Significance	Provided a supply of coal and building materials for Edinburgh and agricultural lime for the surrounding farmland.
Started in	1818
Completed in	1822
Length	32 miles
Draught	3' 6"
Headroom	8' 10"
Lock size	70" × 12' 6"
Number of locks	3 locks; 1 boat lift
Tunnels	1
Aqueducts	5
Goods carried	Coal, bricks, building stone, lime, paving stone, tiles, slates, timber, sand, passengers.
Operating authority	Scottish Canals
Contact details	enquiries @scottishcanals.co.uk

Towpath seat, Ratho

THE NAVIGATION

The canal leaves Linlithgow above the old St Magdalene Distillery, now partially converted to luxury flats. The intriguing beehive-shaped construction beside Manse Road Basin is a doocot (dovecot) containing 370 nesting holes and would have acted as a 'larder', its inhabitants providing fresh meat as a welcome change from salt beef during the long winter months. The waterway heads through an open and largely arable area with fine views to the north over the Firth of Forth towards the Ochil Hills. The countryside is dotted with farmsteads and there are plenty of trees to add variety. In some parts cattle graze and overall it is a very comfortable and verdant landscape. Philpstoun slumbers beside the canal which now takes on an intimate feel, diving between trees and into a shallow cutting. From time to time, usually on bends, there are rows of stones set into the ground lining the edge of the navigation. Opinion is divided as to their purpose, with one

Replica steam packet boat (in fact powered by a 3-cylinder diesel engine) on the Edinburgh & Glasgow Union Canal

SHALE BINGS

The word 'bing' is derived from the Gaelic word 'ben' meaning a hill or mountain and is used to describe the large red mounds which dominate the landscape in this area. A Victorian chemist and entrepreneur, James 'Paraffin' Young, came here prospecting for cannel coal, so-called because it burnt very brightly and was used for lighting. He went on to develop a process for extracting wax and paraffin from the oil-bearing shales that culminated in an industry employing 13,000 people at its peak, in 120 separate works. The United States followed on by discovering the crude oil we use today and the last works in the area closed in 1962, leaving behind this intriguing and colourful topographical legacy.

side supporting the theory that they provided grip for the horses towing the boats. Those of a less prosaic disposition suggest that they were the forerunners of today's motorway 'rumble' strips and served to wake a slumbering horse (dozing from the tedium of a hard day's plodding) before it strayed into the water. Now the waterway winds its way through open countryside, regularly punctuated by the pinky-red shale bings, some spilling down to the banks themselves and lending a curious feature to an otherwise plain vista.

Beyond Winchburgh the waterway nestles into a short, tree-lined cutting that all but shuts out any evidence of the village. The canal then breaks out into wide open countryside and starts upon an expansive series of meanders in order to stay on the contour, often wrapping itself around the foot of a pink shale bing. It has been called the 'Mathematical Canal', a description relating directly to its snaking, contour course, and nowhere is this more obvious than here. The loops are exaggerated and at times the canal seems to double back on itself, so that the views ahead are of a wide and ever-changing, panoramic landscape.

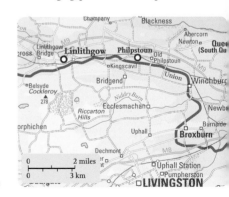

POINTS OF INTEREST

Falkirk A focal point on the Antonine Wall, a drover's town, and a centre for iron founding and coal mining (*see* Forth & Clyde Canal, page 286 for further details).

Linlithgow Occupying a superb site on the south side of Linlithgow Loch, this Royal and Ancient Burgh is the former county town of West Lothian. Robert II held a parliament in the Great Hall of the palace in October 1389, establishing the charter and during the 15th and 16th centuries the settlement enjoyed a monopoly trade along the Forth shores which lie just 3 miles to the north. The Union of the Scottish and English thrones in 1603 started Linlithgow's decline and with the loss of its monopoly trading status to the merchants of Bo'ness, the town gradually slid into obscurity. There are some 280 different spellings of 'Linlithgow' recorded over the years, which makes the origin of its name open to some doubt. However, taken as a description of its site beside the loch, 'lake in a damp hollow' would seem to be as likely as it is apt. Industries in the area have included agriculture, tanning, textiles, mining, quarrying, the making of glue, soap, shoes and candles together with milling, brewing and distilling. St Magdalene's Distillery moved to Linlithgow in the 19th century to be close to the canal for its supplies of coke, coal and grain. It ceased production in 1983 and has now, in part, been converted into luxury flats.

Linlithgow Palace Commissioned by James I in the mid 15th century, it became a favourite residence of all the Stewart Kings. It was the birthplace of Mary Queen of Scots in 1542, although she did not return until much later after her sojourn in France. Destroyed by fire in 1746, it has remained un-roofed but splendid in its location beside the loch.

St Michael's Parish Church, Linlithgow The church was first consecrated in the 13th century and later was closely associated with Mary Queen of Scots. However, it was largely destroyed by a fire in 1424 and most of the existing fabric dates from its rebuilding. There is a beautiful stone-carved altar piece in the vestry and some stained glass by Burne-Jones. Most striking – and controversial – is the laminated timber and aluminium spire, erected in 1964 to replace an open stone crown removed for reasons of safety in 1821. This new structure was designed by Geoffrey Clarke to 'symbolise triumph rising like a spear from the Crown of Thorns' and it is floodlit at night to dramatic effect.

Leamington Lift Bridge, Edinburgh Quay

SWIFTS

A substantial part of the Union Canal's revenue during its heyday came from the carriage of passengers. In the early 19th century it took two days to walk from Edinburgh to Glasgow and one day travelling by stagecoach. The Swifts – fast passenger boats – took 10 hours and travelled between 10 and 12 miles per hour with frequent changes of horses. They carried up to 60 people and were distinguished by an iron swan's neck fixed to the prow and sharpened with an edge capable of cutting through an oncoming bargee's towing rope: useful if their slower-moving vessel was a little tardy in giving way!

Philpstoun A small community on the edge of the oil-rich shale strata that once provided employment for its inhabitants.

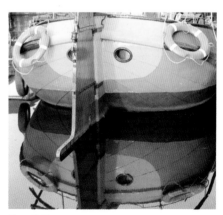

Stern reflections

THE NAVIGATION

By the time the oil shale industry was established, the railway had all but superseded the waterway, leaving it with no part to play in transporting the refined wax and paraffin production. There are views of the Almond Valley railway viaduct to the north as the unwelcome intrusion of the motorway starts to dominate. Thankfully its viaduct is hidden from sight and the navigation passes the Scottish Canals yard immediately to the east of Drumshoreland Bridge. Edinburgh Turnhouse Airport is also in evidence, with the flight path of the main runway crossing the canal at this point.

On its approach to the Almond Aqueduct the navigation enters a shallow cutting before

JOHN SCOTT RUSSELL

A famous Scotsman – engineer, shipbuilder and scientist – who, apart from giving his name to the modern aqueduct over the Edinburgh City Bypass (just to the west of Edinburgh) was a renowned naval architect and designer of the *Great Eastern*. Built in collaboration with Isambard Kingdom Brunel, this iron sailing ship was by far the largest vessel afloat when launched in 1858. He also propounded the Solitary Wave Theory that today has many diverse applications.

The inland boater can observe the phenomenon for himself: when a boat stops suddenly a single wave – or soliton – can, under certain conditions, be seen to roll forward and, gathering momentum, travel a considerable distance along the canal. Boats moored in its path can be tossed about 'in a state of violent agitation' much to the discomfort of their occupants.

launching itself across a second impressive river crossing 75ft above the ground. Below is the Almondell and Calderwood Country Park. Still lined with trees, the canal passes the disused quarry that is now the home of the Scottish National Climbing Centre, making its way to Ratho and the Edinburgh Canal Centre.

There is an attractive picnic site on the towpath side as the waterway leaves Ratho, itself a charming village of rambling old cottages. The motorway is ever present as the canal proceeds through open, undulating countryside with views towards the Pentland Hills. The third aqueduct to be encountered, the Scott Russell Aqueduct, is, in its new concrete uniformity, a striking contrast to its two predecessors and has no need of the tallow and horsehair caulking that is reputed to have been employed in joining sections of the more traditional iron troughing together. Its name honours a famous Scotsman – engineer, shipbuilder and scientist – who propounded the Solitary Wave Theory.

The navigation now finally moves away from the motorway intrusion to become entangled in the colourful, modern housing of Wester Hailes and its succession of new bridges. It weaves its way along a newly created and not altogether unpleasant channel, where there are regular mooring rings available. The approach through the outskirts of Edinburgh is pleasantly green and predominantly leafy. This section terminates with the third of Hugh Baird's splendid constructions: Slateford Aqueduct. Like the Almond Aqueduct, it is 75ft above the river and towers over the city's western arterial road and rail connections. Its eight arches total 500ft in length and it weighs-in as Scotland's third largest aqueduct. It has, by way of a companion, the somewhat smaller Prince Charlie Aqueduct close to its eastern end,

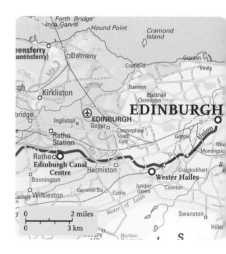

carrying the navigation over a road rather than the Water of Leith.

Edinburgh's western suburbs leave room for parkland, playing fields and plenty of open space, allowing the canal a green and uncluttered entry into Fountainbridge. A section of the navigation here is used for rowing; there are boat houses and the scene is reminiscent of a waterway through a university town. Rowing boats are available for hire at Ashley Bridge, and there are people feeding the ducks and strolling leisurely through the park. National Cycle Route 75 has now joined the towpath on its way into the city from Glasgow. Approaching the site of the old Fountainbridge Brewery (now modern student accommodation), the navigation becomes hemmed in by tenements, making access to the neighbouring streets initially difficult. Ahead is the splendid structure of Leamington Lift Bridge, a fine iron construction recently restored to full working order. Beyond is Edinburgh Quay, currently undergoing extensive development.

POINTS OF INTEREST

Edinburgh Canal Centre, Ratho The enterprise and imagination of one man – Ronnie Rusack MBE – whose combination of business acumen and dedication to the re-opening of the Union Canal has contributed greatly to the Millennium Link we see today. The success of waterway restoration throughout Britain has always initially been down to the vigour and zeal of individual canal societies and the classic strategy is to establish and maintain a high profile through tireless campaigning and, wherever possible, active use of whatever remains of the navigation. The Edinburgh Canal Centre has been a focus for much activity, extending over more than 25 years, all of which served to raise public awareness of the

Edinburgh Quay

canal's potential and Ronnie Rusack can rightly be called 'Mr Union'.

Wester Hailes New development made this one of the most substantial blockages on the line of the Union Canal. However, the waterway had been culverted under roadways and not been built upon, and opening it out was a relatively straightforward task although constructing the array of new bridges must have been a more costly undertaking.

Edinburgh This is a city to be viewed on foot. As the ancient capital of Scotland it has been in existence since the late 11th century when Malcolm Canmore, together with Margaret his queen, adopted Castle Rock as their final abode. Streets run up and down a series of volcanic hills, giving the city an open, airy feel, and Arthur's Seat, overlooking Holyrood Park, offers a marvellous prospect. The Old Town, occupying a defensive position, huddles on the ridge below Castle Rock and strikes a stunning contrast with later Georgian development below, with its series of graceful streets and squares. Over the centuries the city's fortunes rose and fell, losing much of its importance with the 1603 Union of the Crowns; further eroded by the Union of Parliaments just over 100 years later. During the 18th century pomp and circumstance were succeeded by a creative intellectual enlightenment in which the beauties of the New Town were conceived, financed with the proceeds from a burgeoning industrial age. After a lapse of 300 years, history was repeated with the opening of the Scottish Parliament in 1999, housed in a splendid new building near the Palace of Holyroodhouse.

St Giles' Cathedral, Edinburgh Probably the third church to occupy this site with the crown spire, dating from 1495, the only original exterior feature. Completely rebuilt in the 14th century, ongoing restoration and alteration has progressively

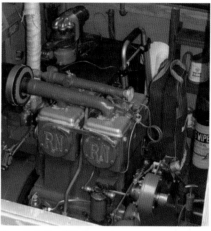

Two-cylinder Russell Newbery engine

changed its appearance and character with the most recent addition being the Thistle Chapel dating from 1911.

St Mary's Episcopal Cathedral, Edinburgh A glorious Victorian Gothic Cathedral by George Gilbert Scott.

POP INNS

Once situated along the length of the navigation providing refreshment to the weary bargee and so-called because they had a door at each end. The boatman had simply to veer away from the horse he was leading, enter through the nearest door, consume a pint while he walked the length of the bar and exit without so much as breaking his stride.

THE INLAND WATERWAYS ASSOCIATION

'Campaigning for the use, maintenance and restoration of Britain's inland waterways' is the slogan adopted by the Inland Waterways Association: activities that they have pursued tirelessly since their formation in 1946.

Two years earlier L. T. C. Rolt, author and engineer, had published the book *Narrow Boat* describing his journey, in 1939, aboard his converted narrowboat *Cressy* around the canals of England together with Angela, his new bride. His encounters with those who lived and worked upon the waterways and his descriptions of their general decline struck a chord with his readers, one of whom – a literary agent and budding author, Robert Aickman – contacted him with the suggestion that they should form a society to campaign for the regeneration of the waterways.

The two men, together with their wives, had their inaugural meeting aboard *Cressy* in August 1945

L. T. C. Rolt on board Cressy

L. T. C. Rolt

at Tardebigge Locks, near Bromsgrove, on the Worcester & Birmingham Canal and both couples soon established a firm rapport. They cruised together and spent time at the Aickman's flat in Gower Street in London where, on 15 February 1946, the Inland Waterways Association (IWA) formally saw the light of day. Tom Rolt was nominated as its first secretary and Robert Aickman was appointed chairman. A prominent canal historian, Charles Hadfield, took the role of vice-chairman and Frank Eyre filled the treasurer's post. The society was soon to attract the naturalist Peter Scott and his glamorous wife Elizabeth Jane Howard who, after four years as secretary (following Tom Rolt's departure after a disagreement with Aickman) went on to become a well-known literary figure.

Aboard *Cressy*, Tom and Angela Rolt led the IWA's first campaign by challenging the owners of the Stratford Canal – the Great Western Railway – over a former drawbridge near Kings Norton, which had been replaced with a fixed bridge with insufficient headroom to allow for navigation. After a question was asked in parliament by Lord Methuen, a recent recruit to the IWA, the company was forced to raise the bridge and a year later, in August 1948, the association went on mount a second, more ambitious campaign cruise in the north of the country. Here the *Ailsa Craig* was hired from R. H. Wyatt of Stone and, in an effort to maintain the rights of navigation along an assortment of waterways, a number of IWA members cruised a variety of northern canals including what was one of the last complete crossings of the Huddersfield Narrow Canal (*see* page 148) before its restoration in 2001.

Subsequent campaigning successes have included the complete restoration of the Kennet & Avon Canal (Milepost 12), the Basingstoke Canal, the River Avon in Warwickshire together with the Peak Forest & Ashton Canals (*see* page 176), the Rochdale Canal (Milepost 24) and the Ripon Canal in North Yorkshire. These are but a random sample of waterways that owe their continuing existence to the unerring perseverance of the IWA both at national level and through their regional membership.

WERGIES

Messing about in the mud has long been the pursuit of little boys (and girls) and is an occupation that some of us have great difficulty in shrugging off, even in later life. Imagine, then, having the opportunity to legitimise this sensory indulgence in the respectable form (in the eyes of some, at least) of canal restoration. There are still many muddy, overgrown ditches festering in their own private world of decay that were once illustrious watery highways. As the more straightforward canal restorations are successfully accomplished, so the more difficult ones become the targets for the doyens of dirty digging, namely the Waterways Recovery Group (WRG). Formed with the express purpose of resurrecting fallen waterways and familiar to many a boater as the driving force behind the old National Waterway Festivals, this organisation is able to dig the dirt with the best of them. There are many navigations, far too numerous to mention, who have benefited from their unstinting ability to mix endeavour with cheerfulness, pleasure with muck and sand with cement.

The Waterways Recovery Group, or WERGIES as they are often affectionately known, are in reality made up from a disparate group of people, generally with the shared aim of restoring waterways and having a really good time – although not necessarily in that order. Often, in their wholehearted pursuit of a muddy and watery objective, it's hard to discern whether it's a matter of self-discovery or waterways recovery. What is, however, abundantly clear is their dedication and enthusiasm for the job in hand, together with the skill and sheer professionalism that is brought to the task.

Originally the brainchild of Graham Palmer, the WRG has become a highly respected and well-equipped member of the waterways scene as can be seen from the accompanying pictures. Without their unstinting efforts many a waterways restoration project would not have reached

Clearing out the Droitwich Barge Lock

fruition, nor would we be enjoying the regular festivals and events – ranging from the National Trailboat Festival to the Canalway Cavalcade – that they mount with such good humour every year.

Current restoration project at Gough's Orchard Lock on the Cotswold Canals

CRINAN CANAL

This is an isolated waterway that combines an air of mystery with great beauty and stunning maritime views. Most aspects of the Scottish countryside are embraced within its short nine mile length, from the often moist weather – in all its myriad forms – through to vistas of soft hills, rearing mountains, bog and moorland. Compared with many of its English cousins, this is a navigation on a extensive scale as befits the terrain it traverses and as such can be enjoyed both for its engineering, as well as for its setting.

This is a piece of waterway history best described by Val Hickin's first-hand account:

'In 1968 it was decided by canal enthusiasts nationwide to hold a "national dig". The venue chosen was the derelict Ashton Canal in Manchester, happily now part of the navigable Cheshire cruising ring. This became known as OPASH and was followed up four years later by a second attack: ASHTAC.'

'Five days before the weekend dig I travelled up in my guise as working party organiser for the South Wales section of the Inland Waterways Association (see Milepost 21) and was kindly accommodated in a rather battered old green caravan on a small patch of waste ground, also used by the locals for soccer practice, etc. They were none too keen on this obstruction appearing on the pitch and one night a small bonfire was lit underneath. The smell fortunately woke me and I was able to deal with it comparatively easily. The next day I managed to contact a member of the law. Mentioning the arson attack, I was told "what do you expect if you put a van on their recreational area".

'My time was spent preparing for the weekend, checking access for lorries and confirming arrangements with the council tip officials for the rubbish. Friday was very busy as most of the plant arrived, with JCBs and dumpers by the dozen,

Some of the debris retrieved during ASHTAC

as well as a couple of cranes that were to be used for removing large objects like old vehicles from the locks.

'And by the evening the "navvies" started arriving in their hordes – between 300 and 600 as I recall. The accommodation was a disused gas showroom, sleeping bags on the floor. Before the dig could start we managed to lower the water level in the canal by about 2ft which showed us just how much had been dumped over the years.

'One of the more interesting sights were the small jetties protruding into the waterway from gardens next to the canal: their illicit dumps becoming ever more obvious as the water level receded.'

Saturday 'The dig started under heavy rain and leaden skies. All the volunteers were despatched to their length of canal – the bigger the group, the longer the length of canal. As only a couple of people had driven up from South Wales, my gang had a very short section, including a fixed bridge into a small industrial estate.

'Throughout the clearance operation, there was always a large police presence, happily ticking off items on their list of stolen motorbikes, bicycles, etc., and we were instructed to report any suspicious finds to them. During Saturday we kept them amused by suggesting that an old bedstead was really an antique and a 45 gallon drum half full of concrete might contain something nasty. All day the rains kept up their relentless efforts, soaking 1½ miles of soggy navvies, but by the end of the day an estimated 250 tons had been removed from the canal. That evening we all went to the pub.'

Sunday 'Still raining and back to site with throbbing temples and under our bridge, which kept the worst of the weather off. Soon, ¼ mile downstream from our site, a JCB hoisted up a cylindrical object with fins on it. There followed much yelling and the site was hastily abandoned

The Ashton Canal drained for ASHTAC

– cordoned off, awaiting the arrival of the bomb squad. Meanwhile the object fell over revealing just the tail of a Second World War bomb, later confirmed by the bomb squad as completely safe. Presumably this was a chunk of metal that the adjacent scrap yard did not like the look of, adopting the local 'chuck it in the cut' philosophy.

By four in the afternoon several hundred soggy volunteers were cleaning their kit and preparing for the long drive home, having removed in excess of 500 tons of assorted rubbish from 1½ miles of canal, reducing the life of the local tip by about three years. With the help of a national paper (the *Mirror*) canal restoration had been well and truly placed on the map.'

FORTH & CLYDE CANAL

Conceived in the second half of the 18th century, this canal was a source of controversy from the very outset, with two conflicting schemes born from somewhat differing concepts of the region's transport needs. The Glasgow faction argued for a 'small' canal on the basis that most goods carried would be going to or from that city, while 'the Wise Men of the East' – the Edinburgh merchants – took a less parochial view, maintaining that the navigation should be 'a proper canal' to serve 'national and universal' interests. It was, ultimately, the proponents of the think big philosophy that won the day.

Bowling Basin, above the Sea Lock

BOWLING
BASIN

BEARSDEN

CLYDEBANK

KIRKINTILLOCH

FALKIRK

GLASGOW

N

BACKGROUND

The Glasgow Bill was given its second reading in March 1767, yet within two months £100,000 had been subscribed for a 'great canal', and the supporters of the small canal agreed to drop their Bill in return for guarantees that a cut would be provided into the city. The navigation, engineered by John Smeaton and surveyed by Robert Mackell, was to be between 7ft and 10ft deep and to run from an entry into the Clyde near Dalmuir to Grangemouth, where the River Carron meets the Firth of Forth. Royal assent for the Bill was gained on 8 March 1768 and work was in hand within the year.

The inevitable shortages of money dogged construction and it was not until 1777 that the Glasgow Branch was completed as far as a basin below Hamiltonhill and the city was effectively connected to the Forth and European markets beyond. The value of the canal was confirmed when potential famine in west Scotland – following poor harvests in 1782 and 1783 – was averted by grain shipped in from Germany and neighbouring countries. However, the navigation had still not achieved its principal aim: to be a sea canal connecting the Clyde to the Forth, funds being insufficient to meet the cost of the final section from Stockingfield Junction (immediately north of Glasgow) to a point near Dalmuir as originally proposed. Robert Whitworth was appointed as chief engineer in 1785 with the remit of increasing the canal's depth to 8ft by raising the water level, upgrading water supplies to meet this increased demand and making the final cut. Finally Bowling, with its newly sunk coal mines, was established as the western entry to the canal and the navigation was eventually opened throughout in July 1790.

The waterway provided a speedy form of passenger transport between Glasgow and Edinburgh via Grangemouth and thence down the Forth to Leith. This peaked in 1836 with approaching 500,000 people carried; the journey time between Port Dundas and Lock 16 was just five and a half hours. The Scottish herring fleet was also able to move swiftly from coast to coast, responding rapidly to the appearance of fish in the firths of Clyde and Forth. Fifty-four boats passed through the waterway in December 1794 alone, all expected to return a few weeks later.

It was railway competition that saw the canal's 20th-century decline, with official closure coming on 1 January 1963. A hundred years earlier dividends paid out of up to 30 per cent painted a very different and contrasting picture. In March 1999 National Lottery Funding was procured to re-open the navigation and the process of decay was reversed: new cuts have been engineered, blockages circumnavigated and more than 30 bridges rebuilt to reinstate the fine coast-to-coast waterway we see today.

The old Sea Lock into the River Clyde at Bowling

THE NAVIGATION

From beside the old sea lock at Bowling Basin the views up and down the Clyde, on a clear day, are stupendous; but the view of Bowling Harbour, in the immediate foreground, is depressing. Decayed and sunken hulks of one-time trim gabbarts settle into the mud and all is dereliction, a far cry from this once-bustling Clyde port, pivotal to the local coasting trade. The basin itself is home to a wide range of sea-going pleasure craft and through the old railway swing bridge, nestling on its mellow pink concrete piers, lies the start of the canal and the first inland lock.

Beyond, the waterway hugs the estuary, offering fine views of the slender, curving deck of the Erskine Bridge towering above Saltings Nature Reserve, with its insects, orchids and willows. By way of an engineering contrast, Dalmuir Drop Lock is soon encountered, offering a unique solution to the mere 20-inch clearance of the busy Dumbarton Road at this point above the navigation. The view of high-rise housing is omni-present as the waterway passes light industry, set in attractively landscaped grounds on the offside.

There are open vistas to the south over the once-prosperous ship-building yards of Clydebank, punctuated by the skeleton of the occasional hammerhead crane, as the waterway suddenly finds itself ensnared in a shopping centre: today's Clydebank! Escape is through a pair of syncopated vertical lift bridges into a green corridor approaching the four Boghouse Locks; the regular appearance of aircraft flying low overhead indicates that this is also the approach to Glasgow Airport on the south bank of the river.

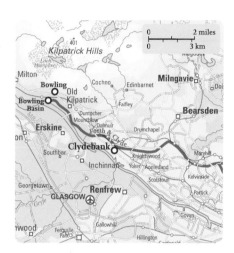

Chief Engineer	John Smeaton, Robert Whitworth
Assisted by	Robert Mackell
Significance	Provided a connection between the firths of Clyde and Forth.
Started in	1768
Completed in	1790
Length	34 miles
Draught	6'
Headroom	9' 10"
Lock size	68' 6" × 19' 8"
Number of locks	39
Goods carried	Timber, coal, tobacco, cotton, grain, sugar, coffee, passengers.
Operating authority	Scottish Canals
Contact details	enquiries @scottishcanals.co.uk

DALMUIR DROP LOCK

In the age of the tram, the former swing bridge on the site of its replacement, the Drop Lock, was a source of constant delays. The lock, an ingenious solution to the problem of passing boats under a fixed bridge, with a clearance of just 20 inches, makes use of an impounded length of water, trapped between lock gates east and west of the bridge. Craft enter this section, the gates are closed and in 20 minutes (give or take) almost 500,000 gallons of water are pumped out, increasing the headroom to 10ft. Once through the bridge, the vessel pauses whilst the water is let back in; the other set of gates is then opened and the boat is free to proceed.

Picnic bench at Bowling

THE NAVIGATION

Above Boghouse Locks the waterway continues its ascent through the five Clobberhill Locks. There was once a large sawmill beside Temple Locks, supplied with exotic hardwoods from around the world through Grangemouth Docks. The waterway then twists and turns, winding through trees and rounding a left-hand bend before boaters are confronted with the imposing Maryhill Locks, forbidding high-rise housing and green, open hillside beyond. The solid masonry of the lock flight prescribes a series of pleasing shapes as each chamber – the whole flight set on a curve – is joined one to another; courses of stonework flow around each circular side pound and the historic dry dock. At the base is the impressive four-arched Kelvin Aqueduct forming the finale to a symphony in stone: a striking tribute to Robert Whitworth, engineer on this, the final section of the canal to be built.

Maryhill Aqueduct leads the waterway to Stockingfield Junction with the choice of a 2¹/₂ mile trip along the skyline of the city to the

Residential moorings at Auchinstarry

terminus of the Glasgow Branch at Spiers Wharf, or an increasingly rural journey in the direction of Falkirk. Here tenements and tower blocks fall away, displaced by the reedbeds of Possil Loch, a nature reserve and a SSSI. Away from the high-rise and tenement housing of Glasgow, the waterway now settles into a placid course with open arable countryside undulating away from the towpath towards distant, rising ground.

At Cadder the views are briefly compromised by a strip of woodland embracing the delightful church and its environs; the shade provided serves to accentuate the opaque inky blackness of the water here. In the summer the contrast between water and the vibrant yellow of the water lilies is most striking. The waterway winds towards Kirkintilloch with alternate views towards the distant Campsie Fells (with their unfortunately placed skyline pylons) and avenues of mature trees. To the south the horizon also grows steadily more distant, and one becomes aware of the great labour that digging the canal entailed as spoil banks loom high running alongside the towpath for some way.

POINTS OF INTEREST

Bowling Once a thriving port for the west coast trade, a coal-mining village and ship-building centre. Now all this is history, enshrined in rotting hulks in the harbour mud and gaunt, derelict buildings on the crumbling quayside. It is the half-way point between Balloch and Glasgow.

Bowling Basin Western terminus for the Forth & Clyde Canal and the one part of the docks where Bowling's maritime tradition is still alive. There are two sea locks here and the basin, once an important transhipment point, is now busy with pleasure craft. The striking late 18th-century Customs House has become the Scottish Canals port office and there is an attractive picnic area beside the disused lock, with marvellous views along the estuary.

Clydebank Some of the most famous ocean liners – *QE2*, *Queen Mary*, *Lusitania* – originated from the great shipbuilding yards of Clydebank which have today become, somewhat incongruously, a vast out-of-town shopping mall. This was also once the centre for the manufacture of Singer sewing machines in this country.

Glasgow In the 6th century St Mungo established a wooden church on the banks of the Molendinar Burn and went on to become the first bishop of the city. In more recent times this stormy Kingdom of Strathclyde settled to trade and commerce in place of feud and bloodshed. Eighteenth-century Glasgow grew rich from cotton, sugar and tobacco shipped across the Atlantic, and from grain and timber from European countries connected by the newly opened Forth & Clyde Canal. The city further consolidated its position and wealth through banking, heavy industry and shipbuilding. By the early 20th century, Glasgow had become a world leader in the production of merchant ships and passenger liners together with railway locomotives, which were hauled by teams of horses through the

The Sea Lock at Bowling

city streets to the docks. Here they would be loaded into vessels by the mighty hammerhead cranes whose gaunt skeletons still punctuate the skyline. Today the city majors on its strong Charles Rennie Mackintosh connection, service industries and is a burgeoning cultural centre.

Glasgow Cathedral The fourth church on the site of St Mungo's original timber building, this Gothic cathedral dates from the 13th century with 15th-century additions. The nave is late Gothic and the Blacader Aisle has decorative ribbed vaulting and carved bosses.

Charles Rennie Mackintosh Arguably the city's most famous son and chief tourist 'pull'. His stunning and very varied output of design and architectural work is well-represented in the following buildings. **Glasgow School of Art** Still

an operational art college, this is Mackintosh's masterpiece. **Hill House, Helensburgh** Everything from the building down to individual items of cutlery designed by the master himself. **House For An Art Lover, Glasgow** Set in attractive parkland and inspired by Mackintosh's original designs. **The Lighthouse, Glasgow** Scotland's Centre for Architecture, Design and the City: the award-winning Mackintosh Interpretation Centre. **The Mackintosh House, Glasgow** A reconstruction of the principal interiors from 78 Southpark Avenue (originally 6 Florentine Terrace), the Mackintosh's Glasgow home. **Martyr's School, Glasgow** Lime-wash plaster, tiling and spectacular roof trusses realised from the pen of the master. **Queen's Cross Church, Glasgow** International HQ of the Charles Rennie Mackintosh Society and the only Mackintosh-designed church to be built. 'Magnificent stained glass and exceptional relief carving on wood and stonework are the highlights of the interior where light and space are used to dramatic effect.' **Scotland Street School Museum, Glasgow** Designed by the maestro himself, opened as a school in 1906 and now a museum of education. **The Willow Tearooms, Glasgow** One of Mackintosh's best-known designs translated into everyday use for everyone: a place to sit and sip tea and absorb the atmosphere.

Spiers Wharf A striking example of an early 19th-century canal terminal basin, established before the requirement for increased water supplies necessitated a connection with the Monkland Canal at Port Dundas, a $\frac{1}{4}$ mile to the east. Today a lengthy run of pleasing tobacco, grain and sugar warehouses has been attractively converted into a mix of residential and commercial premises, making this an inviting place to moor. The elegant porticoed Georgian building, standing on its own, is particularly attractive and originally housed the Canal Company offices dating from 1812.

THE NAVIGATION

Incongruously modern office buildings adorn the offside as, passing the old Hays Shipyard now replaced with the new Seagull Trust boat house, the waterway slips through a wooded defile into the heart of Kirkintilloch and, just as briefly, out again over the Luggie Aqueduct. This fine structure, fringed with delicate iron railings, once interlaced both river and railway beneath its imposing arch; the railway is no longer there. The waterway leaves the town in a side cut, with views across the rooftops of straggling suburban housing to the Campsies, now drawing nearer.

The navigation twists, turns and wriggles its way eastwards pursued along its north bank by the sharply rising ground of the Campsie Fells, now less than 1 mile away, with the infant River Kelvin flowing in the foreground. Twechar, with its new lift bridge, straggles up the hill to the south. At Auchinstarry, before the old coal-loading basin, views briefly extend on the offside before being rapidly obscured by a rocky scarp and the spoil tips of past mineral extraction.

At Craigmarloch there is little to see of its past prowess as a day-trip destination; the basin is silted up and all is overgrown. The next two miles of the waterway take on motorway proportions in both width and straightness. The towpath, as if not to be outdone, assumes the dimensions of a country lane and it becomes apparent that this is the navigation's course through Dullatur Bog. It is a rich corridor for nature in all its myriad forms, forming a SSSI – one of several linked by the navigation in the Kelvin Valley. Water is supplied for the canal from Banton Loch to the north, while across open meadowland to the south there are the occasional glimpses of spoil tips serving as a reminder of the area's industrial heritage. On a dull day the cheerfully liveried Scotrail trains, racing past nearby, add a momentary dash of colour, brightening the scenery.

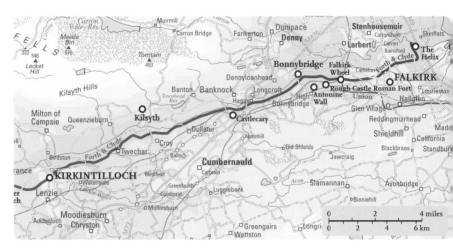

It is almost with relief that, as the ubiquitous high-voltage power line sheers away to the north, the first lock since Maryhill comes into view at the end of a 2 mile straight, followed immediately by a most welcome bend in the navigation. Crossing Red Burn Aqueduct, the canal retains an elevated and wooded position before ducking through the newly constructed Castlecary Bridge.

In common with all the new canal crossings, this bridge is of a cast concrete construction emblazoned with the waterway's bascule bridge logo moulded into the face of the structure, together with the double 'M's depicting the year of restoration. Opinion as to the aesthetic merits of the design and execution of these new crossings will no doubt be divided, but they are undeniably distinctive and bring a continuity and cohesion to the whole project. Other unique characteristics on this canal are the immense proportions of the lock balance beams, hooks in place of bollards at the lockside and the stout vertical posts to restrain an errant lockgate and its flailing beam. Beyond is Bonnybridge, straggling left and right away from the navigation and the new vertical lift bridge.

CRAIGMARLOCH

There is little today to suggest that this was once a popular destination for day-trippers from Glasgow. Pictures from the early 20th century show a floating tearoom (the *Meadow Queen*) and the wooden 'Bungalow' grouped within the basin, together with at least one trip boat; the whole scene is a hive of activity with much merriment in evidence. There were also swings for the children and a putting green for the adults. Outings were aboard a series of boats with the 'Queen' suffix – *Fairy Queen, May Queen* and *Gypsy Queen* – and all operated until the Second World War.

POINTS OF INTEREST

Bishopbriggs Since the Second World War, Bishopbriggs has steadily attracted new housing development and relocated light industry. For many years Wimpey maintained a permanent office in the Kirkintilloch Road and the publisher, William Collins (now HarperCollins Publishers), moved his entire Scottish operation to the suburb in the 1970s.

Cadder Church Set in its charming wooded setting, this building gives little hint of its turbulent past. First established on this site in 1150, the present church dates from 1829 with early 20th-century restoration. However two navvies, their canal-digging activities at an end, decided to divert their attention and skills to excavating bodies for the lucrative dissection trade in the university medical schools, with the newly completed canal neatly solving any transportation problems for Messrs Burke and Hare. To combat problems with such body snatchers', corpses were bolted into coffins and new graves were watched at night. The stone 'hut' just inside the graveyard provided shelter for the watchers who were reputed to have calmed their nerves with spirits (of the liquid type!)

Kirkintilloch An intriguing town that developed from a rural farming community to an inland port in the 19th century with the coming of the canal. It went on to establish a healthy shipbuilding industry – Clyde 'Puffers' were built at Hays Yard just to the west of Townhead Bridge – and become a centre for iron founding: the once ubiquitous red telephone box was produced in its thousands by the nearby Lion Iron Foundry. Cotton spinning and coal mining also played important parts in the local economy, as did coach building for a while.

Kilsyth Once a mining town, its coal deposits are now worked out and most of the evidence of this former activity has vanished. Auchinstarry provided the 'port' where local coal was loaded for Glasgow in the basin which now provides moorings. Immediately to the north of the waterway is a large quarry, source of much of the whinstone basalt which paves Glasgow's streets today. Now closed, the sheer rock faces still provide some demanding climbs for visiting mountaineers.

Castlecary A village on one of the best-preserved sections of the Antonine Wall, Rome's most northerly outpost. Now entwined in the trunk road network of the Scottish Lowlands, Castlecary has, until recently, sat beside the A80 canal crossing that blocked the navigation for nearly 40 years. In 1963 the constructors of the Denny bypass were saved the £160,000-cost of building a lifting bridge by the simple expedient of having a Parliamentary Act passed to close the waterway. In 2000 it cost more than £2 million to provide a new – and navigable – structure in order to re-open the canal.

Bonnybridge As the name suggests, this is a crossing point for the Bonny Burn which rises to the east of Kelvinhead and parallels the canal before flowing into the River Carron. Today the bridge over the navigation is of the 'four-poster' vertical hydraulic lifting variety, no doubt parented by the adjoining pair further west in the Clydebank shopping centre. Bridge lineage aside, this is the best place from which to access Rough Castle Roman Fort.

Maryhill Locks, Glasgow

The Kelpies presiding over the Forth & Clyde Canal

THE ARRIVAL OF THE RAILWAY

Inevitably it was competition from the railway – in this instance the Edinburgh & Glasgow opened in 1842 – that heralded the decline of the two, interconnected lowland canals. Brilliantly engineered, with gradients no greater than 1 in 600, it is one of the flattest sections of track in Britain, 15 miles being dead level. Although a lowland railway, deep cuttings (one, near Linlithgow, an interminable 4 miles long) were constructed, all of which ensured that from the outset neither the Forth & Clyde nor the Union Canal could successfully compete for traffic.

THE NAVIGATION

This section of waterway is heralded by an attractively planted garden which has partially annexed the towpath; dwarf conifers predominate. Once again you are aware of the high-voltage lines which seem to festoon the valleys between the two firths, regularly punctuated by distribution stations. All this is quickly forgotten, however, as suddenly the Falkirk Wheel comes into view and one can only wonder at its conception and construction. At one stroke it embraces function and sculpture, and its bold design cured the Achilles heel of the whole Millennium Link restoration, namely the missing Port Downie locks, lost forever under sprawling urban development. Beyond, the navigation runs straight and non-descript for one mile before its rapid and more traditional descent through Camelon and out to its new connection with the River Carron.

POINTS OF INTEREST

Antonine Wall This dyke and ditch construction stretched for 37 miles, from estuary to estuary, adorning Scotland's slender waist. It is extraordinary to think that the effort required to produce a defensive line up to 12ft high and 14ft at its base, accompanied by a ditch 40ft wide, was expended on an edifice that was so short-lived. Nearby Rough Castle is the best preserved example of a fort still in evidence today.

Rough Castle Roman Fort One of the best-preserved defensive positions along the Antonine Wall, with ditches and ramparts intact. One curiosity discovered during an excavation in 1909 was a series of closely packed pits, or lilia. Sharpened stakes were set in the bottom as a booby-trap, an extremely effective method of breaking a

charge. Other items found in the course of this dig can be viewed in the Queen Street building of the Royal Museum of Scotland in Edinburgh.

Falkirk Wheel *See* the Union Canal page 262 and Milepost 23, page 287.

Falkirk In the 2nd century the Romans established their most northerly frontier with the building of the Antonine Wall, Falkirk lying towards its eastern projection. Within 20 years they had given up on the struggle to subdue the Picts and withdrawn further south, leaving the community to develop over the centuries as an important market centre and focal point for the Highland drovers. In the 19th century large reserves of coal were discovered in the area, which had already become important for iron founding. The Carron Ironworks, one of many along the banks of the River Carron in Camelon, was instrumental in promoting the Forth & Clyde Canal and in shaping its future development.

The Helix Home to the 100ft high Kelpies, this is an exciting parkland development providing activities including cycling, walking, watersports and more.

Is it a bird? Is it a fish? Is it a boat lift? Viewed as a piece of non-representational art it might be either of the first two; as the final link in the £84.5-million chain re-joining Edinburgh with Glasgow, it is very much a boat lift replacing the flight of 11 locks that once reached down to the Forth & Clyde Canal beside Lock 16.

As a starting point the architect, Tony Kettle, saw the canals forming a 'linear, narrow route across Scotland; something akin to a spine'. But this spine was broken and he wanted the wheel 'to be a celebration of it being joined back together again'. Thoughts of a spine conjured up 'elegant, organic structures like fish bones'. So the aqueduct took on 'an organic, spine-like form – boats floating through hoops' – and the wheel was given direction with hooked leading edges on the arms emphasising its rotation. Thus it was as much a sculptural idea as an engineering concept,

The Falkirk Wheel

Leaving the upper gondola of the Falkirk Wheel

with the design of the hooks inspired by a Celtic double-headed axe.

On a more prosaic level this £20-million steel structure raises and lowers craft 82ft. The wheel is 92ft long and 115ft in diameter, while the aqueduct is 328ft long and 67ft above the ground. Each of the wheel's two arms is 4½ft thick and between them they support two gondolas 21ft wide and 5ft deep holding a total of 600 tons of water between them. Fully loaded, the wheel weighs in at 1,800 tons and is held together with 15,000 high-tensile bolts.

The whole construction is powered by ten 7.5kW hydraulic motors, although it is rare for more than four to be used at any one time. Typically it requires little more than the power of two electric showers to turn the wheel and the total electricity cost amounts to little more than £10 a day.

What is something of a surprise, however, is the degree to which what was ultimately just a practical solution – to the problem of reinstating the link between the Forth & Clyde and Union canals – has now become one of Scotland's foremost tourist attractions.

EXPLORING

Wending their quiet way through town and country, the inland navigations of Britain offer walkers, cyclists and boaters a unique insight into a fascinating, but once almost lost world. Fortunately through the vision and determined efforts of many people there are now more than 4,000 miles of canals and rivers to explore, a large proportion in a navigable condition. Canal & River Trust states that half the population of the UK live within 5 miles of a canal or river and many people are discovering that these watery corridors can provide a peaceful haven away from the hurly-burly of everyday life, even in the centre of a large city.

Our canals and rivers can be enjoyed on many levels: from an armchair with a book such as this, aboard a trip boat, by taking a stroll or cycle ride along the towpath, from a sunny seat outside a café or pub, or by hiring a boat and getting onto the water.

There are two main organisations charged with the care of our inland waterways: Canal & River Trust looks after some 2,200 miles of the country's canals and rivers; the Environment Agency manages around 600 miles of river, including the River Thames.

There are books aplenty on the subject, from technical manuals on how to fit-out a boat to

Self-drive motorboats, York

Ratho Princess *at Ratho on the Edinburgh & Glasgow Union Canal*

guides focusing solely on canalside pubs. For a thorough and entirely practical approach the *Nicholson waterways guides*, in print for over 40 years, cover most of the navigable canals and rivers of this country in great detail. Along with factual information for the boater, the *Nicholson guides* also offer a great deal of information on museums and other canal-related places to visit, walks and cycle rides to follow and boat trips to enjoy.

If you are looking for more suggestions on where to go and what to do, an internet search will reveal many websites offering information on a huge range of inland waterways-related subjects. The IWA (www.waterways.org.uk), Canal & River Trust (www.canalrivertrust. org.uk) and Environment Agency (www.gov. uk/government/organisations/environment-agency) websites are good places to start. Tourist Information Centres (TICs), both on the ground and virtual, will be able to supply you with more ideas.

Messing about in boats

Waterside drinking...

The Scottish Waterways Trust (www.scottish waterwaystrust.org.uk) is an independent registered charity helping young people gain the skills and confidence to find work, bringing vibrancy, life and opportunities to some of the nation's most disadvantaged communities, whilst encouraging people to become active and improve their health and mental wellbeing.

There is a National Waterways Museum at three locations: Gloucester Docks, Ellesmere Port and Stoke Bruerne. Each museum has a range of exhibitions and runs regular events throughout the year. Their collections represent a nationally important and unique collection of waterways archive. In London,

...and eating

Hireboats awaiting their crews

(www.tourismforall.org.uk) is a charity dedicated to providing accurate holiday information for older people and the disabled, and offers details of accessible boat trips and the like. Other organisations work specifically to provide access and services on the inland waterways for their local community. More details of these organisations can be found on the National Community Boats website (www.national-cba.co.uk).

For many, their first waterway encounter is through a boat trip. In every town and city blessed with a canal or river, you will find boat

the Canal Museum is housed in a former ice warehouse in Kings Cross. There are countless other canal museums and waterways-related places to visit across the country, run by local canal trusts and other interested parties.

Various waterway events are run by the IWA and used to include the National Waterways Festival, held in a different location each year to promote a particular restoration. In 1989 the focus was Castlefield, at the junction of the Bridgewater and Rochdale canals in the centre of Manchester. Once a derelict no-go area, Castlefield is now visited for Manchester's Museum of Science, archaeological sites, industrial heritage and an outdoor events arena. The restored canal basin boasts al fresco dining and popular bars. Now in its thirty fourth year, Canalway Cavalcade takes place in Little Venice, central London and is the

city's premier waterway event. IWA Trailboat Festivals are held on a landlocked stretch of waterway, again to promote a specific feature or restoration project. The festivals offer a boat rally and trade show and lots of activities and entertainment for everyone. You will find other waterside events taking place all over the country, often initiatives run by Canal & River Trust, canal trusts or local authorities.

Access for all is a vital part of inviting people of all ages and abilities to discover the canals and rivers. Many canals have sections of smooth, level towpath where there is convenient parking and easy access. Boat trip operators and specialist charities offer traditional narrowboats and modern cruisers, wheelchair accessible and adapted for people with special needs, for short day trips and for longer holidays. Tourism for All

Trip boat

trips on offer. Many of the canal trusts run trip boats as a way of raising vital funds and to engage with local residents and visitors. Boats of all shapes and sizes can also be hired, from punts, rowing boats and canoes, through to luxury cruisers and traditional narrowboats. You don't need to launch off for a week's holiday to begin with – many operators hire out boats by the day as an introduction to boating. If the thought of managing locks and steering a boat does not appeal, there are several hotel boat companies offering all the relaxation of time afloat without any of the physical work. British Marine Inland Boat (www.britishmarine.co.uk) represents

Relax, unwind and be pampered

companies offering all types of boating on our navigable canals and rivers.

But exploring the inland canals and rivers does not have to be an expensive business: best of all, it can be enjoyed completely free. For the walker and cyclist, exploring the inland waterways can entail nothing more than a there-and-back stroll or a gentle bike ride. The towpaths offer safe, traffic-free routes and there are many waymarked long-distance and shorter walks and cycle routes, local and national, which take in sections of canal and river. Cyclists can access many of the towpaths, although in some cases a permit will be required (usually free). Just as there is a Countryside Code for walkers, so there is a Towpath Code of Conduct for cyclists which can be found at www.canalrivertrust.org.uk/our-towpath-code.

From their birth as a practical answer to a transport problem, through the high days of 'canal mania', the decline of the past century and into the restoration and regeneration of today, our inland waterways now provide an endlessly fascinating and varied asset, available to everyone.

Canalside cycle track

Customs House, Bowling on the Forth & Clyde Canal

The Rochdale Canal scrambles out of the Piccadilly district of Manchester, past a series of enormous mills – some restored for housing, others still gaping gauntly at the passing navigation – and heads with purpose, if not with haste, for the looming Pennine hills beyond.

This waterway is one of three Pennine canal crossings. It was authorised by an Act of Parliament in 1794 and completed exactly ten years later. With wide locks it was able to handle barges, Humber keels and even small coasters, the latter sometimes trading between the Continent and Irish ports, using the River Mersey and the Irwell Navigation at the western end. However, the Achilles heel of the waterway lay in its requirement for a copious supply of water at the summit pound, together with the sheer physical effort required to operate the three locks per mile averaged over the canal's relatively short length.

The last loaded boat to trade over the canal's entire length was narrowboat *Alice*, in April 1937, carrying 20 tons of wire from Manchester to Sowerby Bridge. The navigation was officially closed by

The navigable culvert under the M62

THE GREAT WALL OF TOD

It has been said by some that the only man-made feature distinguishable on the Earth, when viewed from the Moon, is the Great Wall of China. However appealing the idea, astronauts have shown that it is just a space myth. For a guard detachment, patrolling some of its more remote lengths, it must have been a singularly lonely and, in some cases, solitary occupation. The 'Great Wall of Tod' – the name given to the canalside railway retaining wall on the Rochdale Canal at Todmorden – is unlikely to hold quite such long-standing historical significance. Nor will it become a talking point amongst future astronauts. Owing its existence to the less prosaic function of keeping 'railway out of t' cut', it still remains, nonetheless, one of the wonders of a more local world. Building with brick in the Calder Valley, rather than the local gritstone, was largely down to the advent of the railway: a phenomenon repeated throughout many other areas of the country.

an Act in 1952, while restoration was commenced 30 years ago. Subsequently Canal & River Trust and its partners have completed the work at a cost of £23 million, rebuilding locks, bridges and tunnels and completing many new structures. This investment has only been possible because of projected benefits to the local community over a number of years, totalling in the region of £200 million.

Ingenuity is the name of the game when contemplating a restoration project of this size, following a lengthy period of abandonment. Inevitably houses and roads will have been built on parts of the original line; bridges lowered and sections infilled. On the Rochdale one of the biggest blocks to full restoration lay in motorways, constructed since the navigation's closure and prohibitively expensive to re-route, bridge or tunnel under.

In fact the M60 did require a tunnel and the A627M a navigable culvert. However, it was the passage under the M62, teeming with trans-Pennine traffic day and night, that demonstrated lateral thinking at its best. Close to the original course of the waterway there was a culvert, constructed when the motorway was originally built, to allow the nearby farm access to fields severed by the road. Unfortunately it was rather

too high for its base to align with the canal bed so a lock, originally located 1/2 a mile or so beyond the culvert, was simply rebuilt just before it.

Blue Pits New Lock, moved south of the M62

PLANTS

Himalayan balsam

Japanese knotweed

Knapweed

Himalayan balsam The Himalayan balsam is a serious threat to our native wildlife. Introduced as a garden plant in the early 19th century, it is widely naturalised along river banks and on damp wasteground. It has small, explosive seeds, by which it easily spreads. The plant aggressively out-grows native species in ecologically sensitive areas, especially on river and canal banks, where it can impede the flow of water at times of high rain flow, increasing the likelihood of flooding. During winter this annual dies back, leaving bare banks more susceptible to erosion. Himalayan balsam grows tall (up to 6.5ft). The upright, reddish stems carry leaves in whorls of three or opposite pairs. Pink/purple flowers appear between July and October.

Japanese knotweed Another dangerous invasive species. Fast growing, it reaches more than 10ft in height. It is quick to colonise river and canal banks, roadsides and other wayside places. Large, triangular leaves are borne on red, zigzag stems. Loose spikes of white flowers arise from leaf bases and appear between August and October. Once established, populations are extremely persistent, can survive severe floods and are difficult and expensive to eradicate.

Knapweed This is a widespread, hairy perennial of grassy places. The grooved stems branch towards the top. The leaves are narrow and slightly lobed near the base of the plant. The flower heads appear between June and September and have brown bracts and purple flowers.

Meadow thistle A perennial of damp meadows, locally common in south and central England, Wales and Ireland. The stem is unwinged, downy and ridged. Oval, toothed leaves are green and hairy above and white cottony below. The flower heads appear in June and July: reddish-purple florets and darker bracts on solitary heads.

Meadow thistle

Ragged robin A widespread and common perennial of damp meadows and marshes. The narrow, grass-like leaves are rough, the upper ones in opposite pairs. The delicate-looking flowers comprise five pink petals each of which is divided into four lobes; they appear between May and July.

Teasel A biennial of damp grassland on heavy, often disturbed soils. It produces a rosette of spine-coated leaves in the first year. In the second year, conical heads of purple flowers are borne on tall, angled and spined stems between July and August. The dead heads persists. In flower, teasels are popular with bees; the seedheads are particularly favoured by goldfinches.

Ragged robin

Teasel

Wood sorrel

Wood sorrel A widespread, charming, creeping perennial. Widespread in moist, shady woods, it is an indicator of ancient woodlands and hedgerows. The trefoil leaves, often purplish beneath and which fold down at night, are borne on long stalks. They have a sharp acid taste and were formerly used as a flavouring, like those of sorrel. Lilac-veined flowers are carried on stalks from April to June.

Yellow water lily A water plant with oval, floating leaves. Widespread and locally common. This water lily favours still or slow-moving water and is often found along canals. It roots in mud in the shallows. The flowers, carried on stalks, appear between June and September.

Yellow water lily

295

The Herefordshire & Gloucestershire Canal is typical of those waterways, built predominantly through a rural landscape, without the commercial benefit of any real, local industry. Although started in 1792, well before the dawn of the railway age, its full 34 miles were not completed until 1845, making it the last major through route constructed in Britain and placing it squarely in competition with train transport: a contest it had no hope of winning. Indeed one of its most profitable periods was, ironically, in its run up to closure, carrying materials for the construction of the Hereford to Ledbury railway before finally succumbing to closure in 1881 (to allow part of its bed to be infilled to create the permanent way for the new Ledbury–Gloucester line). Dr Beeching, in his turn, almost succeeded in completing the circle, with the closure of

The restored basin at Over

WATERWAYS UP THE SEVERN

Inevitably an arterial waterway like the Severn encouraged the construction of branch navigations at various points along its course. Near Stourport a canal (*see* Milepost 9) was proposed to run west to the coalfields at Mamble and thence on to Leominster and Kington on the Welsh border. Only the section between the mines at Mamble and Leominster was ever completed. Further south the River Salwarpe, in conjunction with a stretch of canal, was made navigable to Droitwich, whilst the Coombe Hill Canal – just upstream of the city of Gloucester – ran eastwards 2³/₄ miles to aid coal transport to Cheltenham. Nearby, the Herefordshire & Gloucestershire Canal – a truly rural canal started in 1792 and only completed in 1845 – linked the two eponymous cities. Its 34 wandering miles followed a route via Newent, Dymock and Ledbury, required 3 tunnels and 22 locks, and appeared on the canal scene just as railway mania was taking hold. Closed in 1881 to allow part of its bed to be used as a railway (in turn axed by Dr Beeching in the 1960s – only to be reclaimed by the waterway in its current resurrection!), it is now firmly fixed in the sights of a very professional and dedicated canal trust, committed to its complete restoration. Equally important, the trust now has the full policy backing of all five councils along the route who are determined to preserve the line against any future, compromising developments. Now that the comparatively easy canal restorations are complete, or at least well in hand, it is the turn of the difficult ones, considered impossible 10–15 years ago. Some ten per cent of the canal is restored or under restoration. Work is now finished on the first phase at Over, where the canal entered the River Severn and a delightful, landscaped basin complete with the rebuilt Wharf House complements the new housing development. The lock down into the Severn will be the focus for a new phase of activity. The sheer dogged determination and tenacity of the trust, shown in the face of not inconsiderable adversity, whilst meeting a demanding schedule, will surely stand as an inspiration to all those engaged in future waterway restoration.

this railway in 1964, but reckoned without the dogged determination of the Herefordshire & Gloucestershire Canal Trust (H&GCT) who – amongst other projects – are boldly extending their nearby Oxenhall restoration of the canal along the old track bed, running between the beautifully renovated platforms of Newent Station.

Currently a volunteer workforce, under the auspices of the H&GCT, works part-time on up to a dozen distinct sites, spread throughout the two counties, with the twofold objectives of canal restoration itself, together with the equally important aim of raising overall awareness of this derelict waterway. Hand in hand with this goes community involvement, a sense of ownership and a burgeoning understanding of the wide range of benefits that the restored navigation can bring: financial, social, recreational and environmental. By its linear nature this is a local asset that ties together diverse communities, each with their different histories, whilst simultaneously providing a fertile source of history in its own right.

At Gloucester, the Herefordshire & Gloucestershire Canal leaves the Western Channel of the River Severn at Over (currently the trust's *pièce de résistance*) and follows the Leadon Valley in a north westerly direction, rising steadily, before reaching Oxenhall 9½ miles away. The Grade II lock chamber of House Lock has been restored by the H&GCT (but is presently un-gated) and is the upper one of a pair: sadly little remains of its twin (No. 2 Lock) once separated by a short pound. These represent two of a total of 22 locks on the canal. A couple of hundred yards lower down – towards Gloucester – the canal crosses the Ell Brook (once a source of power for a number of local mills) on a newly restored aqueduct and immediately merges with the redundant bed of the old Ledbury–Gloucester Railway: rapidly becoming its new course!

'The Wharf House', Over

Heading further north, the navigation makes its way to Ledbury and thence to Hereford via three tunnels and some very fertile and attractive countryside, skirting the hop yards and orchards encountered along its meandering course. It finds its way through the most skewed of skew bridges, bores straight under Aylestone Hill, before wandering into the city of Hereford. In places it has been infilled and is once again under the plough, whilst other sections hold water and attract the attention of local and WERGIE (*see* Milepost 21) volunteers alike.

One of the many areas, where the trust really demonstrates its strength, is in securing sources of ongoing income that can be relied upon to support restoration work, well into the future. Currently the best example of this diverse (and rapidly expanding) portfolio is the Wharf House at Over. The shell, constructed for the trust by the developers of the nearby redundant hospital site – under a Section 106 planning obligation – has been fitted out by volunteer labour to form a high-class restaurant with equally prestigious bedroom accommodation above. The adjoining basin – once the start of the navigation and its connection with the River Severn – has been restored, providing a high profile focus for H&GCT activities close to Gloucester, with a trip boat and highly attractive landscaping.

This would all have been as aught without a link between the river and the remainder of the waterways system. For a long time this remained somewhat elusive as locks, built to bypass neighbouring weirs on the Severn, had long since fallen into decay and new ownership. The trust's lucky break came when the two Llanthony Lock Cottages and the adjacent derelict lock chamber – now sitting empty but squarely within their grounds – came onto the market, coinciding with a legacy received from a loyal benefactor. The tenanted dwellings provide yet another income stream while the lock, once restored, will ensure that, when eventually

Oxenhall Lock and cottage

completed, the Hereford & Gloucester Canal will once again form part of our connected, cruisable, waterways system.

Ever since Tom and Angela Rolt set out on their pioneering voyage on *Cressy* (*see* Milepost 21) the waterways restoration movement has been spearheaded by dedicated enthusiasts – single minded men and women of vision, most of them unpaid – prepared, where necessary, to devote an entire lifetime to the cause. It is to them that we owe a huge and immeasurable debt of gratitude, both for the waterways system that we see before us today and for what is still to come.

GLOSSARY

Accommodation Bridge Bridge constructed by a canal company to connect adjacent fields severed by the construction of a waterway.

Adit Horizontal shaft into a mine or tunnel bore.

Barge Any craft having a beam greater than 7ft.

Battery boat Boat loaded with batteries (or accumulators) operating in tandem with (and powering) an electric tunnel tug.

BCN Birmingham Canal Navigations.

Beam Width of a boat.

Breach Burst or leak in the waterway bank or bed.

Butty Unpowered narrowboat, towed by a motor and always worked in tandem.

BW British Waterways.

BWB British Waterways Board.

Canal mania Describes the euphoria behind the surge in waterway construction in the late 18th century.

Josher bow

Canal ring Collection of interconnecting waterways that taken together form a circular cruising route, so that the boater ends where he started, without repeating any lengths of the canal previously navigated.

Caisson

i) Watertight tank used to seal off an area on the bed of a river to allow the construction of a bridge pier.

ii) Water-filled, boat-carrying chamber traversing an inclined plane.

iii) The ascending or descending chamber of a vertical boat lift.

Cannel Dull coal that burns with a smoky, luminous flame.

Cill Protruding concrete or masonry section that forms a watertight seal under the top gate of a pound lock (*see* diagram on page 299).

Clyde Puffer Steam powered craft of iron construction, trading around the rivers, islands and inlets of West Scotland.

Cog boat Small rowing boat carried on barges to allow the crew ashore when their craft is beached or moored out in the river.

Compartment boat Steel or wooden craft of crude, rectangular construction. Can be hoisted, tipped, carried on rails or aboard a larger vessel.

Cross-adit Horizontal shaft connecting two mine shafts or tunnel bores.

CRT Canal & River Trust.

Culvert Channel under a waterway carrying a stream or drain, usually of masonry construction. Also means of transferring water from one part of a pound lock to another (*see* diagram on page 299).

Dumb barge Barge without an engine.

Feeder Channel supplying water to a canal (often from a reservoir).

Converted FMC narrowboat

Fellows, Morton & Clayton Large, go-ahead narrowboat carrying company. The first to make serious commercial use of steam-powered craft. Famous for their slender bowed boats, known as 'Joshers,' after Joshua Morton.

Flash Lake caused by subsidence, generally the result of mining.

Flash lock Crude method of enabling boats to change level on a river – operated by drawing one or more vertical, wooden paddles (or shutters) in a weir. The craft either ascended or descended on the ensuing rush of water. Superseded by the Pound Lock.

Fly boat Fast boats – often used for passenger travel and the transport of perishable goods – employing regular changes of horses in the manner adopted by stagecoaches.

Fly operation Non-stop operation of boats by crews working twenty-four hours, suited to motorised craft, rather than those that were horse-drawn.
FMC *See* Fellows, Morton & Clayton
Freeboard Distance between gunnel and water level on a craft.

Gabbart Trim sailing barges designed for the River Clyde.
Gauging Vertical measurement of a boat's freeboard to establish the weight of goods carried.
Gongoozler Canalside spectator.
Grand Cross A concept devised by James Brindley in which the ports of Liverpool, Hull, London and Bristol would be linked through their estuarine rivers (of Mersey, Humber, Thames and Avon) via an intersecting system of canals.

Guillotine gate Vertical gate, moving up and down, employed in locks and sluices, separating one section of water from another.
Gunnel Horizontal section of the deck where it meets the vertical hull.
GWR Great Western Railway (also known in some circles as 'God's Wonderful Railway').

Humber keel Sailing barge, found on the Humber that, minus sails, rigging and mast, travelled along the Yorkshire canal system behind a horse.

Inclined plane Form of boat lift, employing water-filled caissons, travelling up or down a slope from one level to another, performing the role of a lock.
IWA Inland Waterways Association.

Journeyman The next stage up from apprentice: a travelling tradesman.

Leeboard Retractable, vertical wooden board attached to the gunnel of a sailing barge, allowing it to sail close to the wind.
Leggers Men employed to propel unpowered craft through tunnels.
Legging Method of propelling unpowered craft through a tunnel where there was no towpath for the horse.
Lengthsman Waterway employee responsible for looking after a prescribed length of the navigation.
LNWR London and North Western Railway
Lock gate Used in a pound lock to retain water in or above the lock chamber (*see* diagram below).

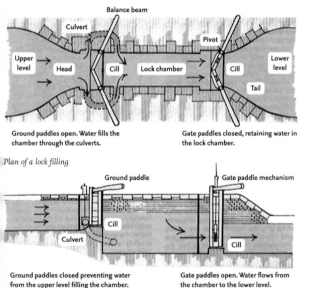

Plan of a lock filling

Ground paddles open. Water fills the chamber through the culverts.

Gate paddles closed, retaining water in the lock chamber.

Ground paddles closed preventing water from the upper level filling the chamber.

Gate paddles open. Water flows from the chamber to the lower level.

Elevation of a lock emptying

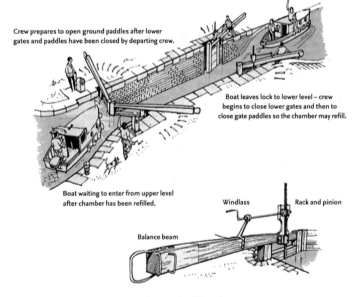

Crew prepares to open ground paddles after lower gates and paddles have been closed by departing crew.

Boat leaves lock to lower level – crew begins to close lower gates and then to close gate paddles so the chamber may refill.

Boat waiting to enter from upper level after chamber has been refilled.

Lock gate with paddle mechanism

Mersey Flat A traditional sailing barge that plied the River Mersey.
Motor Motorised narrowboat often worked in tandem with a butty.

Narrow lock Lock, 7ft wide, built to accommodate a narrowboat.
Narrowboat Narrow beam craft – usually 6ft 10ins in width
Nb Abbreviation for narrowboat.

Paddles Devices set into the side of lock chambers, or into lock gates, to control the flow of water into or out of a pound lock (*see* diagram on page 299).
Paired locks Locks constructed side by side, usually built to speed up passage through a lock flight.
Pond *See* pound.
Pound Length of water contained (or impounded) between adjacent locks.
Pound lock Lock employing a chamber of water trapped between an upper and lower moveable lock gate – or gates (*see* diagram on page 299).
Puddle Process of compacting clay to provide a waterproof lining to the sides and bottom of a waterway.

Reach Stretch of river between, say, two locks or corners.

Severn Trows Sailing boats that traded on the River Severn.
Side pond Small lagoon, set beside a lock chamber, able to 'catch' a proportion of the water that would otherwise be lost downhill during normal lock operation.
Sill *See* cill.
Skew bridge Bridge built at an acute angle to the waterway.
SSSI Often known as a Triple SI, this designation stands for Site of Special Scientific Interest.
Staircase lock One of a series of locks where the flight combines the bottom gate of one lock with the top gate of the next and lower lock.
Staithe/Stather Quay or unloading jetty.
Stop lock Usually inserted where a waterway meets another in order to separate the water 'owned' by one company from that of the adjacent company often with no change in level.
Stop plank One of a collection of wooden planks used to dam a section of waterway so that it can be isolated and drained for maintenance. Also used to contain a breach.
Summit Level/Pound Highest point on a waterway, contained between two, adjacent locks.

Thames Gig Wooden Thames rowing boat that could be fitted with a cover to form a rudimentary tent.
The Potteries Area around Stoke-on-Trent and focus for pottery manufacture, composed of Burslem, Fenton, Hanley, Longton, Stoke and Tunstall.
Tom Pudding Steel compartment boat, towed by a tug in groups of up to nineteen, designed to carry coal along the Aire & Calder Canal.
Tub boat Small, mineral carrying, compartment boat, often of wooden construction.

Warp Fine natural silt dredged from the Trent at Idle Mouth and used as a metal polishing material in the Sheffield cutlery trade.
WERGIES Colloquial name given to members of the Waterways Recovery Group.
Wheelbox Collapsible superstructure (to allow unloaded boats to pass under low canal bridges) giving protection to the steerer.
Wheelhouse *See* Wheelbox.
Wide beam boat Any craft having a beam greater than 7ft.
Wide lock Lock able to accommodate wide beam boats.
WRG Waterways Recovery Group.

INDEX

ACKNOWLEDGEMENTS

Written by Jonathan Mosse
Editor Cicely Frew
Page layout Bob Vickers

The author and publisher wish to acknowledge the contribution made by those researchers and writers who have gone before in the creation and revision of the Nicholson waterways guides.

Grateful thanks are also due to:
Jenny Black, Waterway Recovery Group
John and Jonathan Branford
David Forrester, Inland Waterways Association
Foxton Inclined Plane Trust
Chris Griffiths
Val Hickin for his invaluable contribution to Milepost 22
Paul Hoben, Inland Waterways Association of Ireland
Caroline Jones, The Waterways Trust
Tamsin and Elana Mosse
The inhabitants of Lilac Cottage, Orleton, Herefordshire

Map of Brindley's Grand Cross based on a map from www.thepotteries.org.
Map of Grand Contour Canal based on a map created by the late Dr Mike Stevens.
Wildlife text adapted from *Collins Complete Guide to British Wildlife* and *Collins Wildlife Guide*.

Unless otherwise stated below, all photographs are by the author, © copyright Jonathan Mosse. Photographs marked S are courtesy of Shutterstock. NNSS: GB non-native species secretariat L=left, R=right, T=top, B=bottom.

8BL WRG Navvies; **12** National Portrait Gallery, London; **25**T The Waterways Archive Gloucester; **25**B Inland Waterways Association of Ireland; **25**R, **32–3**, **38**L, **40** The Waterways Archive Gloucester; **42**L National Portrait Galley; **42**R The Waterways Archive Gloucester; **46**R Thomas Bevand; **57**R, **76**T, **77**, **80**L The Waterways Archive Gloucester; **80**R, **81**L WRG Navvies; **81**R The Waterways Archive Gloucester; **82–3** Barn owl S/Glen Gaffney, Goldfinch S/Rick Thornton, Grey heron and Kingfisher S/Tom Curtis, Lapwing S/Gertjan Hooijer; Little egret S/PhotoBarmaley **93**T The Waterways Archive Gloucester; **94–5** S/Tim Curtis; **96** Inland Waterways Association; **98** Helen Dobbie; **112**T, **113**, **116**, **117**L The Waterways Archive Gloucester; **126** Callum Frew; **134–5** Long tailed tit Paul Huggins, Moorhen Paul Huggins, Nuthatch S/Alan Scheer, Reed warbler S/Iuri Konoval, Snipe S/Kaldo Karner, Tree sparrow S/Marcin Perkowski; **155**L Caen Hill Lock flight S/Jane Rix; **155**R S/Jon le-bon; **159**TR, **166**, **169** The Waterways Archive Gloucester;

194–5 Banded demoiselle S/Alan Scheeer, Bumble bee S/Vladimir Sazonov, Comma buttefly S/Willmetts, Glow worm S/Timo_W25, Grasshopper S/Igor Semenov, Holly Blue butterfly S/Robert Hardholt, Ladybird S/Stoupa, Large Skipper S/Steve McWilliam, Marsh Fritillary Frank Lane Picture Agency/Ted Benton, Orange-tip S/Jens Stolt, Speckled Wood S/Christian Mussat; **232–3** Badger S/Markabond, Brown hare S/Pavel Mikoska, Daubentons bat S/Mike Lane, Fox S/Nialat, Harvest mouse S/Isselee, Mink NNSS, Otter S/J Klingebiel, Water vole S/Laurancea; **244** Foxton Inclined Plane Trust; **245** The Waterways Archive Gloucester; **258–9** Bluebell S/Dave McAleavy, Buddleia S/Rainbow, Cross-leaved heath S/Ainars Aunins, Devil's bit scabious S/Andrey Novik, Early Marsh Orchid S/Ainars Aunins, Floating pennywort S/Tom Curtis, Grey Willow S/Cosmin Manci, Guelder rose S/Malgorzata Kistryn; **270** The Inland Waterways Association; **271** WRG Navvies; **277** Chris Griffiths; **294–5** Himalayan Balsam NNSS, Japanese knotweed NNSS, Knapweed S/Gala_Kan, Meadow thistle S/RTimages, Ragged Robin S/Steve Paul Pepper, Teasel S/Michael Woodruff, Wood sorrel S/NatalieJean, Yellow water lily S/Gregory Johnson

Cover image: Shropshire Union Canal (S/albinoni)

FURTHER READING

Collins and Nicholson Waterways Guides

Grand Union, Oxford & the South East

Severn, Avon & Birmingham

Birmingham & the Heart of England

Four Counties & the Welsh Canals

North West & the Pennines

Nottingham, York & the North East

River Thames & the Southern Waterways

Norfolk Broads

Inland Waterways Map of Great Britain